CONFESSIONS OF

A ROCK 'N' ROLL NAME-DROPPER

My Life Leading Up to John Lennon's Last Interview

To Laurie,

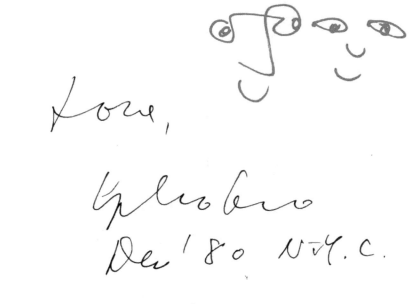

Love,

John Lennon
Dec '80 N.Y.C.

1980

CONFESSIONS OF

A ROCK 'N' ROLL NAME-DROPPER

My Life Leading Up to John Lennon's Last Interview

LAURIE KAYE

FAYETTEVILLE MAFIA PRESS

Cover by Mick Haggerty
Edited by David Bushman
Book designed by Scott Ryan

Published in the USA by Fayetteville Mafia Press
Columbus, Ohio

Contact Information
Email: fayettevillemafiapress@gmail.com
Website: fayettevillemafiapress.com
Instagram: @fayettevillemafiapress
Twitter:@fmpbooks

ISBN: 9781949024586
eBook ISBN: 9781949024593

Dedicated to my loving husband, Curt Fisher, whose encouragement, emotional support, technical help, and belief in my ability to tell my life story leading up to John Lennon's last interview in my unique writer's voice, finally made *Confessions of a Rock 'n' Roll Name-Dropper* happen!

CONTENTS

—FOREWORD—

In her life and work as a journalist, Laurie Kaye mastered the art of rooting out the humanity in her subjects. It's a quality that *Confessions of a Rock 'n' Roll Name-Dropper* demonstrates time and time again. And this aspect was fully in evidence during the final interview of John Lennon's life on December 8th, 1980.

For Kaye, that day had all the markings of greatness. Working with her RKO team, including radio legend Dave Sholin and engineer Ron Hummel, Kaye was elated with the prospect of spending time with Lennon and Yoko Ono. And the experience would not disappoint. During the interview, Kaye succeeded in coaxing Lennon into thinking broadly about his career. In so doing, she prompted perhaps the day's most poignant observation from Lennon. "I always consider my work one piece, whether it be with the Beatles, David Bowie, Elton John, Yoko Ono," he said. "And I consider that my work won't be finished until I'm dead and buried, and I hope that's a long, long time."

Given the sad portents to come that evening, Lennon's remark has taken on chilling connotations. Like many Beatles fans, I have played the interview back numerous times over the intervening decades. Even now, Lennon sounds so fresh and so heartbreakingly alive, eagerly trading quips with Kaye and Sholin, while answering every question with optimism and gusto. But for my money, the best moments don't arrive until the end. The RKO folks have exhausted their questions, and the hour is growing late. With the sands of time running out on his life, Lennon good-naturedly signs autographs and poses for pictures with

Kaye and her team.

Listening to that fateful interview is like an audio time capsule. We know that the engine of John's doom is only a matter of feet away, waiting outside the Dakota's carriage entrance. As John busies himself with a ballpoint pen, futilely trying to autograph Double Fantasy's overly slick cover photo, we hear the telephone ring in the background. "Do you have the car waiting?" Ono asks into the receiver. [As history knows, the limo won't arrive, prompting Lennon and Ono to hitch a ride with Sholin and the crew to the Record Plant. In the spare moments caused by the delay, Lennon will sign another autograph—the image of which will be emblazoned across newspapers around the world in a matter of hours.]

And that's when Kaye presents Lennon with her copy of *Grapefruit*, Ono's 1964 collection of aphorisms and philosophically oriented "instructions." Lennon can hardly contain his glee, autographing the book and tagging it with one of his playful line drawings of the couple. As Kaye thanks him for his gesture, Lennon exudes a sense of warmth. "Oh, it's a pleasure!" he booms. "I'm a fan of people too, you know? I like people to sign their books when they give them to me and all that." It's very nearly the last thing you hear that day, with the audiotape spooling off. But it's the part I play, over and over again, if only to hear the sound that Kaye elicited from a voice whose music transformed the ages.

It's not uncommon for readers such as ourselves to imbue such moments with meaning. We all know what's waiting out there in the night for Lennon. We ferret out these final moments in an attempt to find meaning in all that darkness, to forage for one more hidden gem. It may as well be Marie Antoinette trudging her way to the guillotine or Kennedy's limousines making that final turn onto Elm Street in Dallas. We seek out images of wisdom and hope in these final moments, for something larger and somehow more lasting in those final moments.

What Kaye gave us that afternoon is as impactful, if not more so, than any of them. The simple gesture of asking Lennon to autograph *Grapefruit*—the very book from which he read the instruction that would lead him to compose "Imagine"—yields Lennon's unmistakable humanness and fragility. And it's the very same kind of heartfelt moment that Kaye coaxes out of so many of her subjects, the sort of instance where we feel something greater, more prescient about her interviewees. It's no different, say, than the instance in Kaye's interview with Little Richard in which the rock 'n' roll pioneer rues the manner in which latter-day historians tend to elide his contributions. Or when George Harrison admits his undying awe, even surprise over the imprint that the Beatles left on world culture. And then there's the impromptu moment in which Linda McCartney belts out a line from Chuck Berry's "My Ding-a-Ling."

To be able to mine so much humanity during something as perfunctory as an interview—which is, at its essence, a publicity exercise, after all—is a subtle gift that Kaye possesses in spades. With *Confessions of a Rock 'n' Roll Name-Dropper*, Kaye traces the story not only of how she found herself at the Dakota on that fateful December afternoon, but also how she slowly but surely perfected the craft of making sincere human connections during her interviews.

In a world in which instances of genuine humanity seem increasingly rare, it is a story worthy of its telling. As readers will shortly discover, there is warmth and heart in these pages.

Kenneth Womack
Author, *John Lennon 1980: The Last Days in the Life*
Host, *Everything Fab Four* podcast

—CHAPTER 1—

"Imagine"—My Lead-up to Lennon

On December 8, 1980, I was overflowing with excitement, anticipation, and disbelief as I approached the Dakota Apartments on Manhattan's Upper West Side. I was there to play my part in John Lennon's one and only US radio interview following the release of his and Yoko Ono's brand-new album, *Double Fantasy*, and the voices in my head were telling me that this was without a doubt about to become the best day of my life that I could ever even begin to imagine, and that I was truly the luckiest person on the planet.

Visions of thousands of screaming Beatles fans packed into Dodger Stadium so many years earlier swirled through my brain like milkshake in a blender, and I could barely keep myself from swaggering down the sidewalk as my associates and I approached the security booth area right outside the Dakota's entrance.

I'd flown out one day earlier from the West Coast as part of our three-member RKO Radio team along with an executive from Warner Bros./Geffen Records, and although our RKO trio had already worked together on a number of attention-getting network radio rock specials and interviews over the past few years, including heading off to London just the year before to hang out with Paul McCartney and Wings, this would be an entirely different ball game…after all, we were on the verge of meeting up with someone who'd literally disappeared from the music business for the previous five years—JOHN LENNON!

John had been hunkered down in the role of ultrahappy househusband and attentive father ever since his eighteen-month-long "Lost Weekend"—the time during which he was, by his own admission, miserably separated from Yoko and living in Los Angeles—and he hadn't recorded or released any new music in at least the five years since. But now *Double Fantasy*, the new album created with his often critically reviled wife Yoko Ono, was his way of opening the door to the eighties and a whole new era. No one else in the world could even begin to imagine how it felt to realize that we were about to become the only American radio gang chosen to help John and Yoko usher that era in.

The buildup to our interview had already been somewhat mind-blowing. At one point, while everything was still in the early planning stages, I got a call from someone asking the date, year, and time of my birth, because apparently Yoko was working with her personal astrologer, who was going to take all the information collected and then use it to put together an astrological chart that would then determine the best possible day for our Dakota meetup. Of course, the surprising thing is that even with all that intimate information, and despite the fact that John and Yoko had already planned to head to Hawaii and the West Coast during that time period, somehow Monday, December 8, 1980, a date that will live forever in freakish rock 'n' roll infamy, was chosen.

Our flight to the Big Apple alone had been a total trip, with celebrities like British actor Anthony Hopkins and former heavyweight champion Ken Norton onboard. Although I barely had the opportunity to say hello to Hopkins, who had just starred in the widely celebrated film *The Elephant Man*, I was excited to meet Ken Norton. Standing next to the massive boxer as he towered over me seemed to put my whole life in perspective, and I remember that as we shook hands, it felt like my digits were being enveloped by a huge Hormel ham!

My main goal on that flight to New York was to come up with an amazing list of questions for John and Yoko. We'd been warned well in advance that asking about John's time with the Beatles was a definite no-no, so as I wrote out my thoughts regarding the recording process and inspiration behind the various songs on *Double Fantasy*, I also shuffled through the *Playboy* magazine interview with Lennon that had just hit the newsstands, and with each page I became more and more convinced that I was about to be torn to shreds by my idol. It seemed to me that John had not only been adamant about talking to the writer about not wanting to talk about the Beatles, but his past in general, and I began to get the scary feeling that we were all about to be slammed by his superior intellect and wit.

I knew also that his personality was notoriously complex, and the last thing I wanted was for him to think that I was some foolish, undereducated fangirl who still saw him as "the smart Beatle" while letting stupid questions with obvious answers pour from my mouth.

Fortunately, I was able to get over at least some of my insecurities. That night before the interview, the four of us from RKO and the record company were all sitting up together as though we were having a slumber party in one of our rooms at The Plaza hotel, drinking hot chocolate and savoring the moment as we nailed down last-minute details. This helped me see myself as more than ready. Staying at The Plaza was especially exciting and coincidental considering that nearly seventeen years before, Beatles manager Brian Epstein had booked himself and the band there for their very first US hotel stay, arriving at New York's Kennedy Airport just a couple days prior to their debut appearance on *The Ed Sullivan Show*.

While we waited in John and Yoko's outer office the next day for our interview to get underway, their assistants filled us in on what the couple had been up to so far that morning, letting us know that they were just finishing up with photographer Annie Leibovitz from *Rolling Stone* magazine. Leibovitz had spent the last couple of hours upstairs with them snapping pictures, including one that would become the most iconic shot ever of the famous couple—a naked John Lennon curled up on the carpet in a fetal position wrapped around a fully clothed Yoko Ono, which basically defined the very nature of their relationship.

I'd actually had my own encounter—okay, more like a run-in—

with Annie Leibovitz just a couple of years earlier in Seattle. As a radio news anchor/reporter at KING-AM, the major Top 40 station in town at the time, I had been begged by a local publicist to attend the famous photographer's University of Washington show opening and then do a quick interview with her that would air as part of my newscast the next day. Even though I had to be at work before five o'clock the next morning, I sat in the audience that night throughout Annie's lengthy lecture and then approached her afterward. But instead of being appreciative and accommodating, Leibovitz loudly accused me of lying through my teeth, asking why in the world anyone would book a radio interview with a photographer! I was mortified, and got away from her as fast as I could.

Despite my initial reaction so many months later when I learned that Annie Leibovitz was working right upstairs with John and Yoko, I was certainly not about to let the possibility of running into her at the Dakota dampen my spirits in the least! No worries, though—fortunately I was never forced to encounter the photographer again.

Our team was ushered into an incredible room that turned out to be Yoko's (and, to a lesser extent, John's) private office so that we could get set up for the interview. The first thing I noticed was the fluffy white wall-to-wall shag carpeting, which almost made me wish I was barefoot, and we were all asked to take our shoes off before entering. The next thing that caught my eye was this spectacular, superlong, glass-topped coffee table framed in metal, with serpents winding their way up and around each of the legs. I remember that as I looked at these man-made snakes through the glass off and on during the entire interview, I had this surreal feeling of "Am I really here? With John and Yoko?" No doubt about it: I was living a dream, and I was more than just a tiny bit scared that I'd suddenly wake up to find out I was imagining the whole thing.

RKO engineer/producer Ron Hummel was busy taking out his tape deck and other equipment just as Yoko joined us, introducing herself and seeming very happy to see me, a female, as part of our otherwise all-male team.

I felt a connection right off the bat, not just because we were both women, but also because I'd always been intrigued by her avant-garde approach to art and music, even if I didn't actually understand the meaning of her conceptual art or exactly what she was trying to say with some of her early, experimental music. But I was inspired by the way she'd never back down, even while becoming a controversial figure blamed by 99.9 percent of the rock/pop music-loving public for breaking up the Beatles. In other words, I was in awe.

And so our pre-interview kicked off with Yoko telling us that John was just finishing up with Leibovitz but would be down shortly. While waiting for Ron to mic her up, I whipped out the silly little mechanical windup toy I'd picked up in San Francisco's Chinatown—a fire-breathing dragon that I thought Sean, their five-year-old son, would have a lot of fun with. Yoko was sure John himself would absolutely fall in love with it, and she was totally right on. When John spotted it later, he immediately grabbed it and wound it up, watching the dragon travel the entire length of the glass coffee table top while the two of them laughed like crazy, both he and Yoko saying how much Sean would enjoy it—that is, if they ever actually gave it to him rather than keeping it themselves.

Another item I'd brought along with me was my personal copy of *Grapefruit*, a 1970 edition of Yoko's 1964 conceptual-art and poetry book featuring, as it said right under her glowing portrait on the cover, "Works and Drawings by Yoko Ono" and an "Introduction by John Lennon." I'd picked up the book years before on the bargain table at Cody's, Berkeley's popular Telegraph Avenue bookstore, never imagining that I'd be sitting with the author herself a mere four years later, waiting for her former-Beatle husband to join us.

Once Ron had Yoko's microphone in place, the two of us gals chatted on tape about the relationship between men and women in society and the pressing need to open up a new dialogue between the sexes. Dave Sholin, the RKO executive who'd made sure I was included in the interview in the first place and was naturally just as thrilled as I was to be there, joined in, as did Warner Bros. Records' Bert Keane, who'd been instrumental in pulling the whole event together. And so there we were, the four of us plus Yoko, when suddenly there was a knock at the door. As it opened slightly, just a couple of inches, the first thing I saw was John Lennon's trademark round glasses and his nose sticking through the crack. When he opened the door all the way, I turned toward him and, in my typical, smart-ass fashion, looked right at him and asked under my breath, "Can't you see we're in the middle of an interview?"

He looked at me and laughed out loud, and when Yoko did too, I thought to myself, *Everything's okay! We're gonna have a good time here!*

John introduced himself to our group and sat down right next to me on the small loveseat to join in the conversation. My brain began to explode—ME, sitting next to JOHN LENNON— unfrickingbelievable! How in the world this could ever happen was totally beyond my comprehension, and as I made my best effort to stay in the moment, I realized that this interview could very well be the milestone event that would define not only the rest of my career, but no doubt my entire life!

I had no way of knowing at the time that this was to become John's final interview, mere hours before he was shot and killed just outside this same building later that very evening. While countless books and bios have been published since on the life and times of John Lennon, none of those authors spent that ill-fated day with John and Yoko, nor were any of them confronted later on and literally forced into a conversation like I was with the beyond-creepy character who was about to become his assassin. He refused to get out of my way, stepping right in my path as I tried to walk away from the Dakota hours later, while obnoxiously asking me, "Did you talk to him? Did you get his autograph?" over and over and over.

For years I've beat myself up about this, wondering why I didn't realize there was something seriously off about him and, even more importantly, why I didn't sense that he was at that very moment carrying the gun that he would use to murder John Lennon before the night was over? The guilt has been hanging heavily over my head for more than forty years.

To my mind, this is what makes me the right person to tell her singular story as the half-century anniversary of the tragic event that affected so many lives, including my own, approaches. As a young rock radio reporter/writer/producer sitting at the Dakota that day with John Lennon and Yoko Ono, I'd guessed right about the life-altering nature of our interview, but what I couldn't even begin to imagine was that this unparalleled episode would not only dramatically change the course of my life and career, but my psyche as well. To this day, when I mention interviewing John Lennon on the former Beatle's last day on the planet, the response is nearly always the same—jaws drop, people gasp, and the inevitable question is asked: "When are you going to write your book, Laurie?"

The answer is NOW.

Here I am on ABC *20/20*'s "John Lennon: His Life, Legacy, Last Days," which aired in October 2020, just after I had started writing my book. (Photo by Brenda Rippee)

—CHAPTER 2—

"The Winner Takes It All"

The event that sent me rockin' down my career path and eventually into the Dakota Apartments to meet up with John and Yoko had actually taken place just about seven years before, during my senior year in high school.

It was January 1973, and my seventeen-year-old self and good buddy Allen were sitting in his brother's pickup truck, actually a white El Camino, parked on the street outside our urban West Los Angeles campus midday on a Thursday. We'd both just uncharacteristically cut class to listen to LA's number one FM radio station, KMET, conduct the live drawing for five sets of tickets to the upcoming Rolling Stones Nicaragua Benefit concert—four of which would be for that night at Inglewood's "Fabulous Forum," while the fifth would be for a Stones concert in Honolulu. With fingers crossed, I held my breath, praying desperately that my name would come up as one of the five winners out of what had to be hundreds of hopeful contest finalists. Allen had borrowed the truck from his older brother on the slim chance that was exactly what would happen, as I'd promised to make him my date to the show if I won. No matter how nervous I was about the outcome, or about getting caught off campus and being busted when I was supposed to be in class, I was prepared to sit tight and wait it out until the moment when the fifth and final winning name would be called.

After dragging out his intro to build up as much suspense as possible, the KMET-FM disc jockey finally picked the first winner's name out of the hat. The moment he read it out loud, I began to panic—it wasn't mine. But there were four more to go, I told myself, so no giving up yet! And sure enough, the second name he called out was LAURIE KAYE—I won!

Little did I know it at the time, but thanks to this victory, my life was about to change in ways I couldn't even begin to fathom.

The Stones' *Exile on Main Street* was the rock album of the hour, even if critical response when it was first released back in May 1972 was less than stellar. But die-hard fans and newbies alike were entranced by the band's musical diversity—from rock 'n' roll to rockin' country and back again. And the fact that it was Keith Richards rather than Mick Jagger singing lead on "Happy" was a super big bonus. *Exile* had been recorded in the basement of Keith's mansion on the French Riviera amid stories of massive heroin abuse, so the fact that the album even made it out of the makeshift studio and onto the charts was amazing.

Wherehouse Records in Westwood Village was my local go-to for all the latest albums during those junior high/high school days. My friends and I would run there the minute we heard on the radio that Elton John, Neil Young, a former Beatle, or any of our other early seventies faves were dropping new vinyl. Wherehouse was a huge corner store with attention-grabbing window displays featuring all the latest major-label releases, and we spent hours at a time after school or on weekends digging through discs in the hopes of making a major musical discovery. But I had managed to score my copy of *Exile on Main Street* another way—in a KMET-FM call-in giveaway, one of many I dialed into back in the day in the hope of not just winning whatever it was they were handing out, but also getting to speak with whichever disc jockey was on the air at that time. Those cool FM DJs were my heroes. Not only did their voices sound thick and rich, but these DJs also were exposed to the best music long before I was, and each one of them seemed to take great joy in sharing it with me and all the rest of their LA listeners.

Plus, they seemed to be privy to all the stories behind the artists' studio recording sessions and where they took place. But most importantly, these DJs were able to introduce me to a number of artists whose early output catapulted me into other musical realms and who became some of my absolute favorites—Lou Reed and David Bowie included.

Both Bowie and Reed in particular turned out to be important musical introductions. Not only did I end up seeing Bowie live over the years more than I did almost any other performer, but much to my elation, I also got to interview him later on in my career. And Lou Reed became part of my first major video production gig in Los Angeles, when I was hired to coordinate the shoot for his and Sam Moore's title track for the 1986 movie *Soul Man!*

This music video turned out to be extra exciting, since I was able to not only hang out with both Lou and Sam all day in the recording studio, but also meet up with others who'd been booked, including Cassandra Peterson (supersexy TV horror movie hostess Elvira), Frank Zappa, and Stevie Ray Vaughan. Unfortunately, Zappa wasn't feeling good enough to perform, so we headed over to West Hollywood's Chateau Marmont hotel to work with Vaughan. We waited quite a while before Stevie arrived at the hotel's outdoor pool area, but this was several months before he'd become clean and sober. He was superhigh and claimed he had no idea he was supposed to be taking part in our "Soul Man" music video. As I tried to talk him into it, Stevie looked down at the shoes he was wearing and surprised me by saying, "No way! My boots have more sole/soul than Lou Reed!" Wow!

Unfortunately, during high school I was somewhat limited in my ability to call in to KMET to take part in its frequent contests. My stinker of a stepfather refused to let me have a telephone in my own room. He didn't just deny me my own number, but even went so far as to say no to my multiple requests for an extension phone. When I wanted to talk to anyone, I had to take or make calls on the living room telephone, or if he and and my mother weren't home or happened to be in their bedroom, I was able to drag that phone by its long, tangled cord into my own room, close the door, and finally have a bit of privacy. If I happened to be home late in the day, which I usually wasn't thanks to various after-school jobs, like my stint behind the counter at the local McDonald's, I could dial up a KMET DJ as soon as those afternoon call-in contests were announced. But what actually worked best for me was setting my alarm clock for the wee hours of the morning so that I could wake up at two or three o'clock, even on a school day, and quietly sneak out of bed and into the living room to bring in the phone. I would then turn on the radio, which I almost always had on anyway whenever I was home and hiding out in my room—unless of course I was playing an album—and wait for the late-night DJ to announce a call-in. I soon discovered that competition was much less fierce in the middle of the night. That was how I happened to be the number one caller and winner of my very own copy of *Exile on Main Street*, a recent release that I'd been dying to hear in its entirety, since not only wasn't it getting the airplay it deserved, but it was also a double album with so many songs on it besides its singles that demanded my attention. When the album was delivered, I was in heaven . . . but little did I know how much more was in store.

Not long after that, just before Christmas '72, a huge earthquake hit Managua, Nicaragua, leaving thousands dead and hundreds of thousands homeless. Legendary concert promoter Bill Graham, who just a few years later would become instrumental in my San Francisco live-music experience, decided to stage a benefit concert to bring relief funds to the desperate country. He enlisted the Rolling Stones, which made sense because Mick's wife, Bianca, was from Nicaragua, as was the timbales player in Santana, the band that would become the Stones' opening act. Then Cheech and Chong signed on too, and the Nicaragua Benefit concert was set for January 18, 1973, at the venue known as the "Fabulous Forum" in Inglewood, which was THE major large indoor LA rock concert venue.

Tickets sold like crazy at an average price of under twenty dollars except for the very best seats in the house, which were going for an at-the-time-outrageous price of one hundred dollars per. When those expensive tickets didn't immediately sell out, prices were reduced, and apparently a number of them were turned into KMET giveaways, and the radio station made a huge deal out of it. Not only did all the KMET DJs offer nonstop call-in contests so that their listeners could win a chance to score a pair of tickets in one big on-air drawing to be held the day of the show, but the station also included everyone who had previously called in and won a copy of *Exile on Main Street* in its pool of potential winners, so I automatically had a shot.

I was beyond excited, because in my heart of hearts I somehow knew my name would be called and I would be a ticket winner. The only problem was that the drawing was going to be held mere hours before the show, on a Thursday, a school day. Not only would I have to cut class and find a radio somewhere to listen to the announcement, but I would also need to figure out how to make my way midday to KMET in the Miracle Mile/mid-Wilshire district to pick up my prize.

I didn't have a car or even know how to drive. The same stepfather who refused to let me have my own extension phone of course also had kept me from getting behind the wheel or even, for that matter, taking drivers ed in high school the year before. So I enlisted my friend to help out, with the promise of making him my escort to the show. That was how my buddy Allen became my coconspirator, borrowing his brother's pickup truck and parking on the street that day outside the gates of University High School—aka Uni—so we could both ditch school at the same time, climb into the truck, cross our fingers, and listen to the drawing go down on the radio.

When they announced they were giving away tickets to the Stones' benefit show in LA as well as tickets plus airfare and hotel to the upcoming Hawaii concert, of course I was determined to be the big winner and get an exotic Hawaiian mini-vacation along with a Rolling Stones concert. So when the disc jockey started to pull the names of the ticket winners out of his hat, or whatever he was using to hold what had to be hundreds of bits of paper with contestants' contact info, Allen and I were practically holding our breath waiting to hear the results. At least I was. For a split second I was almost disappointed to hear "Laurie Kaye" called out as the second winning name. Dang it! I wanted to be name number five and win that Hawaii trip, despite the fact that since I was under eighteen, there's no doubt no way I ever would have been able to go. But hey, I still *won*, and the next step would be driving over to the radio station as fast as possible to pick up those tickets!

Allen navigated the streets, and we made it to KMET in record time—just about twenty minutes. We parked right outside the building on Wilshire and dashed inside for what I expected to be a quick exchange—something like, "Hi, I'm Laurie Kaye, I won tickets to the Stones. Thank you very much!" But instead we were told that disc jockey B. Mitchel Reed wanted to hand my prize to me personally ON THE AIR and introduce me to his listeners, which both shocked and thrilled me at the same time. Reed was not just an FM radio pioneer but a Top 40 vet as well, and possibly my biggest hero on the station known as the Mighty Met, which was responsible for introducing me to the album rock radio format. I had no idea that I'd be lucky enough to actually meet him, let alone have him personally hand me the pair of tickets to the Rolling Stones that would have the potential to change the course of my life. While Allen waited in the lobby, I was ushered into the studio, where B. Mitchel Reed—aka the Beamer—stood up to meet me. After asking my name, how old I was, and where I was from, he told me that with a voice like mine, I should definitely be on the radio!

WOW! I thanked him profusely, took the tickets, and floated out of that studio on cloud nine.

By the time I arrived at the Forum in the rain several hours later, my feet still hadn't hit the ground. We managed to make it (admittedly somewhat impatiently) through Santana's set, which was more like a lengthy jam session than a performance showcasing its hit singles, as the bulk of the audience—including me—seemed to believe it should have been. While ready and restlessly waiting for the main attraction, we still found ourselves chuckling along with Cheech and Chong before working our way through a never-ending intermission that seriously seemed to last forever.

When the Rolling Stones finally hit the stage, I was in ecstasy, and not just due to the incredible group of musicians playing and singing their hearts out right in front of me. It was also thanks to the way they looked, especially Mick Jagger in his glam-rock, glitter jumpsuit and headband. As an amateur but quite talented photographer, my friend Allen had brought along his camera and wasted no time in taking a ton of pictures.

To this day, whenever I look at those black-and-white stage shots of his, I'm instantly transported back to that place and time. It also

The Rolling Stones Nicaragua Benefit. (Photo by Allen Lavee)

became a barely believable thrill just a handful of years later to be able to tell Mick during our conversation for the rock radio special I was writing, *Top 100 of the 70's*, just how meaningful his Nicaragua benefit concert event had been to me.

By the time the Stones' cool, commanding set came to a close with an encore of "Midnight Rambler," the crowd had gone crazy.

Yes, the concert that night was incredible. I was no longer a virgin when it came to experiencing the Rolling Stones live, but being invited into the KMET broadcast booth was possibly an even bigger win. B. Mitchel Reed passed away about ten years later, but he still lives on in my heart. Even though I had just met him and barely spent six minutes in his company, he managed to instill in me the confidence I so badly needed to tackle life head-on going forward.

And so it was that brief visit with the Beamer that inspired me to take the next necessary step in my personal evolution—I wasted no time plotting my second attempt to leave home. I'd tried to become a successful teenage runaway once before, but this time I was determined to iron out all the kinks and seriously make it stick.

I began by spending the next couple of months pinching pennies as hard as I could, saving up to get my own place so that I'd be able to get out of the hell house (actually a series of cheap West Los Angeles apartments) I'd been living in miserably since my mother married her domineering second husband almost a decade before. We'd both been fighting with him and each other constantly ever since. I'd already been accepted into a cool, so-called hippie college (UCSC—the University of California at Santa Cruz) starting in September, but that was still months away. I knew I needed to be on my own and free from pointless parental (and stepparental) restraint ASAP. So again, I enlisted the help of a male friend—this time my dear longtime pal Greg, who, along with his family's huge, ancient station wagon, came over after school one day when both my mom and her husband were at work to help pack all my things into that roomy old car and take me to my official new digs.

I'd lied about my age and paid in advance to reserve a spot in a room at UCLA co-op apartments in Westwood just the week before. I even had a UCLA student ID to verify my "eligibility" and help spin my story, since I'd been in a special program for advanced-placement students at Uni High that allowed us to take classes on the UCLA campus. So when my mother came home from work that night, it was fairly obvious that I'd finally escaped. My room was pretty much empty except for the furniture, and all the walls were stripped bare. I'd taken down and rolled up all of my favorite rock posters, including the live shot of Leon Russell that had been hanging over the head of my bed for well over a year despite the fact that my mother said it scared her to death because she thought he looked like Satan.

But now, like my Leon Russell poster, I was nowhere to be found. I decided that all I really needed to leave behind was a brief note letting the folks know that no, I wouldn't be coming home again. I also purposely neglected to let them know when my upcoming high school graduation would be taking place, since I definitely wasn't about to invite them. And I certainly wasn't going to tell them where I'd moved, just in case they tried to send the cops out to catch me, since, after all, I wasn't just a minor but a teen runaway to boot.

In all honesty, even back then I suspected that my mother and stepfather were as eager to get me out of their day-to-day lives as I was to make my escape. And so that was it. My teenage ticket to freedom came thanks to KMET, DJ B. Mitchel Reed, and the prize he had handed me: a pair to the Rolling Stones!

—CHAPTER 3—

"Raised on Radio"

Flashing even further back in time, my story as it relates to the music in my life actually starts with a tiny red plastic transistor radio straight out of my grandparents' Huntington Park (southeast LA) jewelry store. Sure, Nana and Papa's huge shop had plenty of showcases filled with diamonds, rubies, and pearls as well as tons of flashy costume jewelry, but the only thing this pop-obsessed preschooler craved was my very own mini-radio to glue to my ear like all the older kids I saw on the street. I wanted to connect with my early on-air idols—the disc jockeys on AM radio stations KRLA and KHJ, who seemed to know everything about the songs they played and the celebrated artists who made them.

From Papa I got my first taste of female hitmaking: Connie Francis singing "Where the Boys Are" in what he called "that cry in her voice" that he loved so much, coming from the wooden-cabinet radio that sat in the corner of my grandparents' bedroom for so many years. They kept a record player in their living room back then too, with Nana's *My Fair Lady* Broadway-cast album and my own very first 45, Alvin and the Chipmunks' "Ragtime Cowboy Joe," constantly spinning in heavy rotation.

From the time I was born, I'd grown up living with, and being cared for, primarily by my grandparents, sharing a room in their two-bedroom apartment with my unmarried, divorced mother until I was about six. As my grandmother admitted years ago, although the first word to come out of the mouths of most babies is "Mama," she fully expected mine would be "Nana." She was wrong, though—MY first word turned out to be "wamamu," which was the closest I could come as a tot to asking for a bite of my number one favorite food: watermelon. And yes, wamamu is still my fave!

Also to this day, thanks to Nana, I still sing "Just you wait, 'enry 'iggins, just you wait" every time I feed my dogs, exactly like Julie Andrews taught me to do on the *My Fair Lady* album so many years ago. Another thing Nana did quite often was watch TV shows featuring live performances . . . everything from Lawrence Welk's weekly music variety series to a number of broadcasts featuring a one-of-a-kind, rather large female jazz singer she absolutely adored, whose name I thought I heard the show hosts say was Elephant Gerald. Of course, I was wrong; it was Ella Fitzgerald, whom I ended up seeing perform on my own for a number of summers at the Hollywood Bowl when I was older.

My mother was strictly a Sinatra fan, with Frank always blasting from her own large-knobbed rotary-dial radio sitting on the nightstand in our bedroom. But none of those big music machines (or artists) really did it for me. I was a little kid coming into my own at the dawn of the sixties, with an instant crush on those teensy, portable, popular Sonys stacked in the rear display case of the family jewelry store. I wanted one of those radio babies more than anything, and finally, after hinting, waiting, and yep, even begging, I did get a transistor radio of my own. From that day forward, my fate was sealed. Now I could curl up under the covers at night, put my earplugs in, and secretly listen to the music that meant everything to me—an experience I imagine millions of other kids around my age were having at the same time.

I let the music carry me away from the reality of my fatherless existence and into another world, one where the cool kids could teach me how to "twist again like we did last summer" while also reassuring me to "hush my darling, don't fear my darling" because they knew that "in the jungle, the mighty jungle, the lion sleeps tonight." This is when hit song lyrics began to have a profound effect on my life.

My mother spent her daytime hours back then in a series of unsatisfying office jobs, although she truthfully was unemployed more often than not. It was during those jobless days that she was forced to become the babysitter she never wanted to be, tackling the role of sole caretaker of a toddler/preschooler who basically got in the way of everything she *really* wanted to do, whether it was window-shopping at Saks Fifth Avenue in Beverly Hills, hanging out on Hollywood's star-studded Sunset Boulevard., or talking on the telephone for hours on end with her fellow single girlfriends, which she felt comfortable doing only when she could be completely alone in our bedroom.

She came up with some creative ways to keep an eye on me while still having the room all to herself, including one bizarre game she invented that I would eventually look back on as Jesus on the Cross. When she wanted some space, Mom would tell me to lie on my back on the living room carpet with my arms outspread like a crucifix; then she'd pretend to nail me to the floor while informing me that I couldn't get up until she'd pulled out every last nail she'd hammered into me. Then she'd disappear into our bedroom and yak on the phone for what seemed like hours while I lay on the floor too terrified to move even an inch to the right or left, let alone try to stand up. I passed the time by singing to myself, sometimes reaching the point of breaking down in tears.

One early evening, after abandoning me on the living room carpet for an especially long time, my mother was still wrapped up in her phone conversation when my grandparents came home from work. As Nana unlocked the door to the apartment, she heard me crying and calling out my mother's name, so she hurried in and found me lying there sobbing. She demanded to know what the hell was going on. I told her, and rather than a sympathetic response, her immediate reaction was "Get up, you fool!" Then she ran into the next room to chew out her daughter, and as I heard them screaming at each other, I had no one to blame but myself.

Thanks to episodes like this, it was obvious my mother wanted nothing more than to get out of that living situation and into her own apartment. Of course, what she really wanted was to meet and marry a man who could take care of her both romantically and financially so that she would never have to work again, and she was definitely ready to head out on her own to enhance her dating prospects as well. Unfortunately for her, she had me, an almost-in-elementary-school albatross around her neck, to drag along wherever she would end up.

What finally sealed the deal as far as our move away from my grandparents' place was a terrifying event that happened one morning as my mother and I walked from their upstairs apartment down to the building's parking lot facing Venice Boulevard so that she could drop me off at my daycare center before heading to her job in Hollywood. Mom had a beautiful, nearly new Chevy Impala that my grandfather had bought for her at the Felix Chevrolet just east of where we were living. Even back then, Felix Chevrolet was LA's oldest auto dealership, and it famously featured the cartoon character Felix the Cat on a huge, three-sided neon sign standing way up on its roof. My mother loved her giant white car with a passion, and I'm pretty sure it helped give the impression that she was the sophisticated, entitled, twenty-something young woman she so desperately wanted to be seen as.

As we headed over to her car that early morning, I heard my mother scream in horror. Her magnificent white vehicle was littered with at least a dozen slaughtered, oozing rats, with huge swastikas painted in their blood all over the hood, windshield, and sides of the car! Not a single other automobile in the lot had been touched, just hers, as she was possibly the lone Jew parked there (my grandparents had driven off much earlier to their jewelry store). Mom and I headed straight back up to the apartment, and both of us spent the entire morning crying and freaking out before eventually heading over to Earl Scheib for one of the company's infamous $29.95 auto paint jobs, since the Jew-hating bloody mess and rodent carnage had refused to come off in the wash.

That was my first brush with anti-Semitism, followed not too long after by another: a group of second-grade churchgoing girls confronted me at school one day during recess, saying their parents would never let them play with me because I'd killed Jesus. My mother's reaction, when I told her through my tears what they'd said, was to suggest that I go right up to them the next day and admit, "Yeah, you're right. I *did* kill Jesus . . . and *you're next!*"

The week after the auto attack, my mother and I went back to Earl Scheib to pick up what should have been her sparkling, snow-white, nearly new-looking Impala, but that wasn't what happened—what they had waiting instead was a powder blue version of her beloved car. Somehow there'd been a mix-up, with Mom's Chevy becoming the colorful victim of an auto paint error. They offered to make good on their mistake and repaint her car, but to my mother, this was obviously the last straw. No doubt she knew deep down that she could never look at her Chevy Impala again without seeing those hideous bloody swastikas and dead rats, so she decided at that moment to put her car up for sale and start apartment hunting in order to get as far away from any reminder of the scene of that disgusting incident as soon as possible.

Within a couple of weeks, mother and daughter were packed up and ready to move into a tiny one-bedroom on National Boulevard just off of Robertson Boulevard in West Los Angeles—not the best neighborhood at the time by any means, but Mom seemed to think it was affordable, or at least it would be with ongoing contributions from her father. Oddly enough, this was the very same Papa who'd been telling me falsely for years that I was one of the richest little girls in the world. Every time we'd drive by the miles of local oil fields off of La Cienega Boulevard, he would point to one of the oil wells and say, "That one's yours, Laurie. You'll never have to worry about money as long as you live!" Of course, even back then I realized he was pointing at a different well every single time we passed the oil fields, but I had no choice but to believe him—after all, he was Papa.

Nana was dead set against our move, and not just because she wanted to keep her eyes on us, especially my immature single mother, who'd never lived on her own before. Since our new apartment sat directly next door to a gas station, Nana wasted no time in letting us know that one day it would explode and our entire building would go up in flames, probably taking us along with it. We moved in regardless, and—true story—less than a week after we moved out one year later, the gas station *did* blow up! Our apartment building wasn't destroyed, but still, what a prediction.

Honestly, my mother *loved* living next door to the gas station, since it meant that instead of having to double down on the nasty cigarette butts that lived in her ashtrays when she was out of smokes (or, worse yet, the butts she'd thrown in the toilet but had forgotten to flush away the night before), she could hand her six-year-old daughter thirty-five cents on a Saturday morning while she was busy yakking on the phone with one of her girlfriends and send me to the station's cigarette machine to pick her up a pack of Pall Malls. Quite convenient, and no one at the gas station ever batted an eye, even when I lied and jokingly told one attendant the smokes were for me. As far as my mother was concerned, the only problem with having her own apartment was that now she needed to accept one-hundred-percent responsibility for my well-being. There were no more in-house grandparents to pick up groceries, cook dinner, or even watch over me when she wasn't around. When it came to babysitters, I'm sure my mother hated the very concept of paying someone to care for me, especially at night, when all I'd be doing was listening to my transistor radio, watching TV, or sleeping. That's one reason I rarely, if ever, had any restrictions on what I could or couldn't see on the small screen. *The Twilight Zone* and *Alfred Hitchcock Presents* may not seem like suitable programming for a six-year-old, but both shows were regular weekly events for me back then, whether I was watching with my mother or on my own. Another TV show I always wanted to watch was *Father Knows Best*, the popular network series starring Robert Young and Jane Wyatt, but given my mother's disrespectful attitude regarding the dude she married who'd impregnated and dumped her several years before, she referred to it as *Father Knows Nothing* and discouraged me from turning it on. Mom's friends were fairly shocked to find out she'd be leaving me home alone when they were heading out for the evening, and they often encouraged her to make other plans or sometimes even include me in theirs. That's how I ended up one night in the backseat of her best friend's car at a popular drive-in movie theater as my mother and a couple of her pals went to a late-night screening of Hitchcock's *Psycho*. Of course, I was supposed to be sound asleep, but I stayed awake, my eyes wide open, captivated by the entire film. It was this experience that led to my serious fear of showering, which lasted well into my teens.

Fast forward a couple of years: my mother eloped and married her second husband on New Year's Eve in Las Vegas, and our lives would never be the same. Although we weren't under my grandparents' roof anymore, now that my mom and I were living with her new husband she actually felt even more controlled and oppressed, and from the very start I bore the brunt of her new burden.

The stepfather situation proved to be simply the worst. Besides telling me from the start on an almost daily basis that I was a nobody who would never amount to anything and shouldn't even bother to think about wasting money on going to college, he was repressive and downright mean. Rather than speak up for me and risk losing another husband, my mother told me to just shut my mouth and take it, but when it got to be too much even for her, she would run out to her car and sit there for hours convulsively crying, with her head bumping up and down on the steering wheel. Of course I felt terribly sorry for her, and therefore I tried to placate her new husband as much as an eight-year-old could, but still, I never felt I could truly be myself unless I was as far away (physically and/or mentally) from both of them as possible.

One positive thing my new stepfather did bring to the table—or actually to the living room of our first shared apartment—was one of those long, wooden stereo console cabinets that seemed to take up the length of the entire wall. It came complete with a handful of jazz albums, which was a musical genre I'd yet to be exposed to. While he and my mother added some Sinatra to their tiny vinyl collection, there was no music I could really relate to. For that, I relied heavily on my own precious transistor radio as well as the memorable singles and albums owned by my friends, or more likely their older siblings. This was everything from Elvis's double-A-side 45 "Little Sister" backed by "(Marie's the Name) His Latest Flame" to Hayley Mills's "Let's Get Together," with the B side that became my personal favorite, the sweet, sexy "Cobbler, Cobbler," based on a classic British nursery rhyme.

My mother definitely was not an Elvis Presley fan, so I'd have to wait until movies like *Jailhouse Rock* and *King Creole* made it to television before experiencing any of his early films. Fortunately, the original version of *The Parent Trap*, with Hayley Mills playing a pair of teenage twins, was a movie I did get to see in the theater, and when I heard Hayley sing "Cobbler, cobbler, mend my shoe/I've been dancing the whole night through/I've got such a strange romance/Because the boy I love is crazy to dance," she became my first female musical idol.

From that moment on, whenever I heard "Cobbler, Cobbler," all I could think about was how long I would have to wait before I could finally play records myself with a boy I loved and dance with him until my shoes wore out just like Hayley's.

Plenty more early-sixties films followed, since whenever my mother wanted to spend Saturdays hanging out with her girlfriends and/or going clothes shopping, she once again refused to hire a babysitter, instead dropping me off at a local movie theater in time for the midmorning double feature. Not only was this supercheap, but with an audience made up mainly of young kids and their mothers, she no doubt felt that it was a totally safe environment for her own solo child.

My ultimate matinee moviegoing experience came a couple of years later, in the summer of '64, when a few friends and I arrived ultraearly and waited in line for what seemed like hours to see the film we'd been looking forward to for months: the Beatles' *A Hard Day's Night*. The place was packed with teenagers—almost all girls, naturally—and the moment the movie finally started, so did the shrill screaming and sing-alongs. This made it difficult for us to follow not just the film's plot, but also whatever any of the Beatles were trying to say or sing. So some of us hid in the bathroom as the movie was coming to a close and then snuck back in to grab seats for the next show, with what unfortunately turned out to be an even noisier crowd. Luckily, we didn't get caught.

Those unescorted Saturday matinees featuring films like those from the Gidget series, including *Gidget Goes Hawaiian* and *Gidget Goes to Rome*, starring the dashing James Darren as dreamy Malibu surfer Moondoggie, made a lasting impression on me. What a kick to go to high school years later with his son Jim. Although I barely knew him, he was the closest I'd ever come to meeting the original Moondoggie, the sexy surfer of my dreams.

My attraction to surfers and hanging out on the beach even then was pretty much a given. It all started back when I was five years old and my single mother would take me to Muscle Beach in Venice, where she would use me to meet men. Our typical summer-day scenario featured Mom stretched out on her beach towel on the sand, slathering her superlong, shapely legs with baby oil. Then she'd tell me to *get lost*—literally. The idea was to have me walk as far away as I could while looking for attractive guys to ask to help me find my mother, who would then waste no time in showing off her sexy, suntanned gams as she flirted outrageously with them. Rather than feeling like I was being used as Mama's little pimp, I was actually pretty proud of her. In my eyes, she was always the best-looking lady sitting on the sand, and I wanted to grow up and be the exact same type of beach bunny.

But the beach, and even the Beach Boys, whom I'd discovered thanks to their songs on the radio starting with "Surfin' Safari" back in '62, had to take a back seat once the Beatles exploded onto the scene. As a young girl, I would camp out with friends in their bedrooms for entire afternoons spinning singles and singing along with the lads from Liverpool while dreaming of being a teenager and getting kissed by Paul McCartney. Remarkably, this was something I had the opportunity to tell Sir Paul in person many years later, following our 1979 RKO Radio interview in London, where, yes, I got kissed by him!

Like just about every other kid my age, including all my music-loving elementary-school girlfriends, I found that Beatles lyrics became implanted in my brain from the moment I first heard them, whether on vinyl 45s (seven-inch singles) going round and round on someone's portable record player or broadcast over the airwaves on whichever local AM radio station my transistor happened to be tuned to. This would no doubt have been either KHJ or KRLA, my two favorite Top 40 stations in the early and mid-sixties. My friends and I were able to memorize Beatles lyrics without even trying back in those days simply by listening to the same song over and over before moving on to the next—even if, like "Komm gib mir deine Hand" and "Sie liebt dich," they happened to be in German. The truth is, those Fab Four Deutsche versions of "I Want to Hold Your Hand" and "She Loves You" were the real reason I would make German my foreign language of choice in junior high, high school, and even college classes. I guess I figured that if it was good enough for John, Paul, George, and Ringo, who was I to argue, although I suppose I could have made a case for studying French based on their beautiful *Rubber Soul* tune "Michelle" as well.

When it was announced that the Beatles were playing the Hollywood

Bowl in 1964, and then again in 1965, Top 40 radio airwaves were filled with nonstop Beatlemania, and it wasn't limited to music and interviews. The first on-air call-in contest I ever attempted to enter came thanks to an anonymous creative-marketing genius at one of my top-two radio stations. Someone must have paid off staff members or possibly even the housekeepers at one of the hotels or rented houses the Beatles were staying at prior to their performances, which resulted in swatches of Beatles' bedding being given away to a number of lucky fans who managed to get through on the phone line. These tiny pieces of fabric that members of the group had supposedly slept on seemed even more precious to me than the solid gold trinkets my grandparents sold at their jewelry store. I wanted nothing more than my own little bit of John Lennon linen, a patch of Paul McCartney pillowcase, a shred of Ringo Starr sheet, or a fragment of anything at all that George Harrison's head had rested on. Sadly, I didn't win a thing, and to this day I can't help but wonder if those Beatles bedroom treasures were the real deal. It would still be several years before I was allowed, or even able, to buy my own records. I didn't have the money to do so until I started babysitting, which I began at a very young age just for that purpose. I wasn't permitted to even touch my stepfather's stereo back in those early days either, so when I was home and wanted to hear music from a vinyl source, I had to rely on either of the adults in the apartment to play one of their records. This would usually be their copy of *The Lonely Bull*, the first LP from Herb Alpert and the Tijuana Brass, or, a while later, Ramsey Lewis's *Wade in the Water*, which I recall mainly for its cover of the Beatles' "Day Tripper."

One thing I'll always remember is hearing the Beatles' *White Album* at a junior high slumber party when it first came out a couple years later. The birthday girl's sister, a high school senior, had just bought it for herself but began playing it for us barely teenage young'uns while passing around a joint as well—my first time for both!

No doubt about it, music of almost any kind was the best way for me to get away from it all back then, at least until my number one escape opportunity finally came up: summer camp. For two weeks every year for five years straight, I went to Big Bear Mountain to live in a tent with like-minded Girl Scouts at Camp Osito Rancho, where the main activities were singing, hiking, singing, campfires, singing, washing dishes, and yes, more singing.

I was out hiking one hot afternoon with my fellow campers and our head counselor, all of us singing our camp song, "The Little Osito" ("The Little Teddy Bear") when suddenly someone screamed "SNAKE!" Before the rest of us could even react, our counselor had jabbed her forked snake stick into the ground on either side of the coiled rattler's head and taken her mini-axe out of its waistband holster and chopped the snake's head off. From there, she quickly cut off the snake's rattles, cut and peeled off its snakeskin, and then led us all back to camp to build a fire so that we could cook the snake. So yes, I've eaten rattlesnake meat—and yes, it tastes just like chicken (salty chicken, that is).

Actually, my most vivid Osito Rancho memory didn't even take place at camp. It started just before I left home to catch the bus that would take me away for my first summertime adventure. I'd been reminding my mother over and over to please, please, *please* remember to feed Buster, the sweet, bright-yellow parakeet my grandparents had given me, while I was gone. Buster lived in my bedroom in his cage by the window, and my mother swore she would, but to make doubly sure, I continued to remind her by sending postcards almost daily from camp. When I got home to our apartment weeks later, the first thing I did was run into my room to give little Buster some love. There *was* a parakeet in Buster's cage, but this one was blue! When I asked my mother what was going on, she looked at me like I was crazy and said, "What are you talking about? Buster's always been blue." What? I began to question my own sanity, but unfortunately I had no choice but to accept what she said. Then, the next year, after I went away to camp for the second time and returned home, Buster was green. Again my mother insisted my parakeet had always been that color, and again, there was nothing I could do but pretend to believe her. This was pretty much the nature of our relationship from that point on, since I realized even as a child that it was a lot easier to fake it rather than suffer the consequences of contradicting or criticizing her, especially when it came to her emotionally cruel and controlling husband.

One thing I have to admit about my stepfather is that as abusive as he was both verbally and mentally, he never physically struck me—that was strictly my mother's territory. Mom was a hard-core face smacker, and not just in the privacy of our own apartment. I remember being slapped so hard by her once while we were at the local supermarket that I actually fell to the ground, but no one shopping in our aisle even looked up, let alone dared say anything to her. What finally stopped the violence was the day I stood up to her as a junior high school student and said, "Really, Mom? I've been taking phys ed and doing push-ups all year. Don't you think I can hit you back just as hard?" Of course, I was scared to death this would backfire on me and I'd once again be a sobbing mess with a stinging red face, but it must have struck a note with her, because for some reason, she backed off and never smacked me again.

A full-length body shot of my wannabe-supermodel mother.
(Photo by John Robert Powers Modeling)

Obviously, I didn't have the same kind of relationship with my mother that so many of my close friends were fortunate enough to have with theirs, but how many other mothers showed up at their daughter's high school in hot pants, looking better than any teenager on campus? My five-foot-ten mom had been an aspiring fashion model since graduating from high school herself in Detroit. That's when she enrolled in the John Robert Powers talent academy and showed off her svelte physique and unbelievably long, sexy legs in a series of stunning portfolio photos.

Sadly, Mom's modeling career wasn't meant to be. Rather than encourage her, my grandmother insisted that her daughter drop everything and go to secretarial school while spending every free minute at the local Jewish community center looking for a suitable husband.

My mother did find one, or so she thought. He was an older man who fulfilled her number one criteria, which was the willingness to move immediately from Michigan to California to start a new life in the City of Angels, and that they did. Unfortunately, he left her high and dry once he found out just a few months later that she was pregnant. He even tried to push her out of the car when she gave him the news as they were sightseeing on Mulholland Drive shortly after their arrival. The father I never met wasted no time in abandoning my newly pregnant mother, literally taking everything with him when he split, from their car to her personal belongings, including jewelry. She discovered this when she came home from work one evening and found their small apartment ransacked.

That's all I knew about my real father for years. My mother had gone so far as to cut him out of all of their wedding pictures, so I didn't even realize how much I looked like him. Much like John Lennon, I barely had any contact at all with my birth father while growing up— in fact, I never, ever encountered him face-to-face. He did, however, respond to a letter I sent during my senior year in high school via the bank handling his child-support payments. He unexpectedly answered with a brief note, sending me a photo and offering to finally start up a relationship, only to disappear yet again when I answered.

Meanwhile, there was constant conflict with my mother's then-current husband, who refused to acknowledge me for whom and what I'd become in the years since he'd married my mother. Imagine asking a sixteen-year-old straight-A student taking multiple advanced placement classes why she thought she needed to go to college—did she consider herself too good to be a secretary, like her mother? In retrospect, the way he treated me was simply disgusting, which was exactly the nickname my best friend, Alice, gave my stepfather for years, all throughout junior high and high school, whenever she referred to him: *Disgusting!*

—CHAPTER 4—

Rock, Rock, "Rock 'n' Roll High School"

While still in junior high—actually, on the last day of classes before summer vacation—I somehow managed to break three of the metatarsal bones in my left foot by accidentally stepping into a sprinkler hole while heading home from school. My stepfather reacted as though I'd injured myself on purpose just to bankrupt him, since he and my mother apparently hadn't thought it necessary or worthwhile to include me on their health insurance policy. As a result, I had zero coverage, and the medical bill he received from the orthopedist, totaling several hundred dollars, was enough to send him into a fit of rage directed right at me all summer long.

To top it off, I had to hobble around in a cast almost up to my knee and hang out inside our apartment for weeks while all of my friends were off enjoying typical SoCal summertime activities. So I came up with a crazy scheme to keep my mind occupied and my best buddies close to my heart while secretly involving them in an underground game.

From who knows where, I'd acquired several packs of bright-yellow, banana-shaped stationery, which I opened up one morning as I planted myself in front of the ancient portable typewriter my grandparents had given me. I proceeded to write several handfuls of anonymous letters that I then sent to each and every one of my good friends, signing them all "The Mad Banana." I kept up these mystery mailings on a nearly weekly basis till summer came to a close, with my last anonymous note coinciding with the day the cast was finally cut off my left leg.

That's when the Mad Banana invited everyone on her mailing list to the Grand Reveal, or Grand Un-Peel, as it were, at one of our all-time-favorite meeting spots. This was the infamous inverted fountain on the south end of the UCLA campus, which my pals and I always referred to as "the ever-flushing toilet."

Eagerly but carefully, I made my way to meet up with my entire group of friends for the first time since my accident, and as I walked toward them, I could see they were pointing fingers at each other. Every single one of them was convinced they knew for sure exactly who was behind the whole whodunit. I couldn't hold it in any longer—I laughed and let out my secret, admitting once and for all that I was indeed the Mad Banana! That alter ego has stuck with me to this day and, I've always believed, will probably end up being what I'm remembered for the most.

That's no doubt why a little over a decade later, when I found myself at the Dakota sitting on the loveseat next to John Lennon and asking about initial reaction to his and Yoko's first record together, *Two Virgins*, back in 1968, his answer resonated so deeply with me. "That was the start of the whole shebang," John said as he jokingly imitated the critics' response to their avant-garde album and its controversial, naked-couple cover.

"What are they doing?!?!?" John exploded. "This Japanese witch has made him crazy, and he's gone BANANAS!" Yoko giggled as John continued, emphasizing that in reality "all she did was take the bananas part of me out of the closet more, you know, that had been inhibited by the other part."

"And did that help you?" I asked.

"Oh, it was a . . ." John began to answer.

"A *relief*, right?" Yoko said, finishing his thought..

"A COMPLETE relief, to meet somebody else who was as far out as I was, you know?" John said. "That was the real thing."

As the self-proclaimed Mad Banana, I totally understood where they were coming from. At that moment, it seemed to me that despite being born in three different decades in three different countries, John, Yoko, and I had all somehow come from the same bunch of bananas!

My actual "bunch" (my family, that is) made for a less-than-ideal homelife (to put it mildly), but thankfully parents of my closest friends not only encouraged me in my studies and aspirations but also helped me celebrate my love of all things creative, including both music and reading. As an AP English student, I had a lot of required reading to do, but my all-time-favorite books were the popular fantasy novels from J. R. R. Tolkien that had been published decades earlier. Repeatedly reading *The Hobbit* and all three volumes of *The Lord of the Rings* while being cooped up in my bedroom helped keep me from concentrating on my raucous family reality, leading me instead to focus on what Tolkien called his world of Middle-earth "fairy stories." This made it *truly* amazing for me to end up more than thirty years later working in Wellington, New Zealand, alongside director/coproducer/cowriter Peter Jackson, putting together shoots and cast/crew interviews for *The Lord of the Rings: The Return of the King Special Extended DVD Edition*. And I was possibly even more excited less than twenty years after that when Jackson directed *The Beatles: Get Back*, his incredible 2021 documentary series comprising vintage Fab Four footage covering the creation of *Let It Be*, produced by Jackson along with Paul McCartney, Ringo Starr, Yoko Ono, and Olivia Harrison—what a cool, coincidental connection!

Getting back to *my* high school friends and their families, one of my best buddies, Jan, had an upbringing radically different from my own. She grew up with a loving, caring mother and father, two brothers, and a sister, and hanging out with them at their nearby home gave me such a warm feeling that I could barely bring myself to walk out their front door. Jan's mother, Ella Mae, valued her children above everything else and was so kind, welcoming, and generous to all of their friends that we all adored her. Funny thing: when Jan looks back on our high school years, she compares her mom, whom she describes as "frumpy," to mine, whom Jan says she'll always remember as gorgeous, glamorous, and dressed so very cool. Still, you can bet that back then, I was more than jealous of my dear friend's happy home and family life, and especially of her mother and father.

Jan's dad spent much of his week in Sacramento directing research for California's Air Resources Board, the state's clean-air agency. He was an inspiration to me because even with his important government gig and crazy commuter schedule, it was obvious how deeply he cared for his family. Plus, he played guitar, demonstrating his love of pop culture and contemporary music with his song choices, one of his favorites being the 1972 Don McLean classic "American Pie," which sat at the top of the charts back then for weeks. While Jan and I and the rest of her family would be making a racket in their dining room, her father would be sitting in his small home office with the door wide open, guitar in hand, singing along to McLean's iconic chorus, "Bye, bye, Miss American Pie/Drove my Chevy to the levee/But the levee was dry." By the time we'd all quieted down and gathered in his doorway to listen, he'd be up to the line describing "the day the music died," which seemed to totally resonate with him. That phrase was McLean's label for the tragic plane crash at the tail end of the fifties that took the lives of early rock heroes Buddy Holly, Ritchie Valens, and the Big Bopper. After all these years, the irony of so closely experiencing my own generation's day the music died—the assassination of John Lennon some twenty-plus years later—hasn't escaped me.

Jan's father plays a part in my memory of that sorrowful event as well, since he was one of the first people to contact me following my appearance on NBC's *Today* show the morning after the murder, consoling me as no one in my own family seemed to care enough to do. I will always remember that kind, supportive call from him, and I still think of him every time I hear "American Pie." That memory was especially powerful recently when I had the unexpected privilege of attending a local Don McLean concert. I was there with Jan, her younger sister, Bethie, and their mother, and we all danced and sang along emotionally to a song that still means so much to us, even several years after Jan's father had passed away. And these days, when I look up into the sky here in Los Angeles, I think about how much less smog I see and how much easier it is to breathe than it was back in the early seventies, when his daughter and I were quite the team of troublemaking teens, at least partly thanks to him and his work at the

California Air Resources board.

Even though Jan and I were both nearly straight A students, and almost all of our classes together were Advanced Placement, we were two loud, talkative gals who loved to laugh, especially at our own jokes, and we could never quite quell the urge to speak out when the impulse hit.

That's how we ended up getting thrown out of Mrs. Connolly's second-period English class one morning, exiled to the exterior of her Uni High bungalow but still giggling like lunatics as we came up with what seemed like a solid plan of action. We pushed our faces right up against the building's outside air vents, wailing and howling as though we were haunting the classroom we'd just been banished from, repeating "*Repent, Mrs. Connolly! Repent! Repent! Repent!*" as many times as we could before collapsing into hysterics. We began to hear our classmates inside laughing out loud as well, and only then did it dawn on us that those vents must have been wide open, so that every single sound we'd made had reverberated through the classroom, making it impossible for poor Mrs. Connolly to hear herself think let alone teach.

Suddenly, there she was right in front of us, having furiously stomped outside slamming the door behind her and wasting no time in letting us know that she'd had it. "Enough is enough!" she informed us, and she immediately sent us to "social adjustment," otherwise known as detention, for the next two weeks.

Needless to say, Jan and I were totally caught off guard. We'd never before been punished so harshly for what we thought was just our over-the-top but somehow still humorous and therefore acceptable behavior. We served out our social-adjustment sentence with an all-male group of disbelieving and derisive students who turned out to be actual high school hoodlums whom neither of us had ever previously encountered on campus. Eventually, we both went sheepishly back to Mrs. Connolly's English class, only to resume our typical classroom conduct within minutes, as though nothing at all had happened.

I somehow managed to hide the entire episode from my mother and stepfather, no doubt by forging their signatures and inventing stories about having to stay after school to study for upcoming exams.

I can't even imagine what their reaction would have been had I not been able to pull that off. I'm sure I saved myself from a long stretch of being grounded, which might have meant having to spend every single sleeping or waking moment outside of school cooped up in my room. Of course that could have simply served as motivation to leave my family situation behind even earlier than I actually did. Before I finally got it together to run away from home for real, my big escape was music. When I couldn't manage to be as far away from our latest apartment as possible (we moved almost every year because my stepfather always managed to create major issues with our landlord of the moment), staying at a friend's house or putting in long hours at the library or wherever I was working at the time, I would hide out in my room with the door slammed shut, headphones on or my ears as close to the speakers of my cheap little mini-stereo as possible.

Hanging out with music-loving gal pals Alice and Jan just before a sleepover at another high school friend's house.

I'd paid for that small sound system mainly with money I'd made babysitting, earning fifty cents an hour. So no, my stereo wasn't exactly top-of-the-line, but it did the job, and I was grateful to have been granted parental permission to spend my own hard-earned money on it.

One of the bonuses of babysitting, besides getting out of the house, was being exposed to brand-new music that some of the hip young parents I worked for were listening to, which is how I initially discovered both *This Was*, Jethro Tull's first album, and the group's next LP, *Stand Up*. Amazingly, as loud as I played those records on this cool couple's superexpensive stereo system, I never woke up their nearly newborn baby, who always managed to sleep right through it. I'm guessing she must have already been used to earsplitting rock 'n' roll thanks to her parents. What a lucky little girl! Of course, I wasn't allowed to play my own records at home anywhere near as loud. My little bedroom speakers weren't big enough to blast my favorites anyway, so that's how the headphones I'd also saved up for and bought set me free.

Considering all the household restrictions, it seems pretty surprising looking back that I was even allowed out of any of our apartments after dark, let alone permitted to go to late-night concerts like the Stones at the Forum. Come to think of it, maybe I lied most of the time, telling my mother and her husband that I had to work or study at a friend's house or babysit instead. Sometimes, I didn't even bother lying. I would just wait until they were otherwise occupied and then jump out the window or off the first-story balcony outside my bedroom's sliding glass doors and down onto the sidewalk below.

One of the apartments we lived in was on Selby Avenue, right across the street from West LA's massive Mormon temple, and one great thing about the location of this particular building was its proximity to the local May Company department store, which contained the closest local Ticketron outlet and opened weekdays at 10:00 a.m. That's exactly where my buddy Alice and I headed one morning when we should have already been in school, but we were intent on getting the best tickets possible for James Taylor's debut concert at the Hollywood Bowl. Back then, box seats at the Bowl were somehow affordable even for a couple of less-than-minimum-wage-earning teens, and with no one else waiting in line at the May Co., we zipped right in and plunked down our hard-earned cash, jumping up and down for sheer joy. Not only would this be our first major concert together, but we'd be sitting practically right in front of the stage!

I found out years later that James Taylor was coincidentally a neighbor of John and Yoko's in New York in 1980, and the day before John was murdered, James was standing in front of the Dakota when he was approached by a manically alarming creep who wouldn't shut up or leave him alone. That obnoxious dude turned out to be the same scoundrel who bugged me following the interview the next day—John Lennon's murderer, whom James heard that night from his own space firing the five shots that killed John—so horrifying!

Years after his first Hollywood Bowl appearance, Taylor said that playing a megavenue like that gives an artist the feeling he's arrived, which is exactly how excited young concertgoers like my friends and I felt about the shows we were lucky enough to attend there.

Paul McCartney recognized the Bowl's impact as well, having performed sold-out shows there originally as a Beatle back in '64 and '65. He even mentioned the venue in his Wings' song "Rock Show" from the 1975 album *Venus and Mars*, singing "You've got rock 'n' roll at the Hollywood Bowl—we'll be there, ooh yeah!"

There would be other memorable summer-season Hollywood Bowl concerts during my high school years, including Faces featuring Rod Stewart in 1972—a show that kicked off with fireworks on both sides of the stage and continued explosively through the group's final encore, when the band members kicked a slew of soccer balls into the crowd. I hadn't yet become a huge Faces fan, nor was I even really that familiar with Rod Stewart before that landmark Bowl show, but Doug, the boy who'd bought the tickets and asked if he could take me, definitely was, and heaven knows I would never turn down a chance to rock out anywhere, let alone the Hollywood Bowl. I thought of Doug more as my friend the bagel baker than as a potential music mentor, seeing as that's how he earned his paycheck while working next door to the toy store where I'd found my first major after-school job. Doug not only earned my undying gratitude by feeding me onion bagels fresh from his workplace oven, but he also introduced me to the amazing Faces line up: the two Ronnies, Lane and Wood, playing bass and lead guitar, respectively, plus Ian McLaglan on keyboards, drummer Kenney Jones, and of course Rod Stewart, with his one-of-a-kind raspy, scratchy voice. But what I didn't expect, and really had no clue about at all, was how totally sexy "Rod the Mod" would be onstage. Plus, that hair! His trademark style, back-combed and sticking straight up and supposedly enhanced with sugar water, totally won me over. Rod and the band opened with their cover of the Temptations' "(I Know) I'm Losing You," and by the time they got to "Maggie May" just a few songs later, I was sure I was in falling in love—not just with Faces, but with my good friend Doug for bringing me to such a spectacular show in the first place. Even though we never ended up going beyond being best buddies, that was fine for me. We'd still shared an unforgettable musical moment that sticks with me to this day.

Another major Bowl memory of mine came at the tail end of the summer of '73, when Elton John brought his tour to the iconic venue for the first time. His totally outrageous, ultra-Hollywood entrance was amplified by an intro from *Deep Throat* porn star Linda Lovelace along with hundreds of doves that were suddenly released from the stage to fly out over and into the audience. When Elton sat down at the grand piano in his silvery-white cowboy suit decked with feather boas, wearing the giant, outlandish eyeglasses he'd become famous for, the crowd went crazy!

This was quite a different trip from Elton John's California debut just three years earlier at Doug Weston's Troubadour in West Hollywood, the famous club that held maybe a few hundred people back then, compared with the Bowl's capacity of thousands and thousands. His nights at the Troubadour are credited with kicking off his career, as similar gigs at the club did for the careers of so many other performers in the sixties and seventies, including Linda Ronstadt and the Byrds.

Those early Troubadour shows were almost all huge word-of-mouth sellouts, possibly due to massive record-company guest lists as well as the fact that Troubadour admission could be secured back then simply by calling and making a reservation.

That explains why I spent over an hour hiding out in the phone booth in the main hallway of my high school one day, sticking the same dime in the slot over and over until I finally stopped getting a busy signal (remember those?) and was able to make it through to the Troubadour box office. My reward? A confirmed reservation to see former Buffalo Springfield and Poco member Jim Messina in his latest incarnation, performing with singer/songwriter Kenny Loggins. Of course, I had to jump off my bedroom balcony yet again to sneak out of the apartment to make it to the show, but it was definitely worth it.

To a sixteen-year-old back in '71-'72, Doug Weston's Troubadour was the embodiment of cool, the club where not only Buffalo Springfield made its debut, but also where controversial comedian Lenny Bruce was arrested on obscenity charges for saying "schmuck" in front of a live audience way back in 1962.

John Lennon had his own Troubadour ejections to deal with during his "Lost Weekend" in Los Angeles. Lennon had been in LA for a while thanks to his nearly year-and-a-half-long separation from Yoko Ono in the early to midseventies, with March of '74 turning out to be an especially tough month for him. This happened thanks mainly to the second of two heavily drunken nights he'd spent hanging out at the Troubadour, which started with John and his booze buddy, singer/songwriter Harry Nilsson, drinking Brandy Alexanders and heckling onstage headliners the Smothers Brothers. The night ended violently, with Lennon loudly lashing out and then losing his glasses during his scuffle with club staff members.

Of course, when my friends and I hit the Troubadour earlier in the seventies for the Loggins and Messina show, the atmosphere was quite different. The venue was set up with long parallel tables stretching vertically across the main floor to the front of the stage, and as fans sat, drank, and chatted while waiting for the show to begin, I remember looking up and down the length of our table, thinking to myself that this was without a doubt just where I belonged. I was instantly certain that my true family wasn't the people I grew up or even lived with in the apartment I'd made my escape from that night. It was made up instead of my fellow live music lovers and always would be.

Another amazing show that rocked my senior year in high school was David Bowie at the Long Beach Arena in March of '73. This was the follow-up to his original Ziggy Stardust and the Spiders from

Mars concert at the Santa Monica Civic the previous October. I'd caught that show via live broadcast on KMET-FM, hosted by another of my heroes, DJ B. Mitchel Reed, just about three months before I had my life-changing meetup with him at the radio station. I'd been hypnotized not only by Bowie's unique sound and amazing band, but by his overall appearance as well. The photos I'd seen displaying his outrageous, one-of-a-kind fashion sense and style made it all the more important for me to dress appropriately when I finally got the chance to see him live. To my mind, that's exactly what I did, creating my own one-time-only outfit made up of denim cutoff short-shorts; heavily glittered, argyle-patterned knee socks; and my first-ever pair of sky-high platform shoes. Plus, I styled my hair that night with at least six braids, all tied together with different-colored ribbons, and applied more makeup than I'd ever worn before, including bright-red lipstick. Of course, when my traditional-fashion-plate mother saw me, she almost had a heart attack. She wanted to know where I thought I was going dressed and made up like a lunatic, but fortunately my buddy Brian arrived just in time to spirit me away to Long Beach before she could insist I change my outfit or wash my face. Once we got to the arena, I felt right at home, if not slightly underdressed compared with the hard-core Bowie disciples in attendance.

We had great seats, due to Brian's connections. His supportive dad, Ernie Chambers, was a well-known producer at the time whose credits included the *The Smothers Brothers Comedy Hour*, which was a huge—and hugely controversial, due to their outspoken opposition to the Vietnam War and the Johnson and Nixon administrations—CBS success story.

Thanks to Ernie, I was able to look around our section at the arena and see a number of faces I was sure I recognized from album covers and television, including Herbie Hancock and Leon Russell, and suddenly the realization hit me like a hammer that I was about to experience rock 'n' roll history in the making. From the minute Bowie came out in full Ziggy Stardust mode for "Hang on to Yourself," I was totally entranced. One bizarrely beautiful designer-costume change followed another, with Bowie teasing us musically with a taste of his upcoming album, *Aladdin Sane*. In the middle of the show, when the band began to play "The Jean Genie," I felt like my future, along with the future of popular music, had instantly and astronomically changed. To this day, this Iggy Pop-inspired track is among my favorites from Bowie's massive stream of astonishing material. Although it's hardly possible for me to name just one favorite song of his, I still can't hear "The Jean Genie" without jumping up out of my chair and dancing like a wild woman.

If only my teen years could have been filled with one cool concert after another, not to mention a more palatable home life, how different things might have been. Instead, I felt that my very existence depended on establishing my independence and basically getting the hell out of Dodge. In other words, I needed to work on making my move from the latest family digs into the UCLA Co-op apartments while still a high school student at Uni.

My two new roommates were college students who were just about to graduate, one of whom was already excited about starting law school that coming fall. In fact, it's all because of her, Susan, that I completely flushed my grandfather's greatest dream for me down the toilet. He'd always encouraged me to become a lawyer, saying my penchant for debate, along with my ability to argue my way out of anything, meant I'd make a top-notch attorney.

When I first moved into our small room at the UCLA Co-op, Susan was already prepping for the start of her legal education. I remember quite clearly seeing her come home every night for a full week carrying a huge, heavy bag of books, saying she needed to pick them up as early as possible from the student store on campus, before they were sold out. Incredulous, I asked her, "Really? All those books for just one year of law school?" Her answer nearly literally broke my brain: she looked at me almost scornfully, laughed, and pointed at the book bags that took up nearly half of our entire floor space.

"Uh, not quite, Laurie," she said. "*One* class, one semester!" And that was it. Any thoughts I might have had of eventually applying to law school vanished into thin air that very moment. My late grandfather's dream would never be fulfilled—and truth be told, no one was happier about that than I.

High school graduation came and went. I got my diploma and

celebrated with friends, not family, as we looked back nostalgically on our time as Uni High freshman, sophomores, juniors, and seniors.

My Uni High senior class photo, just before graduation in 1973.

The word "prom" had never been in my vocabulary, so as everyone shared their fond, fun memories of that once-in-a-lifetime night, I was thinking of how my friend Bruce and I had simply gone to the movies instead, then hung out at Tiny Naylor's, an all-night coffee shop in Westwood Village, while talking about what life might have in store for us. We ended up making a semiserious suicide pact, saying that if neither of us was involved with the true love of our life by the time we both reached twenty-eight, that was it—we'd get together and end it all. Bruce was a football player who, in his own words, would have, should have attended the prom, but he was also gay, although definitely not out yet, so it made more sense in his eyes to avoid the event entirely rather than take me or anyone else as his date/beard. I also chose to avoid our senior prom like the plague, because attending it, along with becoming a cheerleader and dating a star athlete, was all my mother ever cared about or wanted me to do during high school. She couldn't help but hope her daughter would be the ultrapopular chick that she herself had never been, but in reality, I never could have been that girl either, nor would I ever have wanted to be. Truthfully, I probably would have dressed up and done the whole prom thing if the wanna-be-hippie dude I had a horribly embarrassing crush on had asked me, but I figured it was not something he would be into, so I didn't think twice about it. Imagine my surprise afterward when I found out that not only had he been there, but the girl he'd chosen as his prom date was pretty much the senior class slut—another type of chick I never could be—or ever want to be.

One high school dance I actually DID go to as a senior was the eagerly anticipated sock hop hosted by popular KMET DJ Barry Hansen, aka Dr. Demento. He played plenty of classic fifties and sixties rock 'n' roll radio hits for us all to jitterbug to, and it was tons of fun.

That summer after graduation and before college was an education in and of itself. I learned how to not only live with roommates, but also to take on an almost full-time job at a local pharmacy and spend nearly every waking moment doing whatever I could to celebrate my newfound freedom. This meant everything from having late-night sex on the beach with an older Co-op resident—actually, not quite sex, since when he asked my age right before getting to home plate and found out I was only seventeen, he wasted no time in practically dragging me back to his car for a ride home—to buying tickets to see bands like Jethro Tull at the Forum.

That Tull show will always live on in my heart and brings back one of my fondest memories of what it means to have friends. There we were, my close pal Alice and I, climbing almost to the top tier of the Fab Forum to reach our nearly-nosebleed seats. A guy came up on the stairs beside us with his arms full, struggling as he carried someone who seemed nearly twice his size right past us to the very last row of the venue. We watched as he lowered his load onto one of a pair of empty seats, and we then saw the look of gratitude on the face of the fellow he'd lugged all the way up through the crowded venue. This to me was the ultimate definition of friendship, since the guy doing all the heavy-lifting didn't act at all like his buddy had been any kind of burden whatsoever. That's exactly how I've always hoped the many friends who've carried me in numerous ways over the years look back on our relationships.

And so, Ian Anderson and company helped me musically celebrate my eighteenth birthday, a landmark event, since it meant I was officially, legally, and mentally my own responsibility from that point forward. Finally, I felt totally in control of my own destiny, and on that note I decided I was ready to reach out to make amends to my mother and even, to some extent, her husband. I felt like I was the grownup of the group now, and I hoped we could all relate to, or at least tolerate, one another as adults. Wishful thinking maybe, but still, it took a huge load off my mind and shoulders. I even made a point of dropping by their place every so often that summer just to say hi, since the pharmacy I worked at was located just a couple of blocks down from their latest Brentwood apartment, but I made sure to keep those weeknight visits brief and 100 percent nonconfrontational, which seemed to work, at least some of the time. Regardless, it definitely helped me regain the confidence that had been stripped from me during our last few years as a so-called family unit.

One afternoon, as I was coming home to the Co-op from work, walking the residential streets of Westwood like the world was mine for the taking, a handsome stranger standing with a friend in the middle of the block surprised me. "Excuse me," he said. "Where are you going? Can we talk for a minute?" Of course I stopped, and without hesitating he introduced himself as Dana, an actor who'd just moved to LA from New York. He went on to tell me he was looking for someone that week who could play the role of his dance partner. He described what he was looking for as a classic rock 'n' roll chick to dance with him in a contest hosted by Dick Clark—that's right, *the* Dick Clark. I couldn't believe my ears, and of course I was somewhat suspicious, so I asked him why out of all the girls walking on the street that day in Westwood, he'd picked me. He said he was impressed by not only my sassy, confident attitude, but also my long legs, which suggested to him that I was a dancer, and that was all I needed to hear. Plus, he complimented my look, saying I had that fifties/sixties-vintage rock vibe straight out of *American Graffiti*, the George Lucas film that had just been released. He then asked me to come see the movie with him so we could get to know each other and rehearse some moves, seeing as neither he nor I was a trained or professional dancer.

When we entered the theater that night, we rushed toward the front of the stage before the movie began to do some fun, frantic jitterbugging to whatever was playing on the sound system. As dance partners, Dana and I definitely clicked, and after the movie we made plans for him to pick me up during the day to do our thing together again, this time for Dick Clark. But first I knew I would need to head over to my mom's in the morning to borrow some classic clothes from her closet. She never disposed of anything in her wardrobe, and I was picturing an original fifties-era skirt of hers that I thought would be perfect for the upcoming gig. Although she wasn't very supportive, in fact she thought the whole thing was a scam and that I was way too gullible, she let me take the skirt. And yes, she even told me I looked great in it—possibly almost as good as she did wearing it back in the day.

Dana picked me up, and off we drove to the Santa Monica Civic Auditorium—a venue I'd last visited just a couple of months before to see Paul Simon on his first solo tour, for his album *There Goes Rhymin' Simon*. I loved that show, and what made it especially meaningful for me was that it was my first real assignment as a rock journalist, for a fairly new Florida-based music magazine/*Rolling Stone* competitor called *Zoo World*. I'd approached the editors via a mailed packet a few weeks before, with a letter detailing my love of music, both live and recorded, and included a few writing samples. Words can't express how totally thrilled this high school senior was to not only receive a response, but to actually be told, "You can write up a storm! You have a style that's all your own!" Yes, they were interested, and yes, they wanted me to send them a review of the next concert I attended. So off I went to catch Paul Simon live at the Civic, carrying my notepad and pen. I jotted down every last detail of his stellar performance, which included guest musicians like the South American band Urubamba, featuring a couple of guys playing the charango, a small stringed instrument made from an armadillo. Gospel singers the Jesse Dixon Group brought their special spiritual touch to songs like "Mother and Child Reunion" and the Simon & Garfunkel classic "Sounds of Silence." All in all, it was a tremendously inspirational set.

So now here I was back at the Civic. This time I was there not to hear Paul Simon's "Me and Julio Down By the Schoolyard," but to take part in a dance contest and then meet and get photographed with Dick Clark. Dana let slip on the way there that the competition was supposed to be rigged. His agent had tried to set it up for the two of us to win, and win we did, although I do believe we actually were the best dancers out of all the couples there—at least Mr. Clark seemed to think so. It turned out the event was being held and photos taken to promote a series of ABC TV specials called *Dick Clark Presents The Rock and Roll Years*, in which the *American Bandstand* host would display his love for and knowledge of my favorite form of music. Rocker/dancer Chubby Checker was on the scene as well that day, and when he and Dick chose me and Dana as their winning dance team, I couldn't help but gush about my love for the Twist and how I'd danced along with Chubby every time I'd heard his hit tune on my transistor radio as a kid. That prompted both Dick and Chubby to ask if I was a professional dancer, which sent me straight to rock 'n' roll heaven!

Almost a decade later, when I worked directly for Dick Clark writing both his weekly syndicated radio countdown show and newspaper column, I was amazed to hear (straight from the horse's mouth) that he not only remembered me from that day at the Civic, but that he also still had the photo taken with me and my dance partner. At that point he walked over to one of his many file cabinets, pulled it right out, and handed it to me. That's just one example of what an all-around mensch and amazing human being the late, great Dick Clark was. I was so proud back then, and have been ever since, to have been able to call him my boss.

After Dick's dance contest, Dana and I continued to date, but only in the friendliest sense. It turned out he was nearly ten years older than I was and somewhat paranoid about what he thought of as my schoolgirl crush turning serious enough to make me drop my plans to go off to college, which I was scheduled to do in a month or so. He was

Dick Clark and Chubby Checker chose Dana and me (the couple in
the middle of the back seat) as their dance contest winners!
(Photo by Dick Clark Productions)

right. If we'd started having a truly romantic relationship, I probably
would have, but I enjoyed his attention and company so much it felt
good just to hang out with him, even on a nonsexual basis.

And so my summer of independence in LA was quickly coming to
an end. Soon I'd be off to UC Santa Cruz and a whole new lifestyle,
which would turn out to blow my young mind. I had no idea what was
in store. If I had, who knows? Maybe I would have held my ground
and waited for Dana to finally come around.

—CHAPTER 5—

"Dude (Looks Like a Lady)"

M y high school close friend and confidant and fellow live-music lover Brian and I were all set to take the trek up from LA to Santa Cruz for the September start of our freshman year in college, with him behind the wheel of his sporty Triumph Spitfire. Just the week before, Brian had helped me pick out a spanking-new sound system with super huge speakers at Underdog Stereo in Westwood Village, and it was all boxed up and ready to go and already sitting in his back seat. But shortly before our departure, a major local live-music announcement was made: a handful of industry giants were collaborating and about to open a brand-new, crazy-cool club on the Sunset Strip, on the site of a former strip club called the Largo. This group included Whisky a Go Go founder Elmer Valentine, music exec/producer/artist manager Lou Adler, eventual Geffen Records creator and President David Geffen (who would go on to release John and Yoko's *Double Fantasy* album less than ten years later), and Peter Asher of Peter and Gordon fame, who not only had worked with the Beatles' Apple Records but later produced major hits for both James Taylor and Linda Ronstadt. Their hip new hot spot would be known as the Roxy Theatre, and the first act scheduled to take the stage was Neil Young and his backup band the Santa Monica Flyers.

Although Brian and I had seen Neil's memorable concert with Ronstadt as his opening act at the Forum just that past March, we both would have done anything to see him again, especially up close in a small club. Anything, that is, except miss the upcoming start date of our first quarter at UCSC—or so I thought.

My totally imaginary love affair with Neil Young had begun with his self-titled first solo release once he'd left Buffalo Springfield. His mesmerizing portrait on the album cover alone moved me to write poetry—okay, embarrassingly bad poetry—as only a fifteen-year-old girl with a ridiculous rock star crush—okay, obsession—could come up with. "A New and Younger Dream," I called my poem, with the opening line "Neil with your stare—are you there?" The rest of the poem I'm sure was even more embarrassing, and thankfully lost in time over the years.

As much as I would have literally killed to see my Canadian-born singer/songwriter idol again, tickets for Neil's opening nights at the Roxy were almost impossible to score, as fans were lining up along Sunset Boulevard well in advance with very little chance of even making it up to the box office. But when it turned out that Brian's dad had a connection to get him in, my friend decided to postpone his trip up north with me at least a couple of days so that he could stay in town to see Young's highly anticipated Roxy show. This was something I was just a little too nervous to consider doing myself, seeing as I was a financial aid student and had to check in early to make sure my student loans and work-study job were all lined up and in order. So instead, as much as it depressed me, I bit the bullet, said bye-bye to Brian, and approached my mother and stepfather asking for a lift up to Santa Cruz. I had plenty of other friends who had also been accepted to UCSC, but they all were heading up to school with their own parents, so unfortunately there just wasn't anyone else I could hitch a ride with.

As bummed as I was about having to make the six-hour trip with my mother and her husband, I decided to make the best of it and simply have them drive me up and drop me off, and hopefully there would be no arguments, insults, or negative vibes along the way. It actually worked out well.

When we got to the beautifully scenic and woodsy campus, my

Before leaving for UCSC, my mother and I took farewell shots
together in a photo booth.

mom's initial reaction was "This isn't a school; it's a summer camp!"
I'd already been to UCSC on a tour of northern California colleges I'd
taken with my friend Alice and her father a year or so before, so it was
no surprise to me, but my mom and stepdad were genuinely awestruck.
Although they'd no doubt heard it was California's premier hippie
school, apparently nothing had quite prepared them for the lack of
official-looking structures, let alone the lovely drive up to campus that
took us right through a forest. After parking outside my dormitory—
College V's notorious B Dorm, as I would soon enough come to find
out—they helped me carry my belongings up to my room on the fifth
floor, and that was that. Hasty farewells were said, I turned away, and
suddenly there I was—a college kid!

Right away I met my new roommate, who also happened to be
named Laurie, which must have been some kind of joke courtesy of
the campus housing department. She also had arrived with her family,
but her mother seemed to want to stick around for a while, probably
waiting to see whom her sweet, innocent daughter would be forced to
live with for the next year. True to form, I wasted no time snickering

and making snotty fun of the poster the other Laurie had already hung over her bed. It was one of those pieces of corny seventies wall art featuring footprints in the sand and messages about marching to the beat of a different drummer, which was nothing at all like the trippy black light and hard-core rock posters I had rolled up and was ready to hang over mine as soon as her relatives left.

But despite our apparent differences, Laurie and I got along just great. She was a likable, hippie, folksinger-type teen, and one of my favorite memories of the two of us together back then was our first time hanging out in the stairwell of B Dorm between the fifth and fourth floors. She'd been cooling her heels there for quite a while waiting for me to finally show up so that we could head down to dinner at the College V dining hall, and in the meantime, she'd started singing. Of course I joined in as soon as I heard her voice when I opened the stairwell door: "I'm so tired/tired of waiting/tired of waiting for you!" We both sang and laughed like crazy, continuing to croon as we descended to the first floor. "I was a lonely soul/I had nobody 'til I met you/but you keep-a me waiting/all of the time/what can I do?" And there it was, our roomie relationship in a nutshell, perfectly expressed thanks to classic midsixties lyrics from Ray Davies and the Kinks.

Our wing of the fifth floor of B Dorm was undoubtedly the most highly sought-after residential spot on UCSC's College V campus. This was thanks to previous residents who'd built lofts in many of the rooms, since we were on the dormitory's top floor, which had tremendously vaulted ceilings. Considering how many returning students had requested living space up there, it was pretty surprising that any freshmen at all made it in. Four of us girls did, however, and Laurie, Ginny, Teri, and I all felt pretty lucky to find ourselves hobnobbing in the hallway with some of College V's obviously coolest characters.

The first one to catch my attention was a tall, lanky, arty-looking guy with nearly waist-length dirty-blond hair (just my type!) who had the single room directly across from me and my roommate. Right off the bat, he introduced himself to the two of us first year Lauries as a fifth-year College V senior, so I knew he had to be at least four years older than I was and way out of my freshman league . . . WRONG!

Before my first week on campus was over, he'd already made a point of inviting me over for a handful of late-night gab sessions where we'd sit on his bed and discuss everything from the space race to our favorite music, discovering that we shared a love of the Beach Boys, Beatles, Bob Dylan, and, naturally, Neil Young. His name was Mark, and he was not only a uniquely talented visual artist and painter but a fledgling filmmaker as well, which is why he'd stayed on an extra year at UCSC, since in order to graduate he needed to finish the senior film project he'd started the previous year.

Finally, Mark asked me out on an actual date. He said he wanted to cook me dinner, which he was able to do, since he had access and keys to the College V student kitchen. So that next Friday, Mark and his best friend, Bruce, also an artist, began the evening by serving up cocktails, cigarettes, and joints to me and my roomie, now known as Laurie B., at a table they'd set up in the student lounge on our floor. It was a double date that was destined to go down in 1973 College V history—by the time dinner was served, we were all so loudly drunk and stoned we could barely eat. So Mark decided it was time for us to ditch the dorm and take a walk across our campus and on to the next one, which actually had a name, Kresge. UCSC at the time was made up of eight separate, distinct colleges, including some with no names yet, just numbers like ours, College V, which was known as the creative arts campus, where all of the true wackos lived. And although I had no idea at the time, I was on the brink of becoming heavily involved with one of the biggest, albeit most talented, sensitive, and well-loved, College V wackos of all.

As expected, after we made it back from that lengthy, exciting walk, our night ended in mildly memorable dorm-room sex. Mark told me afterward that this made him my "Breakie Boy," because yes, I was technically still a virgin up to that point. He thought it was pretty bizarre that I'd waited so long to open myself up sexually, since I'd turned eighteen two months before. What Mark didn't understand was that just about three years earlier, I'd made myself a promise that I wasn't going to waste my first sexual encounter on some immature, amateur high school guy. Instead, I was determined to hold out for a much more sophisticated "older man," like Mark.

But at that point, I figured he already saw me as a naive late bloomer, so I was pretty sure our fledgling relationship was over before it could even begin . . . wrong again! Mark made a point of cozying up to me the very next evening and asking me to join him on another walk, this time through the woods behind our dorm. He held me tightly as he told me (and I'll always remember his exact words), "Laurie Kaye, I'm crazy about you!"

So just two weeks in, my freshman year of college was already off to an unbelievable start. I was barely eighteen but had a twenty-two-year-old boyfriend who was the hip and groovy Santa Cruz equivalent of a BMOC-College V at UCSC's Big Man On Campus. Plus, I'd managed to score the most enviable work-study gig ever, which basically involved hanging out late at night behind the counter of the super popular College V Coffeehouse. I was on top of the world!

With Mark, I was also able to progress musically, since he played me personal favorites of his, like John Lennon's "Crippled Inside," along with the entire *Imagine* LP, as well as the Beach Boys' *Pet Sounds*, both of which I'd already been exposed to but not in the context of listening in bed with a boyfriend. And without a doubt, the more time we spent in bed, the more hot sex we had and the better I became at it. He called me his "Cinnamon Girl" as we went at it while playing Neil Young's first LP with Crazy Horse, *Everybody Knows This Is Nowhere*, and my heart felt like it was ready to explode.

Mark also managed to introduce me to music from artists I'd never even heard of before, like the Jim Kweskin Jug Band and Dan Hicks and His Hot Licks, while implying that one of the Lickettes was both a former UCSC student and a onetime conquest of his. Of course, according to Mark, he'd already slept with just about every girl on campus, and it was no doubt this sex-with-students obsession that led him to stage the late-night orgy he'd decided to shoot in our fifth-floor B Dorm lounge for the final phase of his senior film project.

This seemed like the perfect way for me to demonstrate my newly acquired sexual expertise, so I was determined to play a prominent part. As I stripped down along with my fellow participants, getting stoned while spreading oil all over our bodies and rolling around naked and greasy together on a floor covered with piles of tiny Styrofoam pellets, I felt like I fit right in, even as the pellets crept temporarily into every bodily crevice. For the next few days, we all contributed to obvious trails of these foam microbeads leading from B Dorm all the way across campus, and every time one of us encountered any of them on our way to class, we'd burst out laughing just remembering that crazy night.

Not too long after, rumors began to circulate that all along, Mark actually had bigger plans for his X-rated student-orgy footage. Supposedly, he'd approached the notorious Mitchell brothers, San Francisco's original porn kings, to sell what he'd shot so that they could show it at their landmark adult movie palace, the O'Farrell Theatre. Surprisingly, no one at College V seemed the least bit shocked. I somehow turned a deaf ear to all that talk, and when Mark bought us tickets to see the Beach Boys in San Francisco that fall, I knew I'd fallen in love.

Before we headed to Winterland to see the show, Halloween hit College V's B Dorm as hard as a rock. One of our wing's most notorious residents, a lovable guy named Larry who would go on to become an Emmy-nominated comic and magician, dreamed up what came to be known as the Bloodbath. He and his costumed coconspirators drenched our hallway in faux blood as they crawled around on their hands and knees, attacking anyone who dared to cross their paths. This gooey, horrifying mess turned Halloween into a true nightmare, the thought of which still freaks a number of us former residents out like it was yesterday.

Of course, this wasn't the only frighteningly weird thing that went on in our dorm on a regular basis, not by a long shot. Mark and I, being tall and long limbed, joined a couple of similarly built fellow students in the late-night game of stretching our legs out to both sides of the narrow dormitory hallway, then working our way up along the walls almost to the ceiling. With our legs spread wide apart, we hovered there, lying in wait for those students who'd dropped acid or some other hallucinatory drug to come home from their evening adventures. Once these unsuspecting souls were directly beneath us, we'd scare the crap out of them by dropping straight down right on their heads and shoulders, laughing hysterically as they screamed in terror and practically passed out. Yikes!

Another typical B Dorm prank, at least on our fifth-floor wing, was smearing Vaseline all over doorknobs—not just those to individual dorm rooms, but also the knobs on the outer doors of our unisex bathrooms. That was another interesting thing about our special section of College V's B Dorm. Guys and gals not only lived in rooms right next to each other, a rarity on campuses back in the early seventies, but also shared bathrooms and shower stalls. This led to more than a few embarrassing moments, but still somehow seemed surprisingly normal, like we were all one big family. It also enabled couples like Mark and me to shower together, definitely a new experience for this still fairly innocent college freshman.

Mark also introduced me to his other passions, which included dirigibles—blimps and zeppelins—as well as his amazing collection of vintage comic books. The one-of-a-kind artwork he created was almost all tied to zeppelins and their history, specifically the Hindenburg, the German passenger-carrying rigid airship that famously caught fire and imploded in 1937, killing thirty-five of the ninety-seven people on board in less than a minute, as it attempted to dock at the Lakehurst Naval Air Station in New Jersey.

Mark had even painted a breathtakingly handsome portrait of himself as Captain Max Pruss, the commander of the Hindenburg, just before the disaster.

He gave this amazing painting to me early on in our relationship, sweetly signing the back of his piece of art "To WG, Laurie that is. I love you, Mark." WG, his original nickname for me, stood for Wonder Girl, or "LK the WG," as he called me, referring to the classic

Mark's self portrait as the pilot of the Hindenburg.

DC comics superheroine whom he said I reminded him so much of.

I still have the painting hanging in my home, and it continues to serve as a daily reminder that someone buried way down deep in my past once considered me not only special, but super and worthy of being loved. Since this was not something I had experienced much of growing up, I cherish the painting to this day.

My feeling of being underappreciated early on led to massive insecurities that I've not surprisingly had trouble shaking off my entire life, even today. I still can't help but constantly wonder what my life would have been like, and how differently I might have turned out, had I been raised by devoted, supportive parents, as so many of my friends were . . . but really, what's the point? They were who they were, and like Popeye says, "I yam what I yam, and that's all that I yam." Enough said.

One of Mark's other passions was sexy vintage women's clothing. He made a habit of buying me a number of beautiful pieces whenever we had the chance to hit a thrift shop, whether in Santa Cruz or on our trips together down south to my hometown of Los Angeles or up north to his, Seattle, or even when we headed over to the San Francisco Bay Area for one of the many concerts he took me to. The most memorable of these classic clothes was a gorgeous, skintight, black sequined sixties designer dress he begged me to try on at one high-end outlet in LA. This was a garment I may never have had any occasion to wear as a UCSC student, but it was so stunning and fit so well that he insisted on getting it for me, saying it would be a valuable addition to my wardrobe for years to come. Mark even went one step further and suggested we keep all of my newly acquired collectible clothes in the nearly empty closet in his single dorm room, where, he explained, these dresses would remain untouched, with no one able to try them on or damage them in any way. I said sure, why not, feeling like I had my own private, special, secret, safeguarded wardrobe that would continue to grow along with our relationship.

Thanksgiving approached, and against my better judgment I somewhat hesitantly invited Mark down to LA for what I hoped would be a not-too-revealing family dinner.

We drove down in his VW Bug, and from the moment we reached

my mother and stepfather's apartment, I was regretting my decision. For one thing, despite the fact that my boyfriend and I had been practically living together, and certainly sleeping together on a daily/nightly basis, my mom refused to let him share my former bedroom with me during our stay and made him sleep on the living room sofa. This was at least until they'd closed their bedroom door for the night, at which point Mark would sneak into my old room to climb in bed with me. Strangely enough, this scenario repeated itself over Christmas break, when I traveled to Seattle with him to celebrate the season with his folks in their house. I was banished to their basement sofa bed, and Mark got caught by his mother at least twice while sneaking down to spend the night with me.

What made our Thanksgiving in LA so memorable was my boyfriend's crazy plan for the both of us to drop acid right before dinner. Thanks to the LSD, we not only had absolutely no interest in eating a single bite of whatever it was my mother had cooked up, which probably wasn't much of a loss, since she was certainly not the kind of woman who knew her way around a kitchen, but we also had no attention span whatsoever and couldn't carry on an even somewhat normal conversation. At one point during dinner, Mark looked up grinning from his untouched plate of food and, without warning, began loudly singing his version of the theme song from his favorite childhood Disney film. He got as far as "Old Yeller (ARF ARF ARF), come back Yeller (ARF ARF ARF)!" when my mother realized something strange was going on. She ushered him over to the living room couch, sat him down in front of the TV, and turned on whatever big game was in progress for him to watch. Not that he or I could have cared less about football, but as I ran over to join him, I decided then and there that we'd better make a break for it and head back to Santa Cruz as soon as possible. But Mark let me know he'd already planned a surprise trip to Disneyland the following day with a few of our Santa Cruz pals who were also visiting the LA area, and acid would once again be on the menu.

So, the very next morning, before we pulled into the parking lot at the theme park, we all dosed up to get ready for our first Disney adventure of the day. It was going to be the iconic It's a Small World water ride, complete with hundreds of audio-animatronic dolls dressed as children from around the world singing that somewhat obnoxious title track. As expected, the acid kicked in, and we began to hallucinate, and just as we did, the ride broke down! All of the boats suddenly stopped in their tracks, but unfortunately the damn song kept going, becoming more and more irritating as the minutes passed. Tripping heavily by then, we decided to jump out and swim to shore, only to realize as we did that the water we'd been boat riding in didn't even come up to our knees. In order to look legit, we ridiculously mimed the breaststroke just to make it out of there as fast as we could, but the on-site Disney police had other plans. They rounded us up while we stood in the water as all of the other passengers looked on from their stalled boat seats, and our group was escorted by security out of the park. As the guards walked us back to the parking lot, they told us we needed to leave as soon as we felt ready and able to drive, and by the time we started coming down a couple hours later, we couldn't stop laughing.

To this day, that psychedelic adventure is my most memorable Magic Kingdom experience ever, despite a ton more Disneyland visits made in years to come, including one that took place overnight while the theme park was closed to the general public. I was there working from midnight until 6:30 a.m. as part of the team producing promos— TV spots and trailers—for the fiftieth-anniversary rerelease of Disney's 1937 animated feature film, *Snow White and the Seven Dwarves* (aka Doc, Sleepy, Dopey, Happy, Bashful, Sneezy, and Grumpy)!

Speaking of Grumpy, back on campus at UCSC a trip with Mark to San Francisco's Great American Music Hall to see Van Morrison followed not long afterwards, with Van the Man putting on one hell of a show despite his constant whiskey guzzling, snarky between-song comments, and irritation he was obviously experiencing thanks to the massive cast on his foot. Still, it was a thrill to see the creator of one of my all-time radio favorites, "Brown Eyed Girl," up close and personal, and we were seated at such a great table that it seemed like he was practically performing in our laps and sharing cocktails with us.

Then, for Christmas that year, Mark announced that he'd ordered us tickets to what was without a doubt the most anticipated comeback tour in ages. Bob Dylan and the Band were set to play the Oakland Coliseum in February as part of their forty-date Tour '74. It had been eight years since the last major tour, back in '66, and neither of us had ever seen Dylan live before. The Oakland show was totally sold out, with Dylan and the Band performing classic songs that were simultaneously steeped in nostalgia and relevant to the times, both from Bob and the Band together and in separate sets. Fortunately, *Before the Flood*, the double live album recorded during the tour and released shortly afterward, still serves as a souvenir of the night's intense vibe.

With winter quarter at UCSC coming to a close, I was still working late most evenings at the cool College V coffeehouse to help pay my tuition. One night, I managed to get off earlier than usual and ran excitedly up to our B Dorm fifth floor to surprise Mark, who I figured would be in the midst of painting one of his masterpieces. Once again, WRONG.

I flung open the unlocked door to his room only to find him posing in front of a camera mounted on a tripod wearing a full face of artfully applied cosmetics. Not only that, but he had on the same sexy sixties black sequined cocktail dress that he'd bought me just a couple of months earlier and then offered to store for me in the closet in his room. I noticed he also had on a pair of pointy, spike-heeled women's pumps that somehow seemed custom-made for his huge feet, and I must have looked more than shocked, as I had no idea what was going on or what to say. Mark shushed me as I started to talk so that he could finish

A self-portrait by my cross-dressing boyfriend wearing my dress!

taking the series of elegant self-portraits that he'd obviously planned and set up far in advance of this awkward moment.

I waited as patiently as I could for some kind of explanation, and when it finally came, I knew right away that I was in way over my head and that nothing between us would ever be the same. On the other hand, Mark seemed relieved as he admitted to me that wearing women's clothing not only turned him on, but seemed a lot more natural to him than anything else in his closet. Yes, my perfect boyfriend, the one I'd already imagined marrying and sharing a life with in a house bordered by a white picket fence, turned out to be a full-blown transvestite.

I'd been a fan of Lou Reed's "Walk on the Wild Side"' since I'd first heard the single on KMET a year or so earlier. Despite the fact that I thought I'd not only grasped but accepted the concept of "Holly came from Miami, F-L-A . . . shaved her legs and then he was a she," this wasn't New York City, which, according to Lou, was the place where they said, "Hey, babe, take a walk on the wild side." No, this was rural Santa Cruz, hippie capital of California.

Now I clearly understood why Mark had wanted me to keep all those beautiful vintage dresses he'd given me in his dorm room closet rather than in mine, and it cut me like a knife. No matter how hard I tried, and I did, I was simply too young and inexperienced to even begin to have a handle on this. As much as I was sure I loved Mark and most everything about him, I knew in my heart that I would need a lengthy break from his scene and everything and everyone connected to it to figure things out. So I did my best to fight back the tears as I packed my bags and took a leave of absence from UC Santa Cruz, heading back to LA to live temporarily with my old UCLA Co-op roommates, Susan and Judy. They now had a Santa Monica apartment not far from the beach, and they offered me their living room sofa for a fraction of their total rent . . . so off I went.

—CHAPTER 6—

"Those Oldies But Goodies"

Once back in LA, I naturally lost no time in reconnecting with my precollege summertime crush from the year before, Dana. My hope was he could help provide distraction from what had just sent me down the road toward near total teenage devastation and turned me into a short-term college dropout.

Sweetly, Dana tried his best to come through for me, driving all the way in from his home deep in the Valley to pick me up for several wild Hollywood nights when despite my age—I was, after all, still only eighteen—we hung out at bars like Art Laboe's fairly new joint up on the Sunset Strip. Laboe's location had previously been the legendary Ciro's nightclub/restaurant, where Hollywood celebrities had hung out to see and be seen for decades. And just a couple of years after Laboe took it over in the early seventies, it went on to become a larger version of the famous fun zone called the Comedy Store, which it still is to this day.

Longtime radio DJ Art Laboe was credited with being the first to give West Coast listeners their initial taste of on-air rock 'n' roll. He'd moved from his breakthrough late-night request-and-dedication radio shows during which he played big band and jazz records throughout World War II to broadcasting live local rock shows from popular spots like Scrivner's Drive-In restaurant starting back in the fifties, with his radio shows attracting hordes of teens from all over town. Despite the intolerant attitude of the day toward interracial events, let alone mixed-race relationships, playing song requests from listeners of all colors and ages became Laboe's specialty, and hosting popular radio broadcasts and public dances sealed his reputation as a progressive unifier of the Southern California music scene.

Laboe is also well-known for coining the phrase "oldies but goodies," and by the time he opened his own place up on Sunset Boulevard, he was already quite the radio legend. I'm sure Art would have been excited if I'd been able to tell him as soon as I met him that just a few years later, at the dawn of the new decade, I'd be sitting next to John Lennon as the former Beatle brought up his love for "oldies but goldies."

John mentioned this during our day at the Dakota to emphasize how having just turned forty, he was still super excited whenever he heard any of his favorite songs from back in his early rock days, like 1956's "Be-Bop-A-Lula." John told us he could listen to this Gene Vincent and His Blue Caps rockabilly hit "over and over and over," letting us know that "whenever it comes on, I switch up the tape." Plus, John added, after all this time, "I have the record, still!" Not surprising, since John also let us know that he remembered playing "Be-Bop-a-Lula" on stage for the first time with the Quarrymen the same day he met Paul McCartney, in Liverpool back in 1957!

Heading back to our first night at Laboe's club, I noticed right off the bat that Dana was a regular. Art not only greeted him at the door as though they were old pals, but also walked us right over to the bar and sat me down as Dana ordered drinks for us both. He did tell Art that I was several years away from turning twenty-one, but Laboe's reaction was simply to wink knowingly as he himself handed me my first gin and tonic, followed by several more throughout the course of the evening. This wasn't the first time I'd gotten crazy drunk, but still, when we got back to my shared Santa Monica apartment, Dana had to practically carry me from his parked car up to the front door. Not sure how, but he managed to get me inside, after which I immediately passed out on the sofa and woke up several times throughout the night just to plant my hand on the floor, to steady myself and keep from falling off.

And so I became a Santa Monica couch potato, eventually giving up alcohol in order to take a part-time gig at a greeting card store on the city's Third Street Promenade. This outdoor pedestrian mall was a heavily landscaped shopping center as well as a local hangout, with wide walkways, trees, and giant concrete planters. One afternoon as I was leaving my minimum-wage job to head back to the apartment, I saw a familiar-looking guy perched on one of those planters and was surprised when he called out to me to come over and talk to him. I did, and the fellow turned out to be none other than a much longer-haired and slightly older version of Peter Tork of the Monkees! Oddly enough, Peter had always been my favorite member of that preteen/teen-idol band, which had been propelled into stardom by its self-titled midsixties sitcom.

Peter Tork formally introduced himself, after which we chatted for a while on the promenade, and he asked what I was doing later that evening. He told me he would be taking part in a benefit show that night at the Troubadour and would love to have me come down as his guest if I was interested. Of course I was! I didn't even bother to ask who else would be performing, since just hearing the word "Troubadour" worked instant musical magic on my ears, taking me back to my high school years. What also hit me was that strangely enough, this Spring '74 Troubadour visit of mine would be happening such a short time after John Lennon's ejection that past March!

I managed to make it to the iconic West Hollywood club that night minutes before showtime, and sure enough, just as he'd promised, my new acquaintance Peter Tork had left my name on his guest list at the door. Right before anyone hit the stage, I was thrilled to hear that the entertainment that night would include Linda Ronstadt, members of the Eagles, and Jackson Browne—what a rush! Peter himself made a relatively brief appearance on stage and smiled at me as I waved and enthusiastically mouthed, "Thank you!" Sadly, that was the last I ever communicated with him. I waited around for a short time after the show to see if he'd be coming by to continue our earlier conversation, but it was a no-go, since I had a bus to catch if I wanted to get back to Santa Monica before public transpo called it quits for the evening.

All in all, it was a great experience, even if I was a little disappointed in having to leave the Troubadour all by myself. I didn't really have any illusion that a thirty-something sixties TV pop star would want to start a relationship with an eighteen-year-old college dropout, but the incident certainly boosted my confidence during what was an otherwise unsettling and somewhat dark, blurry period in my life.

The recorded soundtrack to those hazy Santa Monica days came courtesy of one of my roommates. Judy, a perceptive young black woman, recognized my sorry, self-inflicted state and wasted no time turning me on to Stevie Wonder's most recent records, *Talking Book* and *Innervisions*. Thanks to Judy and me, both of these amazing albums seemed to be spinning nonstop on the lone turntable in her Santa Monica apartment. In many ways, Wonder, the former child prodigy turned ubersuccessful singer/songwriter/producer/superstar/hitmaker by the early seventies, became my musical savior during those troubled times. Thanks to songs like "I Believe (When I Fall in Love It Will Be Forever)" from *Talking Book*, I felt that Wonder was able to echo my sad, brokenhearted sentiments as well as provide hope for a warm and loving future with someone, somewhere, somehow, someday.

A few years later, I found myself conducting interviews and writing the script for the RKO Radio Network's Stevie Wonder special. Needless to say, I couldn't help but think back on those downhearted days sleeping on Judy and Susan's Santa Monica sofa, and to this day his inspirational music never fails to lift me out of whatever funk I find myself in. So while Stevie Wonder and his songs soothed my soul, I began to plot my return to Santa Cruz by reregistering and making my way back up the coast in time for summer session.

After deciding that inserting myself into a whole new group of friends was the only way to move forward once I found my way back to Santa Cruz, I began my new outlook on life by renting space in a house near the city's not-so-bustling downtown area with a bunch of unfamiliar, non-College V roommates and registering for a couple of classes mostly just to fill the hours in my otherwise empty summer days. Off-campus jobs for UCSC students were few and far between, especially from June to September, and since I knew I'd undoubtedly be moving back up on campus once fall quarter started, I didn't knock myself out looking for work.

Despite my often lonesome solo summer days and nights, this seemed to me to be a major turning point in my life—my nineteenth birthday was approaching, and the closer it came, the more I began to feel the force of age, as though things were progressing way too rapidly and I was already getting too old to continue living with the uncertainty, randomness, and behavior of my recent past. As I'd been warned by Neil Young in a line from "Sugar Mountain," one of my favorite songs of his, "You can't be twenty on Sugar Mountain." I took that cautionary message to heart as I realized that the time to start figuring out my next steps not only for the school year ahead but for my entire future was drawing near.

Just before I got too serious about plotting out the next phase of my life, and exactly three days before my nineteenth birthday, concert promoter Bill Graham presented Bay Area music fans with the second event in his Day on the Green concert series for 1974, once again giving rock fans the opportunity to take over the great outdoors at the Oakland Coliseum. My housemates drove us up from Santa Cruz early that a.m. for a musical Saturday in the sun, and as we started to spread our blankets out on the field and camp out for the all-day show, we also began chugging down beer by the bucketful. It certainly helped having at least one twenty-one-year-old among us, who could stand in line at the stadium concession stand and legally buy the booze that would get us drunk as skunks.

The ultracool concert line up that day included the Band, Jesse Colin Young, Joe Walsh, and headliners Crosby, Stills, Nash & Young. CSN&Y were appearing as part of their much publicized reunion tour, which also had been put together by Graham, and took the group from stadium to massive stadium across the country that entire summer. I was of course most looking forward to seeing Neil Young, along with Crosby, Stills, and Nash, and when they launched into Neil's "Sugar Mountain," I finally felt like my life was about to get back on track and that everything I'd been so worried about was somehow going to work out.

One interesting note about the 1974 CSN&Y reunion tour is that their original drummer, Dallas Taylor, who had not only played on the band's self-titled debut album as well as *Déjà Vu*, their follow-up LP with Young but also performed with the group at Woodstock, their second live gig, had been replaced by Russ Kunkel. A decade or so later, I would be on the way to making my own connection with Taylor, who by then had been through serious drug and alcohol addiction and had even attempted suicide. I'd been recommended to Taylor as a ghostwriter for the memoir he wanted to publish following his lengthy stint in rehab. After our chatty, friendly phone conversation, I headed over to the address he gave me, which turned out to be an apartment in a funky Los Angeles neighborhood. I was there to meet with him and his girlfriend, a woman who had apparently been one of his nurses/caregivers at the rehab facility. It turned out to be her apartment, and from what I gathered that evening, once out of rehab Dallas had moved in with her, since he was broke and homeless—just another perk of longtime addiction. He seemed relieved to have love in his life as well as hope that he was finally on the mend, and he began telling me stories of his days with Crosby, Stills, Nash, and, eventually, Young. He admitted that from the beginning, he had always felt like the guy looking in on them from the rear door, just as the photo on the back side of that first CSN album cover presented him. But the most memorable tale that came from Dallas that evening—one I'd never seen or heard before and haven't again since—was of a bizarre encounter he claimed to have had early on with Jimi Hendrix. Dallas described meeting and jamming with Jimi one evening in a New York club and said Hendrix invited him to a get-together planned for later that night in his hotel room. But when a self-described innocent, barely out-of-his-teens Taylor arrived ready to party and knocked on the door, a buck naked Hendrix answered, and no one else was in the room. Dallas made it quite clear to me that he believed it was a setup. He was absolutely sure Jimi was hoping to seduce him, but instead of waiting to find out, he immediately turned around and left the hotel. I honestly don't know whether I bought that story as Dallas related it to me that night or not, and I don't believe it made it into his memoir, *Prisoner of Woodstock*, which is credited solely to Taylor himself—no ghostwriter. Shortly after our meet up, Dallas did let me know he was going to try to put pen to paper and write his book by himself, although serious health issues ended up postponing his work, which was finally published in the midnineties. Sadly, Dallas Taylor passed away in 2015 at the age of sixty-six, so I guess when it comes to the believability of his Hendrix story, we'll never know.

By the time the Day on the Green show had come to a close and we were packed up and ready to hunt down our car to head home to Santa Cruz, I had to temporarily split up from my small group of friends. This was in order to find my own private trash can and spend some quality time bending over it facedown, throwing up the entire barrel of beer I must have consumed since our arrival at the coliseum. As a matter of fact, I drank so much brew that day, I swore I'd never touch another drop of beer again as long as I lived.

To this day, the only time I've consumed an alcoholic beverage even close to beer since then was when I was in London a few years later interviewing Paul and Linda McCartney and the rest of Wings for RKO. Paul recommended we head to their favorite local pub, located next door to his office, so I could try a glass of Shandy. I figured that since it was a half-beer, half-lemon-lime-soda concoction, it couldn't kill me, but all it took was one sip for me to start feeling just about as sick as I did after my drunken Day on the Green. So I put the Shandy back down on the bar and haven't picked up any kind of brew since.

Back at UC Santa Cruz for fall quarter, I realized it was time to put my writing skills to good use and start working toward my journalistic goals, even if they weren't exactly well-defined at that point. I moved back on campus—this time, into a tiny single room, barely big enough for a twin bed. This space was in College V's A rather than B Dorm, and I almost immediately began hanging out with students who'd barely, if ever, entered my social sphere the year before. I'd been too wrapped up in whatever it was my boyfriend Mark and his group of College V notables were into back then, but now, with him off campus and out of my life, it was MY time, and as I enrolled in creative writing classes I felt like I was reclaiming a long-lost passion.

Unfortunately, misfortune struck just as I was starting what I thought of as my new, productive student life. After a crazy, wild evening in town, some of my new friends and I found ourselves way too stoned to be running like lunatics to catch the last bus of the night to take us back up to campus. This was especially not the smartest thing for me to do on wet grass while wearing my favorite four-inch platforms, the official footwear of the seventies. I slipped, I fell, and I ended up in the emergency room with a seriously broken ankle and foot. For weeks, make that months, I was once again severely restricted by a heavy cast and crutches, and I could barely leave my dorm room, let alone head off campus. I did my best to get to class and keep up my social contacts, but it was tough. I even had to put off working my job at the newly remodeled and expanded College V Coffee House, although it was now actually much less of a hip hot spot and more like an establishment-run chain restaurant serving homestyle meals cooked in a brand-new, fully stocked kitchen.

When my cast finally came off, I still had to hobble around on crutches for quite a while thanks to the bone shards that had splintered from my ankle, and although surgery was advised, I had neither the time nor adequate enough health care coverage to make it happen. Instead, I decided on a course of exercise to rebuild my weakened ankle joint, and when one local instructor suggested taking a Balinese dance class as a way of strengthening my lower leg, I kept that in mind for when I was fully recovered.

Throughout it all, I kept pen to paper, and I eventually, along with a like-minded coconspirator, became founding editor of the weekly campus journal, which came to be known as the College V Newsletter. Not exactly the most creatively titled school publication, but since I'd already tried my best somewhat unsuccessfully to weasel my way into the clique that ran *City on a Hill*, the weekly newspaper headed by students from UCSC's other, more established and more conventional colleges, I stuck with it.

Surprisingly, radio didn't enter the picture at all for me back then. I'd been unimpressed by the campus station and most of the music choices made by the students in charge, so I kept my distance. In retrospect, it was undoubtedly my loss. It could quite possibly have been a great opportunity, but instead I concentrated on writing about campus life, movies, and music for our fledgling newsletter. In our first issue, I reviewed a College V dining hall concert featuring the impressive South American folk singer Mercedes Sosa, aka "the Argentinean Joan Baez."

The actual, North American Joan Baez was apparently a good friend of hers, and both were known for their dedication to a number of causes, including both the plight of farmworkers and the women's movement. Kind of corny, but I called my rave review "Sosa Not Just So-So," and I went on to describe not only Mercedes's magically commanding stage presence, but also her stirring choice of material, even though I hardly understood a single word, considering it was all sung in Spanish.

But to be honest, the bulk of my personal C-V Newsletter journey was about establishing a weirdly comic tone that carried over to our contributors and their weekly columns. One instant reader favorite was "Ask Ultra-Boy . . . Questions and Answers about Your Super-Powers," a Q and A written by Bruce, a former altar boy who coincidentally had been the best friend of my cross-dressing former boyfriend, Mark, the year before. My dorm roommate from freshman year, Laurie B, also contributed to the newsletter, as did her boyfriend at the time. He was a cool graphics guy and cartoonist named Greg who came up with the idea for Kollege V Komix, which featured Filboid Studge, a goofy, fictional C-V student loosely based on himself. Who would have guessed that Filboid—I mean Greg—would go on to become the original bass player for the Call, recording two major-label albums and touring nationally with the likes of Peter Gabriel?

Before spring quarter came to a close, I started looking into the suggestion that I work on repairing my foot and ankle by taking Balinese dance classes. I quickly decided that if that was the road I really wanted to take, I'd be better off going straight to the source. This meant not transferring to UC Berkeley, which had a well-respected ethnomusicology department with in-house Indonesian gamelan orchestra and dance instructors, but instead heading to the far-off island of Bali itself. Thanks to a number of on-campus connections and frequent trips up to Palo Alto, I was accepted into a Stanford University-based program called Volunteers in Asia. This was despite the fact that I wasn't a Stanford student, like every single one of the other members. I soon began making weekly UC shuttle trips from Santa Cruz up to Berkeley to study Indonesian, a surprisingly easy tongue to learn thanks to the fact that the verbs have no tenses. I was also required to take classes in teaching English as a second language, since a TESL certificate would become my ticket to Asia, granting me airfare, lodging, and the oh-so-difficult-to-get visa that would give me the legal right to an extended stay in Indonesia to study Balinese dance.

So before I knew it, to the surprise and, yes, dismay of my family and most of my friends, I was on a flight with my fellow Volunteers in Asia members to Southeast Asia, making our first stops in Japan, while just about everybody else I knew was off to spend their summer breaks backpacking around Europe. My first taste of round-the-world travel included everything from a secluded monastery in the mountains, where we joined a gaggle of young Buddhist monks-to-be in their nearly impossible-to-keep vows of silence, to the loud and crazy skyscraper rooftop bars of Tokyo during happy hour, and I fell in love with it. We went sightseeing in other exotic places I had never expected to visit, but it was our sojourn to Kuala Lumpur, Malaysia, that had extraspecial meaning for me. This was because it was here that I got to meet the pen pal whom I'd been exchanging letters with ever since we were both just ten years old. It was a dream come true to finally visit sweet Yoke Fah, and something I honestly had never expected to happen in this lifetime. We bonded instantly—two girls from different corners of the world with surprisingly similar outlooks on life—and as we hugged one last time before saying our sad goodbyes, the whole trip suddenly seemed to make sense to me.

My eventual drop off point was the capital of Indonesia, Jakarta, located on the island of Java, an urban metropolis that seriously freaked me out from the moment I set out to walk the streets. It seemed like everywhere I went I saw nothing but dramatically disfigured beggars flaunting their filth and lack of limbs in order to get even a handful of rupiah, the Indonesian currency. To say I was completely turned off and scared and beginning to regret my six-month-minimum commitment to Bali, even though it was a different island, would be putting it mildly. Plus, I was approached by a number of frightening individuals who I was sure were about to rob or attack me, so I headed back to my hotel room and stayed put. Just a few days later, I was able to travel over land to the eastern tip of Java, where I finally boarded the ferry that would take me across the Bali Strait and over to what was about to become the island of my dreams.

—CHAPTER 7—

"Bali Hai"—No, Bali High

My late-night arrival on Bali turned out to be strangely perfect timing. Not only did the father of the family I was about to move in with walk right up and introduce himself once my boat had docked, but he also informed me that rather than take me straight to their house in Denpasar, the island's only major city at the time, he'd made other plans. He dragged me to a traditional all-night Balinese shadow puppet show, which, I was about to learn, was called *wayang kulit*. From midnight until the break of dawn, I watched in utter fascination as the puppets, made of carved leather, were rear-projected on a fabric screen, their shadows cast by flickering oil lamps as they acted out dramatic stories from Hindu mythology.

Although my understanding was minimal and I was practically half asleep, it was oddly both authentic and surreal, a feast for my eyes and ears, not to mention a welcome cleansing following my horrifying Jakarta experience. Plus, my new Balinese father introduced me afterward to the puppet master himself, or *dalang*, who welcomed me to his home turf with open arms. He also promised me that when he retired in a few months, he would give me some of his incredible handmade, vintage puppets as keepsakes so that I would always remember my first night on Bali, which he did. Several months later, when I was on my way back to the States, a Korean Airlines security team opened my luggage and took them from me. Those guards were apparently one-hundred-percent sure that the somewhat sharp bamboo rods, which *dalangs* used to manipulate the puppets behind the lit screens, were potentially dangerous weapons that could be used to attack the pilot during my flight. But I stood my ground when my return flight landed and eventually managed to get them all back from Korean Airlines. I've kept them to this day, further engraving the memory of that dreamlike first-night puppet show in my consciousness.

My gift from Bali's best *dalang*—the puppet master's puppets.

One thing for sure: the Bali that I encountered back in 1975 was definitely not the super popular destination that it would eventually become. Tourism there hadn't exploded yet, and despite rumors of superstar rockers like Mick Jagger heading to Bali to escape the massive crowds he found in more popular vacation spots, it was still pretty much undiscovered.

Visitors then to the tropical island, I would come to find out, were almost all Australians, the bulk of them surfers. A handful of Germans and even a few Americans were tossed into the mix. This is what made John Lennon's response to one of my questions just over five years later, as I was sitting next to him and Yoko at the Dakota, so cooly coincidental:

"How do you feel?" I asked, wondering how they came up with certain song statements together, as a couple. "I mean, are you trying to get something across, or . . . ?"

John jumped in and answered, "It's to share it, you know? It's like being somewhere beautiful like Bali, and all your friends haven't been, and you wanna say, 'My God! I was in Bali, man, and it's just the greatest place, and it's really . . .' It's that; that's how we are about things."

And that's exactly how I feel when it comes to my onetime island abode. As John said, Bali was an incredible destination not only to experience, but also to turn one's friends on to. Which is what I began to do almost immediately upon arrival by writing letters to just about everyone I knew.

One of the first memories of my time spent there begins with a band I guess you could say I've always had an extremely rocky relationship with. Actually, maybe nonexistent would be a better way to describe that band bond, seeing as I'd been going out of my way to avoid the Grateful Dead, a group I associated only with dope-smoking, acid-dropping hippies, since junior high school. My bad! At that point, I'd never even listened to a Dead album in its entirety. Their tune "Truckin'" was practically all I knew of them for far too long, until I ended up in, of all places, Denpasar. These were the days before there were any radio or TV stations on the island, so if you wanted to hear any form of popular music, you needed a cassette player. To my surprise, I was lucky enough to find one sitting in my host family's tiny guest cabin, where I was about to live for the rest of the year.

Unfortunately, their previous guest, who'd kindly left behind his portable tape deck, neglected to leave any cassettes to go with it. Or so I thought until I moved a chair and found one lonely tape sitting all by itself on the floor. I was more than excited as I picked it up to check it out, until I realized that, you guessed it, the Grateful Dead had followed me all the way to Indonesia.

It turned out to be a copy of the band's *American Beauty* album, and my immediate impulse was to dump it and run to the local marketplace as soon as possible to pick up music that I actually wanted to hear. Sadly, that was when I became seriously ill with the Balinese equivalent of Montezuma's revenge and couldn't even begin to think of getting out of bed for days on end. The worst part was I felt too sick to even read or write, so I had no entertainment at all other than that lone Grateful Dead cassette.

Desperate times call for desperate measures. By day three of my debilitating, nauseating bacterial infection, I figured it couldn't possibly get any worse, so I decided I was finally ready to take on the Dead. I broke down and listened to *American Beauty*, and what a surprise! From the minute the first song, "Box of Rain," began to play, I have to admit, I was hooked. It was nothing like what I'd expected, and instead of wanting to rip that tape out of the cassette deck, I was totally turned on to Jerry Garcia and company's amazing amalgam of melodic folk rock harmonies with doses of country and bluegrass. Who would ever have guessed that I'd end up playing that same cassette multiple times a day for months?!

But honestly, I was still hesitant about checking out other recordings by the Grateful Dead once my time on Bali came to an end. My love for *American Beauty* would always be my very own musical secret, especially after heading home to the States, where punk rock/new wave was about to explode.

Just over a year later, I was back from Bali and had begun working at KFRC-AM radio in San Francisco. One of the first local celebrities I met was concert promoter, venue owner, band manager, frequent station visitor, and all-around visionary Bill Graham. Remember he had also been the force a few years earlier behind the Rolling Stones Nicaragua Benefit that I'd been lucky enough to win tickets to, and when I told him about my KMET experience, he became incredibly supportive. But no matter how many times Bill Graham generously tried to hand me tickets to see the Grateful Dead at his popular venue Winterland, I always responded with 'Thanks, but no thanks."

I think it kind of drove him slightly nuts that I continued to refuse to accept his offers. After all, he'd been the first major promoter to book the Grateful Dead, formerly known as the Warlocks, at the legendary Fillmore. As his relationship with Jerry Garcia grew, Graham also helped manage and promote the band as part of the Bay Area musical counterculture scene.

It actually became kind of a joke between us for the next couple of years. I'd ask for tickets to see notoriously raunchy rockers like Iggy Pop at the Old Waldorf, a club Bill also owned, and he'd laughingly say something like "Only if you'll take these too" and shove a pair of Grateful Dead tickets in my hand. Embarrassingly enough, I generally ended up giving them away to my radio station coworkers rather than going to see the band myself, but of course Iggy Pop was another story entirely.

It was with unbridled excitement that my date and I showed up one night at the standing-room-only Old Waldorf, Bill's relatively cozy venue, to see one of our idols, Iggy Pop, for the first time. Among his hordes of fans, Iggy was considered the originator of punk rock, and my date and I had no idea if this show was going to be one of his infamous events that involved bottle smashing, chair tossing, peanut butter smearing, chest slicing complete with bloodshed, or even blow jobs.

As we stood not far from the front of the stage digging the show while Iggy got down and dirty, I noticed a haggard, heavyset, strangely out-of-place-looking dude staring right at me, which kind of creeped me out. I gave him what I thought was my best "get lost" look and tried to concentrate on the show, but apparently it served only to encourage this odd guy, because suddenly he waddled right up next to me and tried to start up a conversation.

With obvious scorn, he looked out at the packed house and asked me what the attraction was to punk rock—what I liked about it and why. When I responded with some typical-at-the-time-for-me smart-ass answer, he stuck around instead of moving away, as I'd hoped, kept talking, and then asked me if I wanted to come backstage with him. I couldn't stop myself from being totally impolite as I sneered and nastily replied, "Yeah, right, like they're going to let you backstage.

Who are you, the roadie's grandfather?"

Right then and there my escort turned around to take a good look at whom it was I was being so snarky to. He nudged me with his elbow and said under his breath, "Laurie, don't you know who that is?" I answered, "No, and I don't care. He's a punk-hating pest bugging the crap out of me!"

His response was to get me to look at the weird guy's right hand, which I then noticed was missing most of its middle finger. But this meant nothing to me until my date pinched me and practically spat in my ear as he whispered harshly, "Laurie! That's fucking JERRY GARCIA!"

Beyond mortified, I turned back to my mystery man to apologize, but he was already gone, making his way through the crowd. Sadly, I never, ever got the chance to tell him before he passed away how sorry I was for being such a rude, bratty little bitch. Forgive me, Jerry!

Less than a decade later, when I was back living in Los Angeles and freelancing as a writer for *Rock Magazine*, I got the call to interview Bob Weir in his Hollywood hotel room. This happened in 1984, just as *Where the Beat Meets the Street*, the second studio album from his CBS side project, Bobby and the Midnites, was about to be released. Weir was best known as the rhythm guitar player and cofounder, along with Garcia, of the group that would become the Grateful Dead. When I told him a slightly less self-incriminating version of my Jerry/Iggy story, he nearly fell off his bed laughing.

But it was the look of sweet disbelief on Weir's face when I admitted that I had had to travel halfway around the world—all the way to Bali, as a matter of fact—to discover and appreciate the Grateful Dead that really made my day. As he told me that afternoon, this would actually be the best time for me to finally check out the band in concert. "The Grateful Dead is more alive now than it ever was," he informed me. "We're better at it now. Practice makes perfect."

So why mess with perfection, I had to ask. Why step into the studio with Bobby and the Midnites, a band that, sure, featured some hot talent and a fine producer—Jeff "Skunk" Baxter, best known at the time for his stints with Steely Dan and the Doobie Brothers—when Bob was already part of such a legendary gang of rockers? "It's obvious that I front this band," Weir explained, putting heavy emphasis on the "I." "Look, I'm not interested in being in another band like the Grateful Dead, where I'm just a part of the band. I want the freedom to be able to be the front man in this band!" And so he was . . . even if the last live gig Bobby and the Midnites ever played came just a month or so after our interview.

I finally did break down a couple of years later and head out to see the Dead in Southern California at the Long Beach Arena. This was on the band's first major tour following Garcia's life-threatening diabetic coma the year before. Honestly, I was so put off by the hordes of yuppie Deadheads bragging nonstop throughout the show about how many Grateful Dead concerts they'd been to and how many bootlegs they had, I can't say I was really able to enjoy it all that much. Oh well.

The preshow parking lot scene was another story altogether. It was more like a makeshift hippie shopping center where one could buy everything from tasty vegetarian treats to handmade tie-dye tees and of course plenty of drugs, from opium to acid. I may never have achieved Deadhead status, but I was definitely a compulsive shopper, so that late-eighties evening was still worthwhile.

Back on Bali in the midseventies, I started teaching my English-as-a-second-language classes at the medical center in Denpasar. This basically amounted to me telling stories and asking questions about Balinese customs in English, then handing out crossword puzzles I'd created as homework. Fortunately, most of the med center employees who were my students already had a basic knowledge of English, so my limited ability as an ESL teacher was pretty much ignored. We actually had a good time, and as I made friends in class, I found myself invited to plenty of outings at the island's seemingly endless array of temples and shrines and, of course, the sacred monkey forest.

I definitely felt like I had a way-more-than-decent social life, especially when it came to Hindu holidays. It seemed like every other day on Bali was a holiday requiring time off from work or class, and thanks to my students as well as the Balinese family I lived with, I was able to take part in countless inspirational celebrations.

My favorite Hindu holiday was without a doubt Saraswati Day. This was celebrated in honor of the goddess of knowledge, music, art, wisdom, and learning, aka Saraswati. She was not only a significant creative icon, but also a terrifically talented, four-armed, stringed-instrument-playing, legendary beauty as well. Her day of devotion is also closely related to books—not necessarily reading them, but recognizing them as sacred texts. This was carried out, surprisingly, not just at Hindu temples, but at the beach as well. Strangely enough, most Balinese natives back then almost never went near the ocean, since the beach was considered almost entirely a tourist/surfer attraction. The exception came when they were celebrating and offering prayers to Saraswati before cleansing themselves and, as my Balinese family demonstrated for me, their books in the sea water while hanging out on the sand.

I celebrated my own personal holiday when I turned twenty on Bali. I definitely felt like I'd made my way down from "Sugar Mountain" right on time, just as Neil Young and his song lyrics had warned me would be necessary. It seemed more than strange to be so far away from both my home and from good friends on such a big birthday, but I hung in there. It hit me that at the same time I was saying goodbye to my teens, I was saying hello to a wonderfully weird, wild, and wacky future that could only belong to me.

Given that I had spent so many summers as a teenager on the beach in Santa Monica, specifically right next to lifeguard station sixteen, which was the popular spot on the sand known as Sorrento, it made perfect sense to me to commemorate my twentieth birthday on Bali at the seashore. Kuta was the beach of choice for nonnatives who couldn't afford the more expensive oceanfront resort area of Sanur. So off I went, determined to indulge in a rare day of decadence, since I'd taken time off from both my work and dance duties.

I stopped just short of the beach to eat at a tiny roadside café where, rumor had it, extraspecial mushroom omelets were served, the key ingredient being magic psilocybin shrooms. A group of obnoxiously noisy German tourists sitting at a couple of outside tables seemed to be enjoying theirs, so I sat, ordered, ate, paid, and went on my way—and when I hit the sand, I waited. And waited. And waited. Finally, it happened—a wave of psychedelia overcame me, and it showed no signs of diminishing as the daylight hours dragged on. I was still paralyzed on the sand and hallucinating as the sun went down, and I realized there was no way I could sit down to dinner with my host family without giving away exactly what I'd been up to.

Instead I spent the Indonesian equivalent of about twenty-five cents and rented a room in a local surf shack to try to sleep off my mushroom trip. When I woke up early the next morning, it registered right away that my family undoubtedly had been worrying about me all night. My plan was to somehow get home in time to sneak into my bedroom before any of them woke up. No such luck.

From the minute I made it back from the beach to the main drag in Denpasar, I sensed that a number of locals were looking at me as though they'd been asked to keep their eyes open for a tall, curly-haired, missing American. My reception once I got home was slightly worse than I imagined. My Balinese mother and father were relieved that I was safe, but hugely disappointed in me for what they interpreted as running off and disappearing, and they made me promise never to leave the house again without letting them know exactly where I was going, whom I was with, and when I'd be home. So much for being an independent twenty-year-old adult. Still, it was nice to know that my foreign family truly cared about me, and from that point on, I made sure to keep them fully in the loop.

While teaching ESL and regularly sightseeing across the island, I was also taking Balinese dance lessons multiple times a week. These sessions unfortunately proved to be far more difficult than I could ever have imagined. I quickly realized it wasn't just a matter of memorizing dance movements, but also required that I learn how to express myself at the ripe old age of twenty in the same ways that Balinese babies were taught before they even started learning to walk.

Intense statements made with eye expressions and hand gestures are the key to excellence in traditional Balinese dance. Despite the fact that I was fortunate enough to have a very talented teacher, there was no way I could even come close to performing the one dance I was studying, the Tari Tenun, otherwise known as the Weaving Dance, with the same skill as your average eight-year-old Balinese girl. But still, I made my way from urban Denpasar to my teacher's tiny shack in a remote village outside of town as often as I could.

I traveled part of the way by *bemo*, a sort of independently driven minivan, and then walked the bulk of the distance to her door through endless rice paddies. As I took off my shoes to tramp through the flooded fields, I tried to ignore the slimy feel of the mud and rice crop beneath my feet, but by the time I reached the site of my lesson I was usually shivering and pretty creeped out.

It wasn't until quite a while later, while having dinner at home with my host family one night, that I finally understood what was going on. This wasn't easy, considering their limited English and my less-than-fluent skills in the Indonesian language. As a platter of some unrecognizable, swirly, serpentine-looking food was being passed around the table, I politely asked what it was, only to be answered with a word that meant absolutely nothing to me. When the head of the family explained that the dish was made from a sort of fishlike, finless animal that lived beneath the surface of rice paddies, it suddenly dawned on me that I'd been walking on eels every time I'd taken a dance class.

I felt like I'd just taken a baseball bat to the belly, since for someone like me, with ichthyophobia, aka fear of touching or even looking at fish, especially live ones, this was way too much. I got up from the table and spent the rest of the evening trying to soothe my queasy stomach. Although I had no intention of quitting dance lessons, I knew I had to come up with a plan to get myself through those rice paddies going forward without shrieking and vomiting.

I managed to find some rubber booties that completely covered my feet and helped me ignore what I now knew to be long skinny swamp eels slithering around in the mud beneath practically every step I took. Sadly, it still didn't help my already weak dancing skills.

My teacher did her best to sympathize but couldn't hide the fact that she was still somewhat peeved. She'd been going through tough times of her own since long before I began studying dance with her and therefore found it difficult to understand what she saw as the silly issues of an obviously well-off white girl. Was I anywhere near wealthy? No. But in Bali, my last name was often mispronounced as "Kaya," which translates as "rich" in Indonesian. Therefore, most people just assumed I had money, and plenty of it.

My teacher's own story had been a true Balinese fairy tale, but without the happy ending—at least not as of the time I knew her. Born into the royal family of a remote district on the island, she was named Mas, which translates as "gold." Her family name, Tjokorda, meant "descendent of kings," so her full name, Tjok Mas, stood for the King's Gold, which is exactly how she was raised and looked upon by her family and fellow villagers, who idolized her.

Tjok Mas grew up to become a beautiful and talented dancer performing all over the island for locals and foreigners alike. Her father wanted nothing more than for her to eventually marry her similarly talented dance partner, considered to be the best male dancer on Bali, hoping that together they could possibly join an international performance troupe.

On the day they took part in a special celebratory performance of the great Hindu epic the *Ramayana*, Tjok Mas was never more graceful or radiant than she was as she danced the role of Sita, the divine wife of the story's hero, Rama. The dance ended and the crowd cheered loudly, eager to congratulate the gifted young star. But Tjok Mas failed to return to the stage to acknowledge the audience's applause, and despite her father's frantic searching, she was nowhere to be found.

The mystery was solved when her handsome dance partner finally spoke up, admitting that Tjok Mas had told him just before the show that she was running away afterward to get married. As her father suspected, she had chosen a lower-caste partner with whom to elope. This was considered a big deal on Bali, even though he happened to be the son of a fairly wealthy government official.

Although her new husband's family and fellow villagers were thrilled to accept royalty into their fold, Tjok Mas's father banned the couple from her former home. They were somewhat forgiven once she had her first daughter, but when she gave birth to her second little girl, the real trouble started.

Her husband, Agung, subscribed to the ancient Balinese legend that if a man doesn't have a son, he's doomed in his next life to do nothing but women's work. He also believed in a traditional law that permitted him to look for a new wife to bear him a son even while remaining married to his first.

Agung began spending less and less time with Tjok Mas and their two daughters, and it turned out he'd taken up with an older widow in a neighboring village, making this woman his second wife and impregnating her in hopes of having a male heir.

When Tjok Mas found out, severe depression struck like a sledgehammer. She stopped eating and lost so much weight and became so weak she was barely able to get out of bed in the morning. Her friends, family, and neighbors all avoided her, but she hung on, spending her days praying that Agung's second wife would deliver a daughter, not a son. When that actually did happen, Tjok Mas rejoiced, although Agung became unbearably bitter. She told him she was ready to start over and bear him a son, but her doctor said no, absolutely not, since she would never survive another pregnancy in her weakened condition.

That was Tjok Mas when I met her. She was desperately trying to regain her health and win back the husband who'd all but abandoned her, because even in his twenties, he was already more concerned about his life after leaving this world than he was about his wife and family in the world in which he was already living.

I became her number one confidant while studying dance, and I worried more and more about her during her worst days, when Agung would stay away from Tjok Mas for weeks at a time. Sometimes after one of his rare visits, her mood would improve, and she took great pride in dancing for me, although she still was so thin and frail that it was like watching a feather floating through the air.

My most sincere wish when I left Bali was that Tjok Mas would one day find her fairy tale ending and regain her love of life, her status as one of the island's top traditional dancers, and possibly even her less-than-loving husband. Truthfully, all these years later, I still have no idea how her story was resolved. Hopefully it ended with the words "and they all lived happily ever after," but I guess I'll never know.

Another exciting experience of mine on Bali was becoming infatuated with batik, the centuries-old Indonesian art of fabric design using wax and dye. My fascination led me to a long string of private batik lessons in the artsy Balinese town of Ubud from an older and quite flirtatious local expert. He loved playing Motown R & B hits while not only teaching me how to use a wax needle, but also helping me create my breathtaking snake-filled T-shirt design. I still love and wear it nearly fifty years later!

I wore the shirt I made on Bali using the art of batik to go see this vintage band at the Whisky a Go Go: Strawberry Alarm Clock, with opening act (and good friends) Molly Hanmer & the Midnight Tokers. (Photo by Curt Fisher)

As my adventures on Bali came to a close, I began thinking about everything I'd been missing being so far from home. News was hard to come by in that remote corner of the world, and even when I came across copies of weeklies like *Time* magazine to try to catch up on current events, I found that they'd been government censored. Every single one of them had torn or blacked-out pages, including one issue's photo illustrations teaching readers how to do the Hustle. That Van

McCoy disco tune had apparently hit number one on the *Billboard* charts while I was away, as the disco dance craze astonishingly grew by leaps and bounds. Who would have guessed?

Much more important to me was finding out that I'd be coming home to new songs and sounds by some of my top musical heroes. These included Neil Young and his grief-stricken, anguished album *Tonight's the Night* as well as Bryan Ferry and Roxy Music's latest release, *Siren*, the album that would announce to the world that "Love Is the Drug." *Tonight's the Night* had actually been recorded two years before in response to the drug-overdose deaths of Crazy Horse guitarist Danny Whitten and roadie Bruce Berry, both close friends of Young. As Neil said to his fans on the liner notes of his original album release, "I'm sorry. You don't know these people. This means nothing to you."

Other highly anticipated new releases were also out, including the first album from soon-to-be punk/cult favorite Patti Smith. *Horses*, with its revamping of Van Morrison's "Gloria" and ultracool cover shot by renowned and often controversial photographer Robert Mapplethorpe, was about to totally change the way I looked at and listened to women in music.

Also released during my stint in Southeast Asia were a couple of records that would become turning points in the careers of the artists who created them. Fleetwood Mac's self-titled first album with Lindsay Buckingham and Stevie Nicks and Bruce Springsteen's *Born to Run*, which became his ticket to mainstream popularity, were both destined for major success. It was obvious that in pop culture alone, I was going to have a lot to catch up on.

—CHAPTER 8—

Goin' back to "Alcatraz"

The long, exhausting flight from Bali back to Los Angeles was filled with unexpected stops and delays, meaning that I missed my own "welcome home" surprise party. My mother had unexpectedly thrown this gathering together at the last minute and invited most of my best friends from high school. Not being able to attend the party was actually fine with me, since I was so bone-tired and jet-lagged when I landed that I ended up sleeping more than twenty-four hours straight once I finally made it to my mom's spare bedroom.

I woke up and almost immediately left for UC Berkeley, where I had been accepted starting winter quarter, just days away. My buddy Bruce, who'd been my nonprom date, offered to drive me up north from LA in his cool, classic Camaro. We had quite the adventure once we arrived and realized how difficult it might be for me to find a decent place to live, since I was definitely done with dorm life.

Responding to an ad in the local paper brought us over to a huge house in Berkeley that turned out to be the local headquarters for one of the most infamous cults of the day, the Moonies, aka Korean religious fanatic Sun Myung Moon's Unification Church. We managed to escape the Moonie megacompound just as they were about to lock us in, and after that you can bet I was incredibly relieved to be able to rent a room in the very next place we scouted. This was a funky but beautiful, ancient two-story home on Alcatraz Avenue in Oakland—not the greatest neighborhood at the time, but still just a short bus ride or somewhat time-consuming walk up to campus.

The funny thing is that I didn't even realize until months later, on the day I moved out, as I stood in the middle of Alcatraz Avenue loading my possessions onto the bed of a borrowed pickup truck, how the street must have gotten its name. I finally noticed right then and there that on a clear day, you could actually see straight across the bay to Alcatraz Island, the former home of a San Francisco offshore federal prison. In retrospect, this was totally fitting considering that back in high school, I must have listened to the album *Leon Russell and the Shelter People* at least three times a day, and my two favorite songs were "Stranger in a Strange Land" and "Alcatraz."

So now that I was officially a resident of Oakland, literally right across the Berkeley border, I was ready to finish up my college commitment, as I'd planned during my time in Indonesia.

Actually, the concept of attending the undergraduate journalism school at UC Berkeley had been floating around in my brain for a couple of years, but by the time I was ready to make a go of it, I faced more than a slight problem. The University of California had decided to shut it down, and unfortunately, the very last year of admission had already started while I was still on Bali. Unless I'd been willing to cut my time in Indonesia drastically short, there was no way I could have made it back in time.

I chose to stick it out on Bali instead, so by the time I hit Berkeley for the beginning of winter quarter in early '76, I had to practically fight my way into Journalism 100, the Introduction to News Writing course taught by a respected East Coast reporter turned college instructor named Mike Weiss.

Less than a week into class, when we got back our first graded assignment, centered on the who/what/when/where/why aspect of the journalism game, Mike made a point of calling out to me and taking me aside. He asked me what the heck I was doing there, adding that unlike the bulk of his J-100 students, I already had a handle on news writing, so I was essentially just passing time.

He advised, no, *urged* me to apply for a newspaper internship, which he was certain would help me land a writing job, and sent me running to the bulletin board in the J-school office to check out the posted possibilities.

My other influential teacher that quarter turned out to be David Littlejohn, the well-respected arts critic, author, and UCB J-School associate dean. He opened his Journalism 151 class with a warning meant to scare off any students who couldn't commit to his superlong, literary, and ultraheavy reading requirements. I took the bait and hungrily plowed through everything on his list, from Michael Arlen's *An American Verdict*, an account of Chicago's 1969 Black Panther raid, to Tom Wolfe's groundbreaking anthology *The New Journalism* and Norman Mailer's Pulitzer Prize–winning *Armies of the Night* . . . all titles meant, no doubt, to inspire me creatively as a writer.

But what moved me even more was Professor Littlejohn telling me later, during a meeting in his office, about the novel he'd just written that was rooted in rock 'n' roll. To be honest, his work of fiction had what I thought of at the time as a highly unlikely plot. It was about a murderous grad student seeking revenge against a legendary sixties rock performer and was titled *The Man Who Killed Mick Jagger*. This was of course strangely and sadly ironic considering that less than five years later, I'd be in total shock and disbelief following my own actual confrontation with the man who killed John Lennon.

In the meantime, off I went to the big journalism school bulletin board to see what news internships might still be up for grabs that summer. I was absolutely certain the editors of the *New York Times* were sitting at their desks waiting for me with baited breath to enhance their readership with my incredible reporting skills—WRONG. Even though summer was still months away, all of the prestige internships at major papers like the *Times* had already been filled for well over a year, mostly by UCB's snobby, all male batch of journalism grad students. I'd already noticed that on a daily basis, those guys all seemed to wear the same school "uniform": long-sleeved black cotton turtlenecks, baggy Levi's jeans, and Frye boots. They all carried old-school, wooden tobacco pipes similar to those my grandfather had smoked years before. That look, along with those pretentious, stinky pipes, was a turnoff that made me rethink my desired career as a big-time newspaper reporter. So what next?

One of the first posts I read on the bulletin board came from the government-run Voice of America. VOA offered up news and entertainment radio programming for international audiences. It was looking for journalism students who'd lived and studied abroad to fill positions outside the US, and I figured for sure that with my recent Indonesia experience, I had a good shot at getting a gig. I immediately grabbed an application, filled it out, and submitted it to VOA and then called the home office in Washington, DC, just a few days later to confirm receipt.

I was horrified to hear from some male government human-resources representative that even though I seemed qualified, as a female I would be better off just staying home in the States and having/raising kids. This sexist response definitely squelched any desire I had to ever work for a government agency, and it has stuck with me for all my years since.

Strangely enough, just over a decade later, while working on one of my first television production jobs, I happened to be thumbing through an issue of the *Hollywood Reporter* and came across an ad describing a sex-discrimination lawsuit that had been filed against the US Information Agency and Voice of America. Apparently, for years the feds had been rigging the hiring system in favor of men, even altering test scores to avoid giving jobs to women who were more qualified.

I was able to jump on the class-action-suit bandwagon right away, becoming one of about eleven hundred women claiming unfair treatment at the hands of the feds. I was eventually named one of the top fifty class members as the lawsuit, filed in the US District Court, dragged on for a total of twenty-three years. When it was finally settled in 2000, our suit, known as Hartman vs. Albright, earned the distinction of receiving the largest settlement ever in a federal sex discrimination/gender case: a total of $508 million!

Of course, my share of the settlement was nowhere near that amount, but still, it felt amazing to be compensated for the government's lack of interest in hiring twenty-year-old me as an international radio news writer/editor.

Thankfully, I did see another notice on the journalism-school career bulletin board that stood out from all the rest and seemed to call my name. San Francisco radio station KFRC, RKO Radio's Top 40 powerhouse known for its popular morning disc jockey, Dr. Don Rose, as well as its status as *Billboard* magazine's number one AM radio station several years running, was seeking newsroom interns for the first time.

I snatched the notice off the board and headed home right away to send a copy of my résumé to KFRC. Jan Yanehiro, head of the station's public affairs department, was handling the student-intern hiring process just before her move over to San Francisco's KPIX-TV. When Jan called several days later asking me to come in for an interview, I was in ecstasy. I couldn't fight the overwhelming feeling that I was about to take the first step on the road to my true calling.

But before I could even think about starting my summer internship, I had to maintain my student status and finish up that quarter and the next one at UCB. This meant having to take a number of required classes I'd managed to avoid like the plague while at UC Santa Cruz, including basics like poli sci, which quite honestly bored the crap out of me.

To spice things up while spending time on campus, I started looking for interesting, unusual subjects to write about. That's when I discovered Holy Hubert Lindsey, a Southern Baptist minister who'd made his way to Berkeley and then his mark by preaching to students outdoors at UCB's Sproul Plaza almost daily since the midsixties. "It was a time of chantin' and riotin' against the establishment," Hubert told me. "There were some fifteen thousand riotin' students back then who would have loved the chance to beat me to a pulp." Apparently, that's exactly what they did, sending him to the hospital with serious injuries at least a dozen times. But Holy Hubert managed to recover again and again and continue on his crazed Christian mission. I sensed he'd make a colorful interview thanks to his uniquely funny, exaggerated, and egotistical approach to fire and brimstone.

"My wife thinks I'm the grandest old thing that ever walked in shoe leather," Hubert bragged to me, "and I agree with her!"

We sandwiched a number of Q and A sessions in between Hubert's dogmatic sermons and my less-than-fascinating classes, and when my teacher Mike Weiss read the finished piece, he called it "pretty much perfect" and submitted it to the *Daily Cal*, the Berkeley campus paper.

When my Holy Hubert article ended up on the *Cal*'s front page a week or so later in February '76, it became the door opener to my real journalism education at the university, as well as my penchant for hanging out at lower Sproul Plaza. I soon realized that Sproul had not just been home to Mario Savio and the Free Speech Movement the decade before, but was even now a major center for student activity and entertainment, including the latest in live music.

That's how I happened to be sitting around, kicking back and spending time at Sproul Plaza during lunch one Friday afternoon, watching as a still-somewhat-unknown but radically cool-looking all-girl group of teens began tuning up before taking control of the scene with their raucous brand of rock 'n' and roll. The Runaways had gotten their start in LA thanks to record producer and Sunset Strip regular Kim Fowley, who had graduated from my LA high school, Uni, although nearly twenty years before I got there. By the time the Runaways played their deliciously rowdy daytime show on the Berkeley campus, Fowley had helped them land a major-label record deal. He'd also been instrumental in putting together their amazing lineup, which included lead vocalist Cherie Currie and guitarists Lita Ford and Joan Jett, who's thankfully still out touring to this day with her longtime follow-up band, the Blackhearts. As a matter of fact, in the years since, I've seen Joan Jett and the Blackhearts everywhere from the Hollywood Palace to the Hollywood Bowl, and she's still rocking just as hard as when I was first knocked out by her attitude and performance decades ago.

Right off the bat, the Runaways made that afternoon one of the best school days I ever had at Berkeley. By the time the group reached the chorus of what would become its signature hit, with Currie singing, "Hello Daddy, Hello Mom, I'm your ch-ch-ch-ch-ch-ch cherry bomb," every one of us lucky enough to show up at Sproul Plaza for their gig that Friday was totally sold.

Besides heading out to hear live music whenever possible back then, including shows at local clubs like the Longbranch Saloon, I had two time-consuming part-time jobs to work into my schedule in order to make ends meet. The first was my early-morning shift as a Fruity Rudy's girl, which meant I squeezed fresh orange juice and made smoothies for the masses for hours in a small, two-person minitrailer parked at the south entrance to campus. Lines before classes sometimes stretched out so long in front of my little window that it seemed like I'd be in the cart working my hefty hand-operated juicer all day long. To my surprise, the main positive outcome of that gig wasn't my daily pay, but rather the rock-hard right-arm bicep I developed thanks to that manual machine.

Fruity Rudy himself was an insulting, unpleasant boss who had a few other portable juice bars stashed in different spots all around campus, but he was probably best known for his relationship with one of his former hired hands, Nancy Ling Perry. Perry had been a Fruity Rudy's worker nearly three years before my time, which is when she also became a known member of the Symbionese Liberation Army. The SLA was the left-wing terrorist group responsible for kidnapping and eventually brainwashing Patty Hearst in 1974 and turning her into a bank-robbing coconspirator. Perry was killed later that year along with several other SLA members in an LAPD shootout, though Hearst managed to escape that confrontation because she'd been stopped and held for shoplifting earlier at a local store and thus wasn't at the SLA's Compton hideout when the cops opened fire.

Finding out about the Fruity Rudy/Nancy Ling Perry/Patty Hearst connection, I felt like I was somehow part of that super strange chapter in Bay Area history. This was even before I found out that the KFRC newsroom, where I would soon be starting my summer internship, had been one of the first, if not THE first, San Francisco radio stations the SLA had called to issue its demands after kidnapping Hearst.

The second job I held during my Berkeley student days was also in food service. It was a university work-study gig behind the snack bar at the Lawrence Hall of Science, popular for its amazing exhibits. This meant taking a shuttle high up into the hills above campus and then back down again for every shift. The science center had a planetarium too, but what really knocked me out in terms of technology back then was our snack bar kitchen, home to a huge, brand-new microwave oven, which was the first I'd ever seen. I found out years later, while producing a TV shoot at Graceland, Elvis Presley's Memphis home and tourist attraction, that Elvis himself was also an early microwave fan and owner. As a matter of fact, he'd bought the first microwave oven ever sold in Memphis, paying the outrageous price of $600 for it.

Considering my time-consuming obligations to my jobs, studies, and articles I was writing for the student paper, as well as my devotion to live music and my fascination with foreign film (primarily French), I didn't have a lot of free time to hang out with my Alcatraz Avenue housemates. There was a chore chart on our refrigerator that spelled out who was responsible for what, which was updated on a weekly basis. All six of us split everything from kitchen mopping to grocery shopping to cooking dinner for all of us each night of the week.

My number one memory in terms of being around the five students I lived with was spending early mornings together slugging down crappy coffee and reading the *San Francisco Chronicle*, specifically Armistead Maupin's captivating new column, "Tales of the City." It was actually more like a serialized novel, with eccentric characters and only-in-San Francisco plot twists. The more I read, the more I fell in love with the notion of moving to the city myself as soon as I could to start my own stream of San Fran escapades while hitting all the hotspots I'd been reading about in Mr. Maupin's fictional column.

When my dream finally came true and I earned my position at KFRC, no one was more excited than I was to not only meet the creator of "Tales of the City," but to actually join him for cocktails and conversation. These meetings took place at the French bistro/wine bar Le Central, which was conveniently located next door to our radio station. The opportunity came thanks to the wonderful woman who was to become my new boss and mentor, KFRC News Director Jo Interrante. Jo was a close friend of the writer she introduced to me as Army, and all of us sat side by side sipping her signature aperitif, Kir, an unfamiliar mix to me of white wine and the sweet black currant liqueur Cassis. I couldn't help but think how far I'd come since arriving in the Bay Area following my Balinese adventure just under a year before, and I couldn't even begin to imagine what might come next.

—CHAPTER 9—

"Bony Maronie"

Finally, summer hit, and I became a newsroom intern at KFRC, aka the Big 610—finally! Just being in that exciting, cigarette smoke–enhanced environment was quite the wake-up call.

The office was filled from early morning on with what would soon register in my bombarded brain as normal newsroom clatter, produced by constantly clanging teletype machines and ringing phones. The long row of news-service teletypes, printing out the latest updates from the Associated Press, United Press International, Reuters, and even an emergency national weather wire, stood against the far wall of the newsroom, spitting out top stories nonstop. That's why the rolls of paper inside them always needed to be replaced, and I soon came to learn that feeding those teletype machines, referred to as the "wires," was practically a full-time job itself.

Wires and their upkeep were brand-new to me, and I was taught right away by the station's news editor, Gary, how to watch over them, respond to their frequent bells and whistles, and check for breaking stories. I felt like I was creating a place for myself on the KFRC news team, which thrilled me no end.

The newsroom residents at the time were all guys except for top gun Jo Interrante, who'd made the move from Texas to take over the

KFRC news director spot once Program Director Michael Spears was also brought in from the same Dallas station. This is common at radio stations, since as upper-level management changes, so does most of the on-air talent, whether we're talking disc jockeys or newscasters.

Jo brought way more than just a feminine perspective to her new position at KFRC. Her unique style was not at all limited to her fashion sense and trendsetting platinum-blonde beauty, but also included the way she wrote and reported, making pop music a major part of the station's news programming. That's why when I was given my first writing and production assignment early on in my internship, I did my best to follow Jo's example.

I was asked to create an hourlong show that would run early on a Sunday morning as part of the station's fulfillment of its Federal Communications Commission public-affairs programming requirements. I knew that if I wanted to impress Jo, which, believe me, I did, more than anything, my show would need to be more than newsworthy, topical, and well written. It also needed to include supercool pop music perfectly related to the subject I chose to cover.

Like most basically insecure young gals who hadn't yet turned twenty-one, I was constantly focusing on and worried about my weight and was therefore often on some sort of crazy crash diet. I noticed that Jo seemed to be too, despite her being so svelte and nearly a dozen years older.

One of the daily tasks she wasted no time in assigning was to have me run out at a moment's notice to the small liquor store right across the street to pick up her lunch. Quite often, this would be a meager combination of a can of zero-calorie Diet Dr Pepper and a small pack of salted cashews. Coincidentally, I'd recently seen a local doctor's ad in the *San Francisco Chronicle* promoting a controversial weight-loss program that involved a mere five-hundred-calorie-a-day diet along with injections of human chorionic gonadotropin. HCG was a hormone extracted from the urine of pregnant women and had not yet been spoken out against or even addressed by the Food and Drug Administration.

Without seeking prior approval from Jo or anyone else in the news or public-affairs departments, I called the diet doctor's office and pretended to be personally interested in dropping pounds via HCG shots. I also convinced him that he could score unparalleled free publicity by agreeing to an interview with me, letting him know that the resulting sixty-minute broadcast about weight loss would undoubtedly bring his business even better results than the newspaper ad he'd paid for. The gullible guy fell for it hook, line, and sinker, and when I finally approached Jo with my proposal for this show, which I called *The Bay Area's Fight Against Fat*, she was overwhelmingly enthusiastic.

The day of my interview arrived quickly, and as I waited in the small studio I'd reserved at KFRC for the receptionist to announce the diet doctor's arrival, I went over my list of questions knowing full well he wouldn't be expecting the interrogation I had in store. Of course I planned to put him on the spot—okay, rake him over the coals—about the safety and effectiveness of the weight-loss program he was pushing. This was not only because of his seemingly impossible claim that HCG could reset someone's metabolism, but also because the diet itself was ridiculously calorie deficient and, for that reason alone, potentially dangerous. After his grilling, which ended up lasting well over an hour, the doctor sheepishly left the studio asking me to please point out his diet's success rate in my finished show. Considering that I already had his signed broadcast release in my hand, I would have promised him the moon just to usher him out the door and get down to work on my first radio special.

It turned out the music I was choosing for my show was actually more FM than AM Top 40, but I knew it set the tone for *The Bay Area's Fight Against Fat* like nothing else could. I brought in a few favorites from my personal vinyl collection so that the engineer who was handling the technical production of the special could dub some music for me. This included a tune from one of my favorite Kinks albums, *Everybody's in Show-Biz*. The song, "Maximum Consumption," included lyrics that named all kinds of delicious, fattening dishes, including pumpkin pie, French fries, and pizza, so I knew that thanks to the Kinks, I had a hit on my hands.

Another couple of songs I ended up using were even more obvious choices. Jethro Tull's "Fat Man" from the *Stand Up* LP worked great, and of course John Lennon's version of the fifties classic "Bony Maronie" from his album *Rock 'n' Roll*, which had come out just the year before, 1975, was perfect. Just listening to Lennon cover "I got a girl named Bony Maronie/She's as skinny as a stick of macaroni/Oughta see her rock and roll with her blue jeans on/She's not very fat, just skin and bone" inspired me to no end. This was especially true because *Rock 'n' Roll* turned out to be John's last solo release before leaving the music business behind for a few years to raise his son Sean once he and Yoko had reconciled.

Thanks to "Bony Maronie" and the other featured songs, as well as my writing, fact-checking, and relentless questioning, the special turned out even better than I had expected. Even more importantly, Jo Interrante became a big fan of my creativity as well as my ability to turn what had been considered a throw-away project into something much more substantial. In other words, she was surprised that I was able to make such a splash just a couple of weeks into my summer internship.

The station's new public affairs director, Conni Gordon, was also impressed, and she immediately told me she'd be submitting *The Bay Area's Fight Against Fat* for a number of awards, which was pretty much unheard of for a newcomer like myself. When I listened to the show as it aired on KFRC super early the next Sunday morning, tears streamed down my face even though I was hearing Jo's voice and not mine, and I knew I was in exactly the right place at what seemed to be just the right time.

But now that I think about it, that wasn't actually the first moment during which I felt I'd found my perfect fit at the radio station. That significant point in time had come just a couple of weeks earlier, maybe the second or third day into my KFRC internship.

I'd been sent out by Jo to run across the street and pick up her typical Diet Dr Pepper and salty-cashews midday meal. It was taking me longer than usual because I was also waiting for a sandwich to be thrown together for someone else in the newsroom, who'd asked me to pick up lunch for him as I was heading out the door.

I was getting more and more nervous as I watched the hands of the big clock on the minimarket wall move forward. I knew Jo did not like to be kept waiting, least of all for her can of Diet Dr Pepper, so I impatiently tapped my foot and drummed my fingers on the counter until everything was ready and I could finally pay up and make my way back to the station, hopefully before she noticed how long I'd been gone.

That's when it happened. As I ran across first Kearny and then Bush Street ready to head up the stairs and dash through the front door of KFRC and down the hall into the newsroom with my bag of goodies, I was stopped dead in my tracks by an extremely strange sight.

A long, bright-red carpet stretched down the entire alley next door to the station's entrance, and another piece of that same red carpeting had been rolled out over the few low stairs leading up to the front door. None of this had been there when I'd left the station less than 20 minutes earlier, but before I could even attempt to figure out what the heck was happening, things got even weirder. My eyes widened in disbelief and I stood like a statue at the entrance to the alley, watching as what seemed to be the longest limousine I'd ever seen rolled slowly up almost to where I was standing. I froze, my feet refusing to move. Suddenly, I realized that sitting atop the front of its hood was a huge set of steer horns.

This piqued my curiosity for all of about five seconds, until the doors sprang wide open and out jumped ZZ TOP. Unbelievable! There was That Little Ol' Band from Texas live and in the flesh standing right in front of me: Billy Gibbons, Frank Beard, and Dusty Hill, all looking at me and smiling as though I must be the official KFRC welcome gal.

Before I could get over my shock and greet them, someone else ran out of the station and onto the red carpet to usher in the band. As I headed up the stairs right behind them, with their bluesy breakthrough hit "La Grange" pounding in my brain, there was absolutely no question in my mind: I knew in my heart of hearts I was home!

My next several weeks at the station became the post–high school education I'd always dreamed of, whether I was writing attention-grabbing sixty-second news stories for the anchors to lead with or excitedly answering the constantly ringing phones: "KFRC newsroom, Laurie speaking!"

I'd been hoping since day one that a job would somehow open up for me there so that I could move straight ahead with my radio career without interruption, but sadly, that summer it wasn't meant to be. With tears in my eyes as my internship came to a close, I left the station clutching a handful of amazing letters of recommendation from the news and public-affairs departments, wondering if I would ever again have a work experience that taught me so much in so little time.

Thanks in part to turning twenty-one while at the station that summer, I felt like I'd entered a completely new phase of my life. I also thought I could finally see the road to adulthood laid out in front of me. It was quite clear that I would have to do whatever it took to make it back to KFRC as soon as possible, as my life was obviously depending on it.

For a brief moment, I considered going back to UC Berkeley and finishing up the few credits I needed to earn my degree, but I knew that following everything I'd just experienced, the classroom just couldn't cut it. I decided instead to go full speed ahead with my job search as the summer came to a close, and as I sat at the kitchen table of what felt like a blazing furnace but was actually the Alcatraz Avenue house in Oakland, I did my best. My Sunday-breakfast companion/roommate couldn't tell if I was sweating or crying as I leafed through the classified ads section of the *San Francisco Chronicle*, watching as my growing ring of spilled coffee made most of the ads all but illegible.

"James," I said miserably as I tried to blot up the coffee, "there's got to be a better way. There's not a thing listed for me here under *B* for broadcast, *J* for journalist, *N* for news, or even *W* for Writer. I'm convinced nobody can get a job through a newspaper class ad anymore."

James looked up from the comics section, where he'd been obsessing over Prince Valiant for at least fifteen minutes. "Hmmm," he muttered. "How 'bout *R* for radio, *P* for print, *M* for media? Or even *I* for "interested in becoming a disc jockey?" I couldn't help but laugh as I turned to the next page of ads. "*A* for assistant?" James continued. "*S* for sports? Why not *E* for editor?"

I responded by telling him that I didn't know how to edit, and I continued pawing through my section of the paper as James moved on through the comics to "Hagar the Horrible," telling me, "Laurie, come on now. If you can write, you can edit."

All of a sudden, there it was. It hit me like a ray of light through the gap in the kitchen curtains. The ad said, "EDITOR. Part-time, experienced for News Service. Send resume and writing sample to . . ." BLAH BLAH BLAH.

I was out of my chair and running up the stairs to my room before James had the slightest clue what was going on. After grabbing a copy of my résumé, my front page Holy Hubert interview from the *Daily Cal*, and multiple letters of recommendation from KFRC, I dashed off an introductory note, then sealed the whole packet up and record-timed it down to the nearest mailbox, even though I knew the mail wouldn't be picked up until the next day. Days went by, and then, after I'd nearly forgotten about the entire episode, the call finally came.

The trio on the phone wanted to know all about me. First, they asked, was I young? How do you even answer a question like that unless you already know whether they want a seasoned journalist or a promising newcomer straight off a college paper? I opted for the truth, promising them I was the best of both worlds. I explained that I was young but experienced, experienced but not jaded, and, well, maybe a bit jaded but only to the point where I recognized that the time had come to get out of the classroom and into the working world.

A convincingly presented spiel, I thought, admitting that if it was a degree they were looking for, then they better forget about me and my fascinating résumé. But if they wanted a knowledgeable, informed, hardworking staff member who also happened to be a damn good writer, better bring me in for an interview!

My impassioned plea managed to convince Jon, Marlene, and Bill that I was ready to work myself into a frenzy for them and their company, Zodiac News Service, as the writer/editor of their start-up college newspaper project. I got the gig! Granted, it was only a part-time job in a totally experimental direction for their company, but to me it was so much more. This was about to become my first baby step on the road back home to KFRC.

I wasn't quite ready to tackle San Francisco's elevated apartment rents just yet, but still, I celebrated my new employment opportunity with a move out of the huge Alcatraz Avenue house in Oakland. I chose a tiny, furnished studio space on Berkeley's College Avenue, since East

Bay rents were friendlier. This would be my first experience living solo. I was so looking forward to daily life without relatives, roommates, or even neighbors who were close friends, and I hoped to find a steady boyfriend who would lead to a long-term romantic relationship. Unfortunately, I ended up instead having occasional flings with guys like the bouncer I met at a local bar who I dated for about five minutes. I also went out on a limb and treated myself to a portable black-and-white TV at a pawnshop in downtown Oakland, figuring that local TV news was a must watch if I was serious about working in the field.

The Zodiac office was in downtown San Francisco at Fifth and Howard, above a printing company in a fairly foul neighborhood populated mainly by sad-looking street people, transient musicians, and hordes of born-agains. Panhandlers were never more than a few feet away, and on my first day I was accosted by one who simply wouldn't quit. He needed a dime, he insisted as he followed me down the sidewalk, so he could get a "Lucy." A Lucy? I had no idea what that could be, until I stopped at the local liquor store for a snack and saw a handful of cigarettes in a cup on the counter. A small sign next to it said "Loosies—10 cents," and suddenly it made sense. The next time I saw him, the guy definitely got a dime from me.

Musicians could be seen all hours of the day and night from the Zodiac office window, loading and unloading equipment as fast as they could in and out of the recording studio down the block. Right next door to Zodiac was an establishment called the House of God, a revival-meeting coffeehouse run by and for wayward teens with their own Godmobile dropping off new recruits before meetings. These revivalists made a huge deal out of thoroughly sweeping the sidewalk but being careful to never push the broom beyond their own doorway. So while the cement in front of their opaque, cross-covered storefront window practically glistened thanks to their religious fervor, the rest of Howard Street stayed sooty, smelly, and, in all probability, pagan.

My job at Zodiac was newly created, and I was officially known as editor of the print packet. This meant that the company was now funding, in addition to its regular daily news service for radio stations, which amounted to six pages per day worth of offbeat stories, a biweekly sort of "Son of Zodiac" print version aimed at college and community papers. Basically, it was up to me to translate Zodiac's radio writing into the printed word, which was pretty funny, as I'd spent the entire summer at KFRC doing almost the exact opposite.

I was given a few ground rules and some guidance in the form of corrections to my copy from John Newhall, who had founded Zodiac and served as the editor, but it was mainly his associate, Marlene Edmunds, who proofread and occasionally rejected my stories and titles as overly glib and/or pun excessive. The perfect example was a piece I'd come up with about the reopening of Cuba to American tourists, which I'd slugged "Havanna Body Been to Cuba?" It cracked me up at the time, but Marlene must not have thought so, because she instructed me to substitute a more sedate heading.

I was actually relieved that my writing wasn't going unchecked. I knew that my combination of late-night typing sessions and early-morning, precoffee proofing was destined to lead to typo after typo, especially since, as I'd pointed out from the beginning, I was not an editor. I was definitely learning a lot, though, especially from the third member of the Zodiac team, Bill Hartman.

Bill was a Vietnam vet who'd become Zodiac's business manager and tech expert. He taught me how to do everything from extracting unblurred stencils of my original pages of copy to lifting the claws of the collator when loading in stacks of one hundred sheets or more so that they wouldn't fly in my face when I turned the thing on.

As much as I enjoyed my writing and other work with the three Zodiac principals, it didn't take long for me to realize that their start-up was doomed. It simply wasn't getting the reaction they'd hoped for, and as a result, I found myself going from room to room in the office feeling like a dog who'd been scolded and walked away with its tail between its legs. Still, we persisted, even as I was beginning to feel hitched to a falling star, and when I found out that I needed to take time off to have my wisdom teeth pulled, it didn't help the situation.

A couple of weeks later, I came back to the office with puffed cheeks, relying on warm bullion and icy diet soda for sustenance, prepared to make a noble sacrifice. I was convinced the Zodiac print packet was screaming with potential, but it just didn't seem that enough attention was being paid to marketing and customer contact. Plus, after nearly two weeks of codeine, I felt zapped of my typical spunk. I wanted to keep my relationship with everyone at the company positive, but at the same time I was determined to give the print packet a respectful burial as I walked away with another impressive entry on my résumé and a bit of money in my pocket, which is exactly what happened.

During my last couple of months at Zodiac I'd managed to pick up another part-time gig, this one on the air as a radio ski reporter. This was despite the fact that I'd never been on a pair of skis in my life, and I'd never even been exposed to snow except on a couple of winter day trips up to Santa's Village in the San Bernardino Mountains as a kid. Still, I was hired by All Media, Inc., to research, digest, write, and record sixty-second-plus reports on ski and snow conditions biweekly. I did this using aliases like the one given to me by San Luis Obispo AM radio station KSLY, which identified me as, I'm embarrassed to admit, the K-SLY Snow Bunny.

Luckily for me, before the ski season dragged on much longer, I received a surprise call from KFRC. Jo Interrante was letting me know that their news editor position had just opened up, so she was offering me the job starting as soon as possible. Wow! My longtime radio dream was about to come true.

The cool satin jacket that came with my first full-time radio gig, at KFRC.

—CHAPTER 10—

"You Turn Me On, I'm a Radio"

Once I reentered KFRC, I found myself back in the fold with not only my original inspirational associates from the newsroom, but also with others who'd made a huge impression on me as an intern. Music Director Dave "the Duke" Sholin and Production Engineer Ron Hummel were at the top of my list. I had the utmost respect for the two of them and wasted no time in letting both Dave and Ron know that I wanted to branch out and work with them on anything music related as much as possible. Program Director Michael Spears was also a major influence, as was his eventual replacement, Les Garland, who took over a few months later when Spears moved on to KFRC's RKO Los Angeles sister-station, KHJ-AM.

I was totally thrilled to be back in the exciting and unpredictable Big 610, Top 40 atmosphere. On any given day, something would happen that totally blew me away. One morning, for example, I found myself walking out of the newsroom and nearly tripping over hitmakers Daryl Hall and John Oates, who for some reason were sitting against the wall on the station's hallway floor. Definitely a typical KFRC type of surprise!

Work quickly became so much more for me than just handling

news editor responsibilities. I now had the opportunity to get to know popular disc jockeys, including superstar morning man Dr. Don Rose as well as the station's lone female jock at the time, Sally Adams. I was also able to check out a lot of the new music that the crew of colorful local record promo guys would lay on Dave Sholin when they came to see him once a week hoping for his airplay approval.

It was all mind-blowing, especially the multihour RKO Beatles special that I was about to become extremely involved in, admittedly in a very strange way. I had just started again at KFRC and was telling Dave a little about my background. I let him know that I was a SoCal gal from Los Angeles who couldn't wait to leave high school and head north to attend UC Santa Cruz and later UC Berkeley. Right away, Dave asked if my family still lived in LA and if I was planning on heading home for a weekend anytime in the near future. If so, he wanted to know, would I consider doing him a big favor while I was there? I could barely believe the Duke was asking me for help, and of course I said yes. His face lit up when I said, "Sure, Dave. What can I do for you?"

That's when he let me know that he'd been told there was a box of vintage tapes that had been sitting in the vault at KHJ for ages just waiting to be picked up. It was believed to be a collection of Beatles-related interviews conducted at the station since the early sixties that no one at KHJ had neither the time nor the inclination to listen to, or possibly they didn't even know exactly what they were.

The idea of heading over to Hollywood with an admission ticket to the offices of KHJ excited me to no end. I'd grown up a huge "Boss Radio" fan, so first and foremost for me it would be like rediscovering my childhood. And being trusted with what turned out to be a carton full of original Beatles interview tapes was even more thrilling—I definitely felt I was now part of the RKO family!

I flew home to Los Angeles that weekend and immediately called the KHJ contact that Dave had set me up with. When I got to the station, I followed him into what looked like an age-old storage closet and picked up the shabby-looking box of tapes the station seemed all too eager to hand over. I brought the box back to KFRC upon my return to San Francisco, and Dave Sholin eagerly headed into the newsroom and started going through it. As he checked out all the tape reel cases, he brought up exactly what I'd been hoping for: turning those tapes into a multihour RKO Fab Four special.

News Director Jo Interrante was on the scene too, and Dave immediately asked her not only what she thought of the idea, but also if she would be interested in writing the show. Jo was super positive about this being a terrific opportunity and potentially an attention-grabbing accomplishment for RKO and whoever ended up working on it, but she was also honest and direct. She explained that she was simply too busy running the news department and being a single mom caring for her two young kids to tackle a massive project like this. Then, to my never-ending amazement, she looked Dave right in the eye and asked, "What about Laurie?" She suggested that I would be perfect for the gig and no doubt do a killer job—WOW!

Right away, I began researching and writing about the early Beatles, actually known as the Silver Beatles back before they had achieved international success. This is when they were making a number of lengthy trips to Hamburg, Germany, practically moving there to get their act together onstage. That's when I found myself considering a move of my own, to Mill Valley, the fairly affluent suburb across the Golden Gate Bridge from San Francisco, miles away in Marin County.

I certainly hadn't ever planned on living all the way out in Marin. However, when a nice gal not much older than I was in the station's accounting department told me she'd found a cool house just a few blocks from downtown Mill Valley and needed a roommate to make the rental happen, I drove out with her to check it out. One big plus in my book was that she had a car, so it seemed like most of the time, I'd be able to hitch a ride to and from KFRC with her. That was before I started tackling extra projects, going out with new friends after work, and sometimes even dating.

Looking back, I probably should have taken into account how conservative my soon-to-be roommate was. She was a sweet person, but we had next to nothing in common except that we both totally fell for the house she'd found on Circle Drive. For me, this happened the minute the front door opened and I caught my first glimpse of the wall-to-wall, leopard-print shag carpet. So I bought a foldout futon and a couple of pieces of inexpensive vintage oak furniture, including a fancy vanity with a huge mirror and padded bench. I also found a classic, gigantic desk that doubled as our dining room table, and before I knew it I was on the verge of becoming a Mill Valley resident living just down the street from members of the Jefferson Starship.

I was also excited to have access to a number of intimate music venues in the area, like the original Sweetwater and the Old Mill Tavern, both within walking distance of my new home, where one would be sure to see locals like Dan Hicks hanging out onstage or at the bar. But socializing in Marin County couldn't help but take a backseat to my tons of work, especially as preproduction on the show originally called *RKO Radio Presents The Beatles* intensified and it became apparent that we were about to create a major rock radio special. Eventually, we would be able to use the far more descriptive title I'd come up with—*The Beatles from Liverpool to Legend*—but first, as a fourteen-hour show, it would be released on reel-to-reel tapes to air only on RKO stations across the country in one- or two-hour blocks each night over a one- to two-week period.

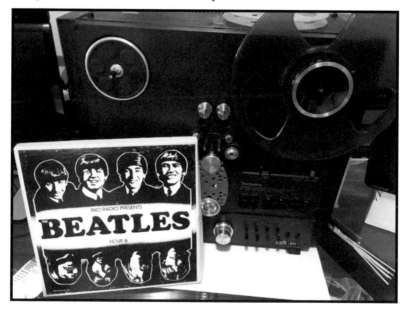

RKO Radio Presents the Beatles—the original, 10.5-inch tape-reel box
containing hour six from our total of fourteen hours

This was before we expanded it first to fifteen, then eventually seventeen, hours and it was sold in syndication, sent out on vinyl discs, and aired just about everywhere! Right away, the project required endless research, outlines, production notes, interviews, and script writing, all on top of my already hectic full-time day job in the newsroom. What that meant for me was working long into the night, either in the production studio with engineer Ron Hummel or solo in front of the brand-new IBM Selectric typewriter at my newsroom desk. From the start, I would often need to spend the night at the station, since I'd work long past the point of being able to catch the last Bay Area Rapid Transit (aka BART) train back to my Berkeley apartment in the East Bay. Once I made my somewhat silly move to the leopard-print-shag-carpeted house in Mill Valley, the public transportation situation got even worse. Those over-the-bridge bus schedules were even less accommodating, and since I had no immediate plans to buy a car or even get my drivers license, I had no choice but to make KFRC my second home.

That's also what led to my drug use hitting an all-time high, and I'm not just talking about marijuana. This was despite the fact that there happened to be a particular pothead news anchor/reporter whom I absolutely idolized (but who shall remain nameless) who could regularly be found in between newscasts smoking joints outside in the alley. He inserted himself into the line of cute, young, downtown San Francisco bicycle messengers who were lighting up while on their own breaks, and though I was invited and honestly quite tempted to join them, there's no way it would have worked for me.

Instead, it was both cocaine and crystal meth that began to play a major part in my early radio days. I turned especially to the latter fairly often after passing out on the sofa super late at night in the funky little KFRC ladies' room lounge. I would set my alarm to wake up extra early the next morning so that I could snort some speed and finish up a batch of Beatles work before raging full steam ahead on my editorial responsibilities in the newsroom for the entire rest of the day.

Believe it or not, I looked to John Lennon himself to justify my crystal meth consumption while I spent all those months working on *RKO Radio Presents the Beatles*. In pieces of the interview one hears in the first hour of our show, John talks openly about his need to do drugs during the Silver Beatles' excursions to Hamburg. This was primarily so that he and the rest of the band, including Paul and George, who was just a teenager at the time, could make it through the often all-day/all-night sets they performed.

The following transcribed, truncated excerpt from hour one of *RKO Radio Presents the Beatles* tells the story, written by me and narrated by KFRC midday DJ and National Disc Jockey Hall of Famer John Mack Flanagan, who did a great job voicing the entire fourteen-hour script. This particular hour was heavily interspersed with 1960s interview bites from John Lennon.

Flanagan: "In Hamburg, the Germans were well under the rule of rock 'n' roll. The group's 1960 residency was the first of five enlightening Hamburg gigs. The lads were about to learn valuable lessons in endurance and stage presence, and had they been a little quicker to hit Germany, they might have taken some in-person tips from an American sergeant named Elvis Presley. The Silver Beatles played their hearts out at Hamburg's Indra Club, a scruffy establishment that brought out the band's true raunch, encouraging outrageous antics and wild onstage behavior."

Lennon: "It was a good experience, but it was sooo—we wouldn't like to do it again! We'd start about five in the evening, or weekends at three in the afternoon, and you get the younger people in, and then we'd play an hour, then have an hour off and then a new set—people could come in and just buy one drink and stay all night, but they just came in and out, so you've got a hundred different audiences all night. And it just went on until about six the next morning, when you fell asleep. But we didn't play all that time, we played on/off, on/off, so we used to go to bed for two hours, then get up and play again, then go to bed half an hour and get up and play again."

Flanagan: "The boys were pressed upon to lose any trace of aloofness in their act, as they played the raucous German dance and drink clubs. The Silver Beatles gained a reputation as a bunch of rowdies, but the Germans loved it and egged them on, urging them to '*Mach schau, mach schau!*' ['Make a show, make a show!']—and they did, making quite a show. According to a German booking agent, John Lennon and company pulled off a number of stunts, like the time John appeared onstage in just his swim trunks—pretty risqué for 1960. Or when Lennon came on with a wooden toilet seat around his neck. The locals loved it, and the Silver Beatles went even wilder. They began aping Hitler and doing the goose step in between guitar solos, only to drive the crowds crazier. The club's late-night clientele seemed to thrive on the mock violence on stage, leading the Beatles to actual acts of outrage like John and Paul's attempts at interior decorating—setting fire to the wallpaper in their dingy Hamburg hotel room, for which the two were deported. George was close on their heels, asked to leave because at seventeen he was under the legal age for cabaret work. But when the lads left Hamburg, they took with them a sense of showmanship. Their Indra Club gig was spent either on pills or on stage—they had to maintain that crazed performing pace, which often meant eight to twelve hour sets—marathons of madness!"

Lennon: "Drugs were around then, you know. People were smoking marijuana in Liverpool, and I wasn't too aware of it at that period, when we were still kids, 'cause all these Black guys were from Jamaica or their parents were—there was a lot of marijuana and that stuff around. The beatnik thing had just happened, and the first drugs I ever took, I was still at art school with the group—we all took it together—was Benzedrine from the inside of a Benzedrine inhaler. And a beatnik, sort-of British version of Allen Ginsberg came up from London and was sort of turning everybody on to this inside of an inhaler, and everybody talked their mouths off for a night and thought, *Wow! What's this?*

"In Hamburg, 'cause we had to work six or seven hours a night onstage with no rest, the waiters always had these pills called Preludin and various other kinds of pills, but I remember Preludin 'cause it was a big trip. And all the waiters were taking pills to keep themselves awake, to work these incredible hours in this like a Vegas-type place— you know, it's an all-night place. And so the waiters, when they'd see the musicians falling over with tiredness or with drink, they'd give you the pill and say, 'Here! If you take this, you can work—you know, you'll be awake!' You'd take the pill, you'd be talking, you'd sober up— you know, you could work almost endlessly until the pill wore off, then you'd have to have another. So by the time we got back to Hamburg, we weren't junkies, but we certainly had a supply of pep pills, as they called them in those days."

(Note: This particular John Lennon sound bite was followed in hour one by the Beatles' version of "Slow Down," the 1957 song by New Orleans native and R & B performer/producer Larry Williams, which had been part of the band's repertoire since 1960. This was a while before they recorded it in six quick takes in the studio in '64. The next year, the Beatles also recorded a cover of Williams's hit single "Dizzy Miss Lizzy," with Lennon again on lead vocals. This was the song that had been the A side to Williams's "Slow Down.")

Flanagan: "Slow Down" was the one thing the Germans didn't want the Beatles to do! The audience, always in a frenzy, were the best teachers the boys ever had. West Germany would definitely leave its mark on the Beatles, but at that time, it wasn't going to be the monetary kind."

—CHAPTER 11—

"Love in an Elevator"

O ddly enough, my Mill Valley move ushered in an almost instant and completely unexpected sexual awakening period.

This was possibly because I finally felt far enough removed from the East Bay, which is just a short trek from the UCB campus, meaning I was meeting a lot of guys who were students. This reminded me way too much of my days as a high school virgin. But now I was suddenly able to reach beyond my educational experience and encounter all kinds of interesting dudes either on the job or while bouncing around downtown San Francisco, which was still a fairly new social scene for me.

One would have thought that the time it took to travel across the Golden Gate Bridge from San Francisco to Marin County would have made me less likely to attract men living and/or working in the city, but that turned out not to be the case. Instead, it was almost as if my Marin homebase made me more mysterious, seductive, and fascinating.

What also helped me move forward sexually was having a boss who took an interest in my personal life. When she wasn't teaching me her top tricks for writing brilliant radio news copy, Jo Interrante was in many ways becoming not just a mentor, but also a kinda-sorta-although-much-too-young-to-be mother figure. Jo went out of her

The gang from KFRC's news and public affairs departments: John Winters, Kimberly Safford, Daphne Poingsett, Mike Colgan, Robert McCormick, Jo Interrante, Laurie Kaye, Ron Rodrigues, Paul Fredericks, and Conni Gordon. (Photo by KFRC)

way to guide me in developing my own sense of style. She advised me to take advantage not only of my youth, but also the unique opportunities presented to me by working at KFRC.

One memorable evening after the final newscast of the day, Jo turned off the lights in the newsroom to keep me from spending the next few hours pounding out more pages of the Beatles' script at my typewriter. She then literally pulled me out of my chair to physically drag me to a cocktail party she'd been invited to at a local hotel.

Drinking on an empty stomach got me giggly and tipsy, so when Jo pointed out a good-looking guy halfway across the room and grabbed my arm to lead us both over to where he was standing, I didn't have it in me to protest. Even when she hauled off and pushed me into him, there was nothing I could do or say, since she quickly ran off and disappeared back into the crowd.

Embarrassed as I was, I had to admit Jo had exceptional taste in men. Immediately after regaining his balance and laughingly introducing himself as Rick, my new friend/victim took my hand and kissed it. He continued to clutch it tightly as he asked if I'd had enough of that hotel cocktail party scene while leading me to the nearest elevator.

A make-out session like nothing I'd ever experienced followed. Rick blocked any potential passengers from jumping in along with us as we rode all the way up and then all the way down again and again while getting closer and closer to making "Love in an Elevator." "Livin' it up when I'm goin' down" is how Steven Tyler would describe it vocally a dozen or so years later, and we finally did give life to his future Aerosmith hit by actually "Lovin' it up 'til I hit the ground."

From there, we raced out to Rick's sporty red car in the hotel parking structure and drove off to the San Francisco waterfront. We parked for nearly a full night of cramped, crazy, and scenic screwing and chatting before he offered to take me home to Mill Valley for more of the same. But my dedication to my job prevailed, and I asked Rick instead to please just drop me off at the radio station so that I could go right to sleep and get up extra early the next morning to make up all the writing time I'd lost. He looked at me in disbelief, but took me back as requested to my home away from home. Although he politely asked for my number, I can't say I was surprised to never hear from him again. It had been a weird way to connect in the first place, to say nothing of my decision to end our night of semipublic passion in favor of prepping for all the work I still had to do.

Following that somewhat freakish sexual encounter, I found myself involved in a succession of flirty flings and short-term relationships. This was fine with me considering that the combination of my commute and workload meant I simply didn't have time for anything more intense.

When I needed a break from my constant late-night writing sessions at the station, I found myself acting out the popular local phrase "Meet me at the St. Francis." This meant scurrying over to the bar in the lobby of the infamous hotel in Union Square for a quick cocktail and sitting beside its much publicized, giant grandfather clock. That beautiful antique timepiece had served as a lovers' meeting place for decades, and true to local legend, I did end up meeting a surprising number of men there. It became kind of like having my own personal dating service long before the days of online digital sites like Match.com.

One guy I met there appeared different from the bulk of the one-night-stand dudes I was approached by at the bar at the St. Francis. He was a part-time Stanford student from a wealthy family back East, and he seemed to specialize in crashing expensive silver sports cars while maintaining just enough of his student status to inherit his humongous trust fund. There was something about him I really liked, though, and we ended up having a number of wild adventures together, from heading down to Stanford just before he totaled his latest silver Porsche to attending a big-money San Francisco Opera benefit featuring well-known local performance artist/entertainer Winston Tong. Winston began his set in a huge, private downtown loft by carrying out a big basin of water, which he used to slowly wash and then wrap the bare feet of one of the city's major opera donors in a long bandage-like cloth. During the foot bath, a number of big, thick joints were lit and passed up and down the rows of curious and amused onlookers, including those of us seated high up in the balcony.

My date and I welcomed the huge spliffs and happily took a number of hits off them. Neither of us had any idea that these doobies were heavily angel dusted, which meant the marijuana had been laced with the hallucinogen/horse tranquilizer PCP to boost its potency. We both ended up losing quite a bit of time thanks to this unexpected psychedelic trip; in fact, I missed an entire day's work at the radio station. When I woke up a full twenty-four hours later, I found myself in an unfamiliar apartment without even knowing where I was or how I'd gotten there.

That kooky relationship ended shortly thereafter when my rich-kid Romeo killed it. He quickly moved on to meet and then marry an adorable up-and-coming actress who was right on the verge of becoming famous. Then, when she did, sure enough, she dumped him. From there, I didn't waste much time in turning to the radio station as my primary dating/matchmaking source, beginning a couple of brief flings with guys who, although they didn't actually work at KFRC, were often there to either promote projects or meet with my fellow employees. My favorite was a talented visual artist associated with the well-known Bay Area-based nonprofit drug rehab organization Delancey Street. Ray had apparently seen me in the hallway and asked his KFRC public affairs contact, Conni Gordon, about me, then handed her his business card so that she could give it to me and make sure I called him. So I did, and not only because Ray was tall and good-looking, but also because I was both flattered and intrigued by his interest and had a feeling he had quite the story to tell about his days as a drug addict and convict. He most definitely did, and although our relationship was another relatively short one, there were some memorable moments, including his recollection of being arrested for robbing a gas station while high-as-a-kite, as well as my own first attempt at treating a date to a romantic, home-cooked dinner in my house in Mill Valley. Poor Ray. I thought I was being so health conscious and trendy by starting off with what I was sure would be a delicious spinach salad, but my guess is I was so nervous about pleasing someone I really liked that I forgot how diligent one has to be when washing fresh spinach. If you're not, the sand trapped inside the leaves stays put, meaning the spinach will taste dirty, with a grainy texture. Sweet Ray tried his best to hide his reaction but ended up having to spit it all out, and naturally I felt so stupid. But strangely enough, even though our dinner date got off to a rather gritty start, we had a lovely night and stayed friends long after the romance fizzled, and the spinach salad episode has served as an important life lesson for me ever since. With my work on the RKO Beatles special wrapping up, I began to have more free evening time, so once again I started meeting men in bars, realizing I had less to lose if they weren't connected to my workplace. The exception came one hectic afternoon in the newsroom when I got a call to come over as soon as possible to sign paperwork for the station's accounting department, which was a few floors up in the building next door.

I rushed over to the elevator and jumped in amid a group of female accounting employees who all knew me, and we started to chat. As the door slid shut, I noticed a hip, attractive, but unfamiliar man standing behind them and silently staring at me, and I couldn't help but stare right back. I watched his eyes travel the entire length of my body, from my toes to the top of my head, as he smiled seductively and asked if I worked in the building. Just as I began to explain that I was coming from next door, we reached the third floor, and the gals in the elevator started to push me out, saying, "Here we are, Laurie!" But before I could take a step out the door, my handsome stranger looked me right in the eye and said, "Nope, you're coming with me; we're going up to the fourth floor." My coworkers were all shocked, but I sure as hell didn't care. I stayed in the elevator as my new fan told me his name was

Jim and that although he worked as a driver for the printing company upstairs, he was actually a musician.

As soon as I knew he was a bass player, it all made sense, since I'd felt he was supercool from the minute I first saw him. Then, when Jim quickly took a pen out of his pocket and held up his arm, asking me to write my name and phone number on it so that he could call me to set up a date, I was secretly thrilled. Here I was, once again experiencing love in an elevator, although this time it wasn't the physical kind—at least not yet. I was shaking slightly as we stood outside of his workplace making small talk, wondering if he would really call and if so, when. We gazed at each other longingly and finally said goodbye as I headed back down to the third floor, where the women in accounting looked at me as though I were some kind of harlot and asked if I was okay. "Are you kidding?" I said. "Everything's perfect!"

I took care of business, then hurried back to the newsroom, walking in just as the phone at my desk began to ring. It was Jim! He said he'd love to take me to dinner the next night, Friday, but I already had plans, so we made it Saturday instead and arranged to meet right outside the radio station. Almost immediately after hanging up, I found myself wondering why I was planning to go to a Friday night client party I had little or no interest in when instead I could be spending time with my exciting new elevator enchanter. I asked my boss and confidant, Jo, what she thought.

Jo told me it was always a good idea to not be too available right from the start, which made sense in a game-playing kind of way. Instead, I began to anticipate my Saturday night date with Jim like I hadn't looked forward to anything in ages.

As expected, Friday evening's client event was nothing special, and afterward a few of us decided to wind things up by heading over to Enrico's, the outdoor North Beach bar on Broadway where cocktails and people watching went hand in hand. The place was, as usual, packed, so we joined a couple of strangers at a big, round table. I found myself seated next to a wild-looking dude with crazy red hair. He bought me a drink and began telling me all about the apartment he was about to leave in San Francisco's Haight-Ashbury district, the neighborhood made famous by the hippie movement in the sixties and that was once home to so many famous musicians, including the Grateful Dead and Janis Joplin. Coincidentally, I'd been starting to think about apartment hunting in the city myself, as I'd had just about enough of my judgmental Mill Valley roommate and lengthy, Golden Gate bridge commute. So when the wild redhead asked me to come check his place out, it seemed like a possibly perfect opportunity.

Before I knew what was happening, he stood up, stepped off the curb, and flagged down a cab, and off we rode to his place in the Haight. Yes, I realized on the way that I'd technically just become a cheap pickup, but the alcohol inside me kept me from feeling remorse. Even when my new pal Paul ushered me into his apartment in the middle of the historic hippie district of San Francisco and headed straight for his perfectly appropriate, if somewhat corny, king-size waterbed, I couldn't help but giggle.

We woke up around noon, and it dawned on me that I would really have to rush to make it back to Mill Valley, get cleaned up, and then head back to the city to meet Jim in time for our date. But first, Paul wanted to take me on a quick walk around his neighborhood so that I'd get an idea of what it was like to live in the Haight.

At the time, there were a number of demolitions going on of vintage Victorian homes that while beat-up, were still beautiful. One that we were about to pass was on the brink of getting bashed by the wrecking ball when the lunch whistle blew and the construction crew instantly put everything on hold. Without missing a beat, Paul pulled me in through the open door to look around, and we saw that the place was completely empty except for a single poster on the wall. It was a beautifully designed graphic of Diana Ross & the Supremes commemorating their show at New York's Lincoln Center back in 1965. When he saw me staring at it, Paul wasted no time in pulling out the thumbtacks in each corner and rolling up the poster for me before we ran out of the house like a couple of hardcore criminals. Laughing like crazy, I held on to my new artwork as I bid him farewell and hopped on a bus heading downtown, where I then had to catch another one to get me across the Golden Gate Bridge and back home.

Unsurprisingly, I never saw Paul or his apartment again, but the poster he rescued for me from that about-to-be-destroyed Victorian home turned out to be an iconic, ultrarare piece of sixties art by designer/illustrator Joe Eula, which I eventually had framed and which still hangs on my living room wall to this day.

I managed to make it back to Marin County with what seemed like just enough time to shower, change, and maybe even take a short nap before returning to the city. However, I hadn't taken into account weekend public transportation schedules, so to my embarrassment I was more than forty-five minutes late as I walked up the block to meet Jim in front of the radio station for our date. Checking him out from a distance, I surmised that he seemed seconds away from being super pissed off and sure that he was about to be stood up, so when I called his name and ran up the stairs to where he was sitting just outside KFRC's front door, he was so relieved and glad to see me it was both heartwarming and super sexy.

We hopped in the printing company pickup truck Jim used for work and headed to what he told me was his all-time favorite place for dinner. Surprisingly, it was not a restaurant in San Francisco, but rather a seafood establishment in Berkeley that had been around for decades. A beautiful, comfortable evening followed as we knocked back a cocktail or two and enjoyed delicious roasted crab. We talked about everything from my new friend's days as an up-and-coming LA session musician in the early seventies to the bond we shared over having escaped our hugely dysfunctional families as teenagers.

Following dinner, we headed back across the Bay Bridge to the city, ending up at Jim's cozy Noe Valley studio apartment, which was right above a corner liquor store/market. Good thing the shop was open 24-7, because the only way to access his pad was by entering and walking all the way to the back of the store, then up a narrow flight of stairs to Jim's front door.

Exhausted as I was from my late-night activities of the previous evening, I passed out almost instantly the minute my head hit the pillow on Jim's futon floor mattress, but not before I saw him turn on his cassette player. I was expecting some sort of slow, sultry music to come from the speakers, but instead out came a steady stream of weird whale and ocean noises.

Jim immediately apologized for the haunting humpback moans and watery whooshes, explaining that it was the only way for him to be able to fall into a deep sleep. As our relationship blossomed, I did a bit of research and found out that the song of the humpback whale is often used not only by people who suffer from insomnia, but also by male whales themselves to bring about hormonal changes in female whales once they've reached sexual maturity. Who knew?

It must have worked, because hormonally, sexually, and emotionally, I found myself becoming more and more attached to Jim as the weeks went by. I spent every free hour I had with him at his apartment, local clubs and bars, and my Mill Valley home. He helped convince me it was time to make my move to the city, and he took me driving around San Francisco neighborhoods to hunt for an affordable apartment. I finally found one on my own not far from Fisherman's Wharf, Russian Hill, and my favorite hangout, North Beach. It was a surprisingly decent-size rental that I could actually make work even with my relatively low budget.

Moving day came quickly; I was incredibly excited, feeling like a true Frisco gal at last even though I knew to never, ever use that f-word if I wanted to be taken seriously by San Francisco locals, especially natives.

I shopped for just the right furniture to fill my new space, but more importantly, with Jim taking the lead, we found the perfect pair of speakers to bring my home stereo system up to the next level. The JBL L26 Decades were instant classics, the closest to the company's studio monitors that I could afford and that would fit in my new apartment. To top it off, the speakers were actually on sale for less than $300. Even though this was way more than a month's rent, it was well worth the investment considering that I still have these vintage sound system elements set up in my home office. Yes, they've been lovingly refurbished, but they still sound terrific and remind me all these years later of the wonderful, music-loving man responsible for bringing them into my life.

Practically from the moment I met Jim, I was super excited at the thought of introducing him to my Jo, since she'd lately been encouraging me to stop randomly screwing around and instead try to find someone with actual relationship potential. I was one-hundred-percent sure that was the case with my latest lover, and I wasted no time in referring to him as my boyfriend while bragging about his good looks, magnetic personality, and musical expertise. Jim had been an ambitious studio musician following in the footsteps of older, more experienced session players like the Wrecking Crew while living in Los Angeles, and he'd also performed at live shows in backup bands hired for rockers like Chuck Berry. Plus, Jim had exceptional taste when it came to music in genres I knew next to nothing about, like hardcore funk and reggae. He introduced me to artists who changed my perception of recorded music, everyone from New Orleans funk band the Meters to Jamaican roots reggae performer Burning Spear. To this day, whenever I hear "Cissy Strut" or "Slavery Days," I can't help but think of my dear Jim.

After meeting him, Jo acknowledged that Jim was not only attractive, but also had quite a seductive personality. Considering that she was also romantically involved with a musician at the time, I expected her to be encouraging when it came to my budding relationship. She was, to a certain extent, but to my surprise, Jo also made a point of telling me that I might be better off in the long haul dating someone who could actually help me with my career.

Coincidentally, while shopping at a used-record store in North Beach one day a short time later, I happened to meet the son of the general manager of another major San Francisco radio station—this one, an FM outlet. Although I initially hesitated when he asked me out, a little voice inside my head (possibly Jo's) prodded me to say yes. And there it was, the beginning of the end of my romantic relationship with my dear friend Jim.

Although this new record store connection didn't work out very well at all, I was thankfully able to maintain a strong, loving friendship with Jim that lasted for years even as we both married others, moved to different parts of the country, and changed the directions of our lives. Throughout our time as a couple, our mutual love of live music created treasured memories that we relived almost every time we got together and talked about the past.

Tom Petty and the Heartbreakers' first Old Waldorf show, back in August of 1977, was one experience Jim and I revived again and again over the years. We were both so blown away by the band's hard-rockin' performance and stage presence that it stuck with us for decades. As usual, our tickets came thanks to concert promoter, club owner, and all-around musical entrepreneur Bill Graham, still a true hero and friend to all at KFRC, including me. The Waldorf was just one of the famous San Francisco venues associated with Graham, along with Winterland and the Fillmore West, but it was my favorite during that time. This was because of not just its smaller size and cozy layout, but also the breathtaking array of talent that was booked there. Everyone from Australian hardcore rockers AC/DC to American punk and new wave pioneers Blondie, Talking Heads, and Iggy Pop played the Old Waldorf back in the second half of '77—plus British bands Elvis Costello and the Attractions, Eddie and the Hot Rods, and the Jam and soulful California keyboard artist Billy Preston. Preston was well known for playing with the Beatles during their last live performance, on the rooftop of London's Apple headquarters, and also on numerous albums and tours with the Rolling Stones. The list of cool Old Waldorf concerts continued to grow for the next few years, until Bill Graham closed it down in 1983.

Luckily, our KFRC-based RKO production team was right on schedule during this same time period as we approached the late-summer deadline for finishing up the network's fourteen-hour Beatles special, set to air in the fall. Top RKO executives had been passing on extremely positive comments all along to Dave, Ron, and me with the exception of one bigwig who criticized what he referred to as our overemphasis on George Harrison's 1971 Madison Square Garden back-to-back benefit concerts. He reminded us with tongue in cheek that the show was called *RKO Presents the Beatles*, not *Bangladesh*, so we went ahead and tightened up that particular live-music segment, laughing as we did so and loving the idea that the product of our many months of extracurricular hard work was about to go public.

—CHAPTER 12—

"Elvis Is Everywhere"

Less than a week after Tom Petty's Old Waldorf gig, I found myself all alone in the KFRC newsroom on a Tuesday around 1:30 pm while waiting for the rest of the news team to return from their fairly late lunch.

Out of nowhere, it seemed as if the wall against which our teletypes sat suddenly up and exploded, and the somewhat-easy-to-ignore clacking that normally emanated from the machines was replaced by bells and buzzers that began to blare and bang on my ears like crazy. Typically, several inches of paper rolled out of just a couple of machines at a time; now huge lengths of printed material started spewing nonstop from the mouths of each and every teletype in the room.

I jumped up from my desk and ran over to see what in the world could be causing such a commotion, and right off the bat I found out: Elvis Presley had passed. His live-in girlfriend had found him facedown and unconscious on his Graceland master-bathroom floor, after which Elvis was rushed to the hospital and officially pronounced dead.

I tore that printed sheet out of the teletype as fast as I could and hurried straight down the hall and into the jock booth, handing the copy to the midday DJ, who wasted no time in informing his listeners of the shocking news.

Strangely enough, Elvis's death played an important role in my own future. This was primarily because not long before Elvis passed away while sitting on the toilet that day, August 16, 1977, I had begun to pat myself on the back for working in radio for well over a year (including my internship). However, for some reason I couldn't seem to understand why KFRC, *Billboard's* top-rated AM station in the country at the time, wasn't about to offer a relative newcomer like me an immediate on-air position. So foolishly, right after Elvis died, I decided to shop around and see what other types of employment I could come up with. That's how I ended up turning my much needed and long-awaited weeklong vacation from the station into a trial run for a reporting job at the headquarters of the *National Enquirer* in Lantana, Florida—just a hop, skip, and jump from Palm Beach geographically, but light years away in other ways. While Palm Beach is primarily known for luxury homes and billionaires, Lantana immediately struck me as a not-so-secret center for drug dealing and prostitution, as I was reminded practically nonstop from the minute my flight landed. Everyone from the airport exit security guard to my cab driver wasted no time in asking me what kind of drugs and/or companionship I was looking for, and once I reached the beachside hotel the *Enquirer* was putting me up in, the bellboy joined in. He offered to come back later that evening in exchange for what he called a "generous tip," saying he could bring me drugs and spend the night. No thanks!

This was back when the *Enquirer* was in the hands of Generoso Pope Jr., the owner/publisher who was responsible for turning it into a tacky tabloid years earlier. After initially focusing on sex scandals and sensationalist headlines, he eventually toned the content down somewhat so that the publication could be displayed at supermarket checkouts.

My personal contact with Pope was, thankfully, limited to one brief encounter. I thought I was all alone as I sat at a table in the back of the *Enquirer* newsroom early one Sunday morning when all of a sudden I witnessed a strange sight: a middle-aged man wearing a bathrobe and slippers entered and started sneaking around, going through anything and everything that his staff writers had left sitting atop their desks. It turned out to be Generoso Pope Jr. himself, and what he was looking for, and then dumping into the trash, were any brightly colored paper clips he might find. Apparently, as a publisher, he allowed only old-school, plain-metal paper clips to be used by anyone in his offices.

But that was nothing compared with the meeting I was called into shortly afterward with a top *National Enquirer* editor in his private office. He hit the ground running by asking me what I thought would be the most attention-getting way for the tabloid to cover the death of Elvis Presley. Before I had a chance to answer, he smiled smugly and opened the top drawer of his desk, swearing me to secrecy while pulling out a photo and boasting that it was about to appear on the cover of the *Enquirer's* upcoming issue. Needless to say, it was the freakish and soon-to-be infamous shot of Elvis in his coffin. I was more than horrified, and I determined then and there to leave that yellow journalism joint as soon as possible and race back home to KFRC, which I did.

The weird thing is, three years and a few months later, I was sickened to see that the *Enquirer* had done it again, this time with its cover featuring a similar photo of the just-murdered John Lennon, taken at the New York City morgue not long before he was cremated. Lennon's photo was more of a close-up than Presley's and also in color, compared with Elvis's black-and-white, but almost the exact same wording would appear: "EXCLUSIVE," "THE UNTOLD STORY," and "THE LAST PICTURE" . . . so very creepy and tabloid typical.

Nearly a year and a half after my *Enquirer* encounter, in December of '78, when our RKO team was looking to expand and update our Beatles special from the year before, I was given the opportunity to schedule a solo telephone conversation with George Harrison. Like both of the other former Beatles I would have the good fortune to interview in the three-plus years following Elvis's passing, George had an emotional way of paying tribute to the King of Rock 'n' Roll.

"It was a surprise to me, as it must have been to the rest of the world, when Elvis died," George told me. "I felt a bit sad because just like with anybody who's been that much in the limelight, they've had so little private life, and it's just the same as, say, Keith Moon." The Who drummer had passed just over a year following Elvis, overdosing on a prescription drug meant to relieve the symptoms of alcohol withdrawal.

"I feel sad when any of those people die because in a way, if you want to talk about the spiritual thing, the real goal in our life is to have self-realization, and I feel sad when somebody dies appearing to be a little premature because, you know, they miss out on the full potential that is there," George said. "But I think in a way it's just part of our lifestyle. It must have been quite lonely for Elvis. At least with the Beatles, or the Fab Four, we had each other to sort-of hang out with. The four of us had to share the experience, and I'm very pleased about that. I wouldn't have liked to have been Elvis or Elton John or some solo performer who went through that experience alone."

Just a few months later, in June of '79, Paul McCartney would share similar thoughts during our RKO interview with him, his wife, Linda, and the latest lineup of Wings in London while reminiscing about favorite rockers who had passed away.

"It's a drag about people who died," Paul said. "I think the point is, if they'd have been here now, they wouldn't have known what to say about it if we were talking about someone else—the same as us."

Like George, Paul brought up the Who's drummer: "When you talk about someone like Keith Moon," Paul mentioned, "who was a good mate of ours, he probably would have just been here loonin' as usual."

I understood right away what Paul was saying about Moon, because moments after his death at the age of thirty-two in September of '78 was first announced, I went on the air on KING-AM in Seattle and referred to him as "Moon the Loon," his longtime nickname. I was surprised that the station got a couple of calls almost immediately afterward from listeners who'd heard my newscast, criticizing me for what they thought was disrespectful name-calling. I felt terrible that anyone would think I'd make up an insulting moniker for one of rock's top drummers!

"He was a great fellow," Paul continued, "but if he would have been here now, he would just be laughing and joking—I don't suppose he'd like anyone to start taking him seriously just because he died. Same with Jimi Hendrix or someone like that, he who was another mate – they were great, you know. They got burned out via various things, and I'm not the man's doctor, so I don't know what it was, but they were great people, and I'd like to just remember them for what they were. For me, he was the all-time guitar player, Jimi. I've seen a lot of guitar players, and I've sat in front of him in a club, and he was just a monster! I remember down in a club one night, me, Townsend, and Clapton all turned up to check out this new talent—he was great, and he was a friend of Linda's too. She remembers him saying to her, when he was going to his first tour in America, 'Do you think we're going to be able to go in by the front door this time?' It was kind of poignant, really, because like everyone, he was insecure. Well, you know, the thing is, they go to where all good rock 'n' rollers go."

Turning specifically to Elvis, I asked Paul if he thought there would have been more great Presley material if he had lived.

"Oh, yeah, of course there would," Paul instantly responded. "I mean, ELVIS! One thing people don't seem to notice about Elvis is he was like the world's—one of the world's—greatest vocalists."

Coming from Paul McCartney, this was quite an expression of admiration.

"Everyone thinks, *Oh, well, he was a star, he wore all those sequins, and he got fat*, and he did all that, but you listen to a record like 'Jailhouse Rock,' and he's pretty amazing. He was always one of my favorites, Elvis. But things catch up with people. Some people get into things that you're not going to get out of, and it seems that Elvis got into a bit of that. I haven't heard the inside story, so I don't know what happened at all, but from what I can guess, it's just supposed to have been drugs. For me, I can't even imagine Elvis into drugs. I'm from the era when it was all the clean living things about Elvis, so it was a bit of a kind of a shock to hear that's what he was supposed to be into. But anyway, I don't care, 'cause he's dead, and everyone's going to be dead one day. And he was gorgeous while he was alive, and I love him. And he's still one of my faves, so I just like to remember him like that—I don't particularly get into the fact that he's dead. For me, he's sort of still alive, knocking around."

Years later, while honeymooning in Memphis specifically to visit Elvis-related locations like Sun Studio and Graceland, I began to understand exactly what Paul was saying. Yes, Elvis was definitely a rock 'n' roll icon, but it did almost seem like he was being remembered as much for his weight gain as anything else. The Graceland wardrobe display of his flashy onstage outfits came in a wide range of sizes, depending on how many of Elvis's favorite peanut butter, bacon, and banana sandwiches he was eating at the time, and was both freakishly funny, sad, and—I might mention—totally relatable for me.

The wall outside Graceland where millions of Elvis fans, including me, left messages for the late, great King of Rock 'n' Roll

My afternoon at Sun Studio, the small recording facility where Elvis was able to make a name for himself thanks to producer/studio owner Sam Phillips, was inspiring. Jerry Lee Lewis, Ike Turner, Howlin' Wolf, Johnny Cash, Carl Perkins and many other major musicians all recorded there at one time or another.

Loved my visit to the legendary Sun Studio in Memphis.

George Harrison, who had a special fondness for Elvis's Sun Studio days, repeated the story we'd featured in the original version of our RKO Beatles special when I spoke with him alone: as a teenager riding a bicycle around his Liverpool neighborhood one memorable afternoon, his entire perception of popular music changed.

"That's when I first heard Elvis," he told me, his enthusiasm obvious. "I think it was coming out of somebody's house. They had the record 'Heartbreak Hotel' . . . and I remember it was very strong at that time. It was the best thing I'd ever heard! I think Elvis really influenced all of us musicians who were around in the late fifties and early sixties. Elvis was definitely, well, he had the best songs and the best voice and the best backing. Those old Sun Records were just fantastic, especially they're really more fantastic if you were in a place like Liverpool at the time."

Almost exactly two years later, during our interview at the Dakota, John seemed to feel the same way. He was still inspired by the vocal style of one of his all-time musical heroes, even citing Elvis's influence on one of the songs from his and Yoko's recently released album, *Double Fantasy*.

"I started out to do rock 'n' roll because I absolutely liked doing it. So that's why I ended up doin' a track like '(Just Like) Starting Over.'" John began to sing it out loud in a funny fifties style—"WEH-ELL, WEH-ELL!"—adding, "It's sort of ala Elvis, and I hope people accept it like that. I think it's a serious piece of work, but it's also tongue-in-cheek, you know? I mean, I went right back to me roots! All the time we were doin' it, I was callin' it 'Elvis Orbison,' and, you know, it's not going back to being Beatles John in the sixties; it's being John Lennon whose life was changed completely by hearing American rock 'n' roll on the radio as a child. And that's the part of me that's coming out again and why I'm enjoying it this time."

Elaborating on his love of classic rock, John told us, "I have the records still. If I hear Elvis—I heard him singing 'I Want You, I Need You, I Love You' the other day—I mean, I was just in heaven. Of course I was goin' back to my youth and remembering the dates and what was goin' on when I heard that music."

What was going on back on January 24, 1958, when John was just seventeen, was that he and Paul were making their first pre-Beatles Cavern Club appearance together in Liverpool, as the skiffle group the Quarrymen. That same day, Elvis Presley's "Jailhouse Rock" jumped onto the UK charts, becoming the first record ever to enter at number one. Another first (and only) for the Beatles and Elvis came in the summer of '65 when the band took time off from its second North American tour. They ended up staying for several days in a supposedly secluded Benedict Canyon mansion that their manager, Brian Epstein, had rented for them from Zsa Zsa Gabor prior to their August 29 and 30 Hollywood Bowl appearances. The idea was to hide the Fab Four from fans while giving the band a break from its nearly nonstop performance schedule, and a major event during this minivacay was their one and only meetup with Elvis Presley, at Presley's Bel Air home on the twenty-seventh, thanks to Elvis's manager, Colonel Tom Parker.

Ed Leffler, who was identified as a Beatles management representative in our RKO special and ended up working with an assortment of other hitmakers, had this to say about the band's 1965 visit with the King in hour five of our show.

"They were invited to Elvis's house with the one understanding from both sides that there would be absolutely no publicity whatsoever. We went over there, and it was very strange, because Elvis and his people were sitting on one side of the room and the boys sat down on another side of the room, and they'd brought their guitars—and Elvis obviously had his in the house. Just sitting there, no one saying anything for what felt like an hour—I'm sure it was about five minutes, but everyone was studying each other, and finally Elvis took his guitar out and started to sing, and the boys did the same thing. It was incredible."

In each and every version told of this rock royalty get-together, it's agreed that although the conversation between Elvis and the Beatles was initially awkward, the impromptu, unrecorded jam session that finally followed loosened things up quite a bit. Sadly, there's no audio or visual souvenir from this once-in-a-lifetime evening, but for those who were there, it's the memory that matters.

While reminiscing about Elvis was just a small part of each of the John, Paul, and George interviews, I was able to conduct one session within the same time period in which the sole topic of conversation was Elvis. This was with his stepmother, Dee Presley, who'd left her husband to marry Elvis's widowed dad, Vernon, back in 1960. She and her three boys revealed their version of life with the rock star in 1979's *Elvis, We Love You Tender*, a book that was met with mixed reviews but still inspired an interesting and well-received on-air newscast feature series for me.

"They loved Elvis," Dee said of her sons. "He spent many hours playing with them, more time than any man, even Vernon or their own father. In '69, when he opened at the International Hilton in Vegas, that was the very first time my sons ever saw Elvis on stage, and at that very moment they decided they wanted to be with Elvis."

All three of Dee's boys then hit the road, touring with Elvis from that point forward, though none of them had any idea how wild and rocky that road would become. "It wasn't that I resented their love for

Elvis," Dee continued. "Not at the time I didn't, but I grew to resent it when I saw what was actually happening. Things were getting out of control."

To hear Dee Presley tell it, the dream life that her sons envisioned when touring with Elvis quickly became a nightmare when he informed them, "I'm the teacher now." He and his Memphis mafia introduced them rather prematurely to sex, drugs, and rock 'n' roll. Dee told me she blamed Elvis for her son Ricky's addiction and for the dissolution of his own marriage to Priscilla, but she nonetheless sang his praises as well.

"In spite of all that happened, there's a certain part of Elvis that I still hold up as very good," she claimed. "Basically, he was a very fine person. He took all the criticism, he did not fight back, and he gave so much of himself to the people. It was not Elvis those last few years—it was something else. He had changed . . . I don't believe they'll ever stop loving Elvis." It was hearing those words that inspired me to wind up the final episode in my Dee Presley feature series by saying, "A legendary rocker, an incredible human being—Elvis, we love you tender."

But it's the following chorus from this 1987 song and video by MTV psychobilly star Mojo Nixon and his recording partner, Skid Roper, that I've since come to believe says it all in regard to Elvis Presley's everlasting appeal:

"Elvis is everywhere/Elvis is everything/Elvis is everybody/Elvis is still the king!"

Yes, without a doubt and still to this day, Elvis is everywhere.

Coincidentally, Mojo Nixon is too, since he happened to be the nondenominational officiant at my first wedding, which took place five years later, in 1992.

Mojo was a last-minute replacement for Little Richard, who'd promised me during my interview with him for *Rock Magazine* a few years earlier that whenever I was ready to tie the knot, he'd take the reins at my ceremony. Even though the late, great Little Richard Penniman did end up dropping out, Mojo made an awesome substitute. In retrospect, I only wish he'd offered to sing "Elvis Is Everywhere" as part of the celebration, since it would have made that marriage more memorable, and in a much better way.

That early-'85 Richard Penniman interview, celebrating the release of his bio, *The Life and Times of Little Richard, The Quasar of Rock*, really opened my eyes when it came to the reality of rock 'n' roll in the fifties. "The Quasar," as Richard defined it for me, is "the brightest star in the universe." As I wrote in my article, "To God-fearing, righteous American parents with rebellious teenagers, Little Richard was the dancin', prancin' black devil himself. And he insists that's why his well-earned title, the King of Rock and Roll, was taken away from him."

"The system did not like it," Richard explained to me. "Here's a black boy that was going Top 40 all the way, and white girls screaming over him. So they put Pat Boone on me, to cover 'Tutti Frutti.' Then they threw Elvis on me, HE did 'Tutti Frutti'—they threw him on me heavy! Then they started calling him 'King,' and he had never written a song! NEVER! I have written many. He told me himself that I was the greatest, that I inspired him to be a star. ELVIS!"

And it didn't stop there, according to Richard. "Here are the Beatles telling the world that I'm the King! Mick Jagger! David Bowie saying that I made him go out and buy a saxophone—if it weren't for me, he wouldn't be no star! Here's Otis Redding saying, 'If it weren't for Little Richard, I would never be on the stage.' Here's James Brown saying, 'He's my Idol!' Here's Michael Jackson saying, 'He's one of my idols!' Here's Prince saying, 'He's my TOTAL idol!'

"But it's been hid from the public," Little Richard added sadly.

He told me about a dream he had had in '57 in which he saw a one-way ticket to Hell with his name on it. This was followed by a real life airplane incident in which one of the two engines caught fire. As I summed it up in my article, 'The plane landed safely, but not before a higher power extracted a promise from Little Richard to leave his life of sin."

"I came from rock 'n' roll to rock of ages," he said.

Shortly after that, he went back to school in Huntsville, Alabama, where he earned his BA and became an ordained minister for the Seventh Day Adventist Church, a fire-and-brimstone denomination. Richard also married a stenographer named Ernestine and was prepared to settle down to a lifetime of religious servitude when he received a call from a British promoter named Brian Epstein, who offered him 50 percent to take on a group of lads from Liverpool. The almost-former rocker admitted that he turned Epstein down because he thought the band didn't stand a chance, but he did agree to tour with them anyway.

"The Beatles had never seen a famous person in their life. They just wanted to touch me—Paul IDOLIZED me. I threw my shirt into the audience, and he went and brought his shirt to me, and he was just so honored for me to put on his shirt! He said, 'The King! The KING!' and he just had a fit."

Little Richard followed his Beatles tale with stories about the days he spent with both the Rolling Stones and Jimi Hendrix early in their careers, and he added that even in the mideighties, when I was conducting the interview, he had devoted famous fans.

"Prince is ME in this generation," he said. "Michael Jackson is too. Michael is me with his flamboyant dressing—whooo!'— his make-up, the sequins. I could design some outfits for Michael that would shake this world!"

No doubt about it, Little Richard Penniman had been shaking this world since he first shouted out "AWOP-BOP-A-LOO-BOP-A-LOP-BAM-BOOM" in his 1955 landmark rocker, "Tutti Frutti." Elvis Presley's '56 cover may have featured altered lyrics and a different vocal style, but both versions captured the energy and essence of the song, crowning both Little Richard and Elvis as the Kings of Rock 'n' Roll.

—CHAPTER 13—

"The Long and Winding Road"
—to Omaha

As the fall '77 premiere of our marathon Beatles presentation grew
closer, my excitement knew no bounds. The original, fourteen-
hour show (soon to be extended to fifteen and eventually to seventeen)
was scheduled to air in different formats on RKO stations across the
country. Some would be featuring two-hour blocks every night for a
week, while others planned on playing just one hour a day, stretching
the special out over a two-week period.

Still unbelievable in my mind was that there I was, all of twenty-
two years old, with barely over a year on the job, and yet I had a major
national radio broadcast event about to hit the airwaves. I was in awe
of every bit of work we'd all done and couldn't wait to hear my name
on the air in the final credits, voiced by John Mack Flanagan.

"The Beatles, copyright RKO Radio Productions. Produced at the
studios of KFRC in San Francisco. . . . Executive producer, Paul Drew.
Produced by Dave Sholin, Ron Hummel, and Laurie Kaye. . . . Special
assistance, Michael Spears. Written by Laurie Kaye."

Just the idea that I could be mentioned in the company of such
highly regarded radio notables as Paul Drew and Michael Spears,
plus successful up-and-comers like Dave Sholin and Ron Hummel,
astonished me. I was equally ecstatic when Drew and Spears, who'd

each held the title of KFRC program director previously in his career, sent congratulations not only to Dave, Ron, and me on our work as a team, but also to me individually on my script. And then, when RKO President Dwight Case chimed in . . . WOW! But I have to admit that in my heart of hearts, what I was really looking forward to was my own mother hearing, recognizing, and being impressed by my work. I hoped she might even let her husband know that despite his years of negativity throughout my childhood, her college-dropout daughter had actually managed to amount to something. But sadly, Mom said no, not a chance—there was no way she'd be tuning in to KHJ in LA to catch the show; she just wasn't interested enough in the Beatles (or apparently her own daughter), she admitted, to take the time to listen. Although there was a part of me that wasn't surprised, I couldn't help but be deeply disappointed. Sigh.

I really hadn't planned on revealing this embarrassing tidbit to anyone I worked with, but I found myself sharing the truth about what my mother had told me to John Mack Flanagan shortly before *RKO Presents the Beatles* hit the airwaves. As he was about to enter the DJ booth one afternoon, he said something to me about how proud my family must be of my latest accomplishment, and I just couldn't hold back. Flanagan's response was completely in line with the kind, considerate, supportive friend I'd found him to be during our past few months of working on the special together, and that same day, after his air shift ended, he handed me a personal note that he'd jotted down on a sheet of KFRC stationery.

"Laurie," he'd written. "I like you. You know why? You care about other people, and you want to be the best at what you do—you will be. I like you, and a lot of other people do too. Thanks for making 'The Beatles' a Killer! You did it."

It was this kind of encouragement that made it all worthwhile and got me past the fact that my own mother didn't seem to care at all about what her daughter had been dedicating herself to for so long or where she might be heading next. My KFRC coworkers and associates had become the family I'd always dreamed of, and it was thanks to their support that I was able to continue my climb up the stairway to a kind of personal redemption through my accomplishments in rock radio.

Some of the most treasured, uplifting comments about my work came from Dave Sholin one day in December of '77 as he entered the private studio of KFRC morning personality Dr. Don Rose—or the doc's "personal palace," as Dave put it. This happened a couple of months after we had finally finished our Beatles special and just as I was nearly reaching the tail end of my interview with the Ramones, quite possibly my favorite punk band of all time. Dave had been looking forward to coming in and welcoming these influential rockers to the station, and he took the opportunity to deliver flattering remarks about me too.

"Laurie's doing an incredible show here," Sholin told guitarist Johnny and bass player Dee Dee, referring to the exciting "new music" special I'd been interviewing the Ramones for. Lead singer Joey would have been there with us in Dr. Don's studio too, but he was still recovering from the second-degree burns he'd suffered just three weeks before in New Jersey when a humidifier blew up in his face as he was doing his preconcert warm-up vocals. Like a true rock 'n' roll trouper, Joey still managed to make it through the band's entire set, injuries and all, but he then had to spend a full week at a New York hospital burn center, followed by even more rest and recuperation before he could resume his role as front man. Dave sent his regards to Joey and then continued complimenting me.

"Laurie was the force behind the Beatles show," Dave informed them. "The biggest Beatles special ever done!" The guys seemed quite impressed, especially since the inspiration behind their own band name had come from the pseudonym Paul McCartney had during his Silver Beatles days, when he would check into a hotel as Paul Ramon while on tour. Plus, we'd just been talking about the Ramones' major musical influences, with Johnny telling me, "Mostly, we collect old records," which came as something of a surprise to me. "Beach Boys, Beatles, a lot of the bubblegum music that was out in the midsixties. We listened to everything—heavy metal too. We just absorbed it all."

"I'm putting together this special on punk, new wave, the problems of labeling it and what kind of music it really is," I let them know.

"They can call it whatever they want," Johnny Ramone responded.

"I guess if anybody's punk rock, WE'RE punk rock! But rock 'n' roll's always been punk. When it first started, parents right away said, 'This is awful; it's noise. I don't want you listening to this; it's going to make you sick!'"

"And then the Beatles came out, and people were against the Beatles and the Rolling Stones," Johnny continued. "So whoever's good in punk rock will succeed, and whoever's not won't."

This made perfect sense, especially considering the Ramones had already proven themselves to be not just good but GREAT punk rockers thanks to their intense live shows, filled with relatively short, catchy, hot-tempo tunes, and their self-titled first album, for Sire Records, which became a smash hit with critics even if it was nowhere near a chartbuster. By the time the band had released album number two, *Leave Home*, less than a year later, I was completely captivated by their stage presence and studio sound. But that's not all. The record company had also miraculously come up with what had to be the spiciest and most instantly collectible piece of rock 'n' roll swag I'd ever seen: a pearl-handled, switchblade-style letter opener with the words "RAMONES LEAVE HOME" printed in all caps and the teeny-tiny Sire Records name and logo underneath. And yes, I still treasure my nearly mint condition, forty-plus-year-old super swag switchblade to this day.

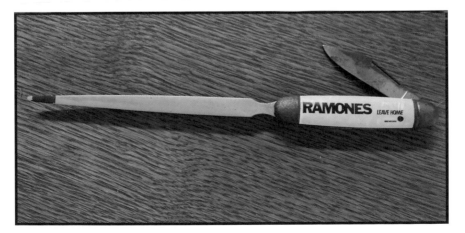

My much cherished Ramones *Leave Home* letter opener.

Johnny, Dee Dee, and I talked for quite a while about the origins of punk rock as well, with the Ramones crediting CBGB's as New York's (and the nation's) primary punk outlet.

"It's just a little bar in the Bowery—it's where the derelicts hang. Us and a couple other groups started there playing for, like, NO ONE, and it just built up."

I had to ask the one question that's still hotly debated to this day: who came first, British or American punk rockers?

"It started in New York three years ago," Dee Dee emphasized, "and we were the first group they started calling punk rock. And we went over to England and were really big there already, before we even had an album out! Groups there started after they came down to see us, and now it's popping up all over, but we find New York more unique. The groups in England have a lot of similarities among each other—like they all had the same influences—us, New York Dolls, Stooges."

They also brought up what they saw as another big difference between themselves and the Brit rockers, specifically between the song that would become their biggest hit, "Rockaway Beach," which was written by Dee Dee Ramone, and the Sex Pistols' "God Save the Queen."

"You've got to have a sense of humor, you know? We want to be entertaining, and keep things lighthearted. Things are grim, yeah, but so what? We've already had our political era in music, like in the late sixties. . . . Politics and music are two different things," Dee Dee insisted. "Somebody wants to sing about politics, they should just become politicians."

As the interview drew to a close, I could hear some serious stomach rumbling coming from one of the band members. I asked if they were hungry, and both shook their heads, with Dee Dee saying, "No, I just ate, and I'm NAUSEOUS!" Turns out they'd just had lunch at a notorious spot called Dragon Burger, which was right up the street at the entrance to San Francisco's Chinatown.

"Oh, no," I said sympathetically. "I would have warned you against that. It's solid grease."

"As long as it wasn't dog meat or anything," Dee Dee responded, apologizing over the next few minutes as he made a number of freaky faces and admitted, "Oh, my stomach is growling away. Must have been those french fries." Poor guy.

Although I'd seen the Ramones perform several months before at a local punk hot spot, Mabuhay Gardens, aka the Fab Mab, the band's upcoming Old Waldorf gig was on my calendar as well. In the years that followed, I was lucky enough to catch Ramones shows in nearly every city I've lived in.

My obvious affection for the group and its music prompted Dave Sholin to stand singing in his office doorway once the boys in the band had left the station. The two of us laughed out loud as he altered the lyrics to one of the coolest Ramones songs while I walked down the hallway heading back to the newsroom.

"Laurie is a punk rocker," Dave vocalized to the tune of "Sheena Is a Punk Rocker." "Laurie is a punk rocker, Laurie is a punk rocker now-ow-ow!"

I may not have truly been the Sheena type punk rocker the Ramones were singing about, but I for sure felt the same sort of rush when it came to new music, and much like Sheena herself, who "just couldn't stay" and "had to break away," I was looking to make my own big move, from what most people would have called the perfect job and living situation.

What I wanted more than anything was to be on the air, and not just anywhere, but in front of a live mic in the studios of KFRC San Francisco. Though I'd been spending my free time recording news and voiceover demos, I knew that what the station's latest program director, Les Garland, was telling me was one-hundred-percent true. When it came to on-air reporting, Les explained, I would have to cut my teeth in the news department of some other, much less prominent radio station.

And so, with the great Les Garland's support, I began to accept my fate and apply for news anchor/reporter positions at stations across the country that he would scout out and recommend me for. Les's promise to bring me back to the West Coast within six months sealed the deal, but still, I decided to postpone my move for just a bit longer. First, I was going to take advantage of the opportunity at KFRC to conduct a few interviews that had already been booked, some with authors I was really looking forward to speaking with.

I was able to meet up with a real variety of bestselling writers on book tours, among them psychologist Dr. Joyce Brothers; Arnold Schwarzenegger; President Carter's mother, Lillian; and, a bit down the line, Linda Lovelace, star of the X-rated film *Deep Throat*. They all looked forward to coming to the station to spread the word about their recently published work, and I was the grateful recipient of their time, insights, and writing tips, no doubt realizing that one day, no matter how many years later, I might be in the same spot—promoting my own memoir.

Surprisingly, it was Schwarzenegger's 1977, soon-to-be-smash-hit autobiography, *The Education of a Bodybuilder*, that made the biggest impact on me. A huge mass of muscle, he showed up at KFRC in good humor, as almost every woman I worked with uncoincidentally came up with an excuse to hang out in the hallway. As we headed to the studio for our chat, Arnold thought he was being funny when he grabbed one of the tiniest of the gals who'd been standing there staring at him, lifting her high over his shoulders and roaring with laughter. She was totally taken by his move, but it honestly left me rather repulsed, which I admitted to him after we'd settled into the studio, saying I was there to hear how he'd worked his way up the ladder of success, not to watch him flirt.

"That's great," he told me respectfully. "You always have to move right along, no stopping. I'm a strong believer in that. You shouldn't settle for less; just always go right up to the top."

And so, with Arnold's advice ringing in my ears, I began our question-and-answer session with what I was sure would be one of his favorite subjects: self-esteem.

"Do you think everybody who wants to be great, no matter in what field, has to have that ego, that drive?" I asked.

"It depends on how good you want to be in a particular area," he responded. "The idea of being the most muscular man in the world impressed me, so I just jumped into that at fifteen. Two- to three-hour workouts a day for five years, and finally, when I was twenty years old, I won the Mr. Universe competition—five years in a row!"

Arnold had no problem admitting that he was using bodybuilding only as the means to an end. "The end for me was getting into acting, and getting enough confidence together in all this other stuff that carries me on to other things," he added. But of course acting *wasn't* the end, because he eventually jumped into politics, serving as California's Republican governor from 2003 to 2011.

When I asked if his folks had backed his bodybuilding goals from the start, our stories really seemed to connect.

"I'm a strong believer that parents should give their children a lot of support, but I didn't have that," he confessed. "The idea of using weight training for getting muscular and becoming Mr. Universe was very strange to my parents, and therefore they didn't support me, which just made me more strong inside and gave me more willpower to show them that I can do it."

At that point in the interview, it seemed like Arnold was almost telling my own story without realizing it. Next, he somehow managed to highlight, again unknowingly, one of the key differences in the way the two of us had been raised, saying that when he won his first trophy, at the age of eighteen, his mother and father jumped on the bodybuilding bandwagon by taking it from him. However, they didn't hide or trash it, like my mother and her husband might have done, but instead went running around town with it to show off what a great son they had. Lucky Arnold!

Strangely enough, it was when I changed the subject and asked if he minded being a sex symbol that the world's most famous muscleman addressed what he seemed to consider the number one aspect of feminism.

"I think the body is extremely important when we're dealing with the opposite sex," Schwarzenegger told me. "Due to women's liberation, it just got to the point now where women also can be attracted to a man physically, rather than just for other qualities. It's always been a man's position to just look at a woman's body and say, 'Well, I like this chick because she has great breasts and a great ass'— to really just look at her body and nothing else, whereas women were never allowed to do that."

This, he said, was unwelcome news for some men. "Now the fat slobs who are running around know they have to straighten out, because women do not give them the attention that they maybe used to get. Women just turned around and did the same thing to men as men have been doing to women for so many years."

And on that note, I began to wrap up our discussion, thinking to myself that I had plenty of provocative sound bites to work with—definitely one of my most attention-getting author interviews to date.

Just ten days before my Schwarzenegger encounter and a week prior to sitting down with the Ramones, I welcomed Talking Heads, a fairly new band at the time, for one of their first West Coast radio interviews, scheduled for the same day as their premiere San Francisco performance at the Old Waldorf.

As I enthusiastically walked to work that morning, I stopped in front of one of my favorite downtown stores to window-shop and ended up heading inside to check out one of the items.

Although it was partially hidden under one arm, I was carrying my promo copy of the band's recently released debut album, *Talking Heads: 77*, which I'd played practically nonstop the night before to help prep for my interview. Almost immediately, I was approached by a wide-eyed salesman who, obviously fascinated by the LP, asked to check it out and started questioning me about it. When he saw that it was a promo copy straight from the record company, he assumed I had some connection to the music business, and within a couple of minutes he had me revealing that I would not only be meeting the band at my radio station in just a few hours but also seeing them onstage at the Waldorf not long after. He asked if by any chance I had an extra ticket, and when I admitted that I didn't have a date yet, he began jumping up and down with joy, begging me to make him my "plus one," which I impulsively decided to do. It made me feel special to be able to bring someone such happiness by sharing new music that was already so important to me, and it led to a friendship that even if it didn't last a lifetime, was still worthwhile.

Talking Heads did put on a unique, terrific show that night, as my interview with band members David Byrne, Jerry Harrison, and newlyweds Tina Weymouth and Chris Frantz had foreshadowed. Once they were all seated in the studio, I started out with my typical opening question, about labeling music as one genre or another, asking if calling their music new wave and/or punk hurt or helped.

"It does both," Weymouth, the group's bassist, answered. "When people lump us all in with new wave, it's like a sort of name-dropping process. But then when they see us, we're not like punk bands that they might have seen before or heard on record. So it doesn't hurt us, but it doesn't help us either."

Lead singer/primary songwriter/guitar player David Byrne turned the table on me, asking what the other bands I'd been interviewing had to say about it. I told him that some San Francisco groups, like the Nuns, detested the term "punk," saying it applied more to the audience than to their music. Then I brought up what seemed to be the most frequently used label when it came to the Talking Heads: "art school rock." Byrne agreed, adding, "But that's just because we didn't keep it a secret that we went to art school. We're not embarrassed about things we did like going to college, and we're not trying to cover that up and pretend we're a bunch of street kids that grew up on the Lower East Side of New York."

Drummer Chris Frantz added, "Sometimes we get an audience who haven't heard our record or anything, and they're expecting us to be like the Sex Pistols or the Ramones, and there's a period of adjustment. But generally they seem to be more open-minded, so I think that's good."

Looking ahead to the band's gig that night, I asked how they felt about audience participation.

"It's nice when they yell things at us," David said as the others giggled in agreement.

Tina took it a step further, admitting "We don't like it when they stay reverent like they're in church. It's actually more fun for us when they get a little rowdy. At CBGB's they get quite rowdy, but there's no room to dance—so people get excited, but they do it in their seats."

"Sometimes, the way kids dance, you think they're gonna hurt themselves," keyboardist/guitar player Jerry Harrison said. "There was that one girl who was dancing as if she was being hung!" The whole band began cracking up at the memory. "She was sitting down, and someone was holding a neckerchief that was tied around her neck, but if she'd made a big mistake and fallen off her chair, it would have hurt!" As Jerry began jokingly imitating their female fan's moves, Tina spoke up, reminding him that this was a radio rather than TV interview. "Nobody can see you, Jerry," she said, and the band members laughed all over again.

David talked about what went into their songs, mentioning real-life emotions, feelings, events. When asked specifically about "Psycho Killer," which had just been released as a single, he explained, "That song is an exercise in looking through someone else's mind's eye. In other words, I've never killed anyone, so I can't say it's from experience. It's fun to play, and people seem to enjoy hearing it—maybe THEY want to kill someone!"

As his fellow band members cackled, they also made it clear that they themselves listened to nothing but Top 40 back home while driving from one gig to the next because, as it turned out, they had only AM radio in their vehicle. "It seems like the mixes of so many songs are all the same," they told me, "and we also know, now that we've finally been in the studio and made a record, that there are people that you can buy who will make a hit record for you. They'll give you that sound—a lot of Fender Rhodes and a lot of congas mixed waaay down in the background, so you can just sort of nod to it. The way most hits are made is by production, by picking the right guys to back up the right voice, and that's it."

Tina took it a step further, saying, "One thing we've never believed in is such a thing as the average listener, and keeping that in mind, we never tried to do anything with a song saying, 'Oh, this is going to make it more commercial.' We just do what we like, and it seems there are people who like it, so we just play for them—and we're going to keep doing that."

And so they did, turning Talking Heads and their totally original sound into a super successful band and eventually leading to the filming of *Stop Making Sense*, their amazing mideighties concert movie directed by Jonathan Demme. I was Dick Clark's head radio and print writer at the time and was given front-row seats to Hollywood's Pantages Theatre for each night they performed and shot there in December of '83 so that I could feature it in Dick's syndicated weekly newspaper column. It was quite the concertgoing/moviemaking experience and one of the best live rock flicks ever made.

About six months after our interview at KFRC, Talking Heads released record number two, *More Songs about Buildings and Food*. It featured the hit single "Take Me to the River," the ultracool Al Green cover that helped catapult the album to gold-record status. The LP marked the band's initial collaboration with producer/performer Brian Eno, who'd worked with such megastars as Roxy Music, Robert Fripp, and David Bowie. Eno also went on in 1979 to join David Byrne on his first project minus Talking Heads, *My Life in the Bush of Ghosts*.

After leaving San Francisco fairly early in 1978, I ended up finally returning to the Bay Area in mid-'79 for my long-awaited on-air position at KFRC. I was back working in downtown San Francisco, across the street and just down the hill from the entrance to Chinatown and the main office of Pacific Telephone, and one day as I was walking up to Chinatown to grab some lunch, I couldn't believe whom I saw exiting the phone company—none other than Brian Eno and David Byrne. Each held a handle of a huge, heavy bag of what appeared to be a ton of telephone equipment, and both were grinning, giggling, and literally skipping down the sidewalk like a couple of deliriously happy kids.

I was tempted to follow them, but ultimately I didn't. It would be a while before I found out that the two of them were living in town while recording at Different Fur Studios, although their album wouldn't be released until early 1981 because of legal issues regarding various vocal samples and the voices of radio personalities whom Byrne and Eno had included in their project. When *My Life in the Bush of Ghosts* finally did come out, initial critical reaction ranged from barely average to top of the crop. Although originally considered a cult favorite, the album has, over the years, come to be considered a groundbreaking experimental masterpiece by some. I know I've always loved it.

Before I could take off from KFRC for what was about to become my first on-air news anchor position, I felt the urge to wrap up my new music special, to which I was adding local punk pioneers as well as the nationally known groups. San Francisco-based bands and Fab Mab regulars like Crime, the Nuns, and Leila and the Snakes all made the cut. It was totally cool to be able to invite them to the station for interviews, especially Jane Dornacker, aka Leila, who would later become a KFRC radio personality herself before moving on to New York as a traffic reporter in the mideighties. That move to Manhattan ended in tragedy when the helicopter she was reporting from one afternoon crashed and sank in the Hudson River, causing her death. So very sad.

I'd seen the Nuns a number of times, including once months earlier when they opened for the Ramones at the Mabuhay. I was really looking forward to their upcoming Winterland set along with the Avengers; both bands had been booked to perform before the much anticipated appearance of the Sex Pistols on the controversial British band's first US tour. This show would turn out to be the Pistols' last until their first reunion in the midnineties, and unfortunately, the entire experience didn't at all live up to the hype, as their album *Live at Winterland 1978* proved.

Still, it turned out to be a night to remember—not as much for the music as for the hurling. Not just fans tossing things up on stage, but also lead singer Johnny Rotten throwing insults at the audience, including his final words before uttering his nasty farewell: "Ever get the feeling you've been cheated?" he asked. Yep, definitely.

On that note, I was finally ready to formally accept the job that KFRC Program Director Les Garland had convinced me would help me build a career on air in radio news. WOW-AM Omaha, the fifty-thousand-watt station famous for giving Johnny Carson his gig as morning show host before he turned to TV and eventually took over *The Tonight Show*, was about to become my new home away from home. I can't say I was thrilled to leave California, but as I began planning my goodbye party, packing up my possessions, and preparing myself mentally for my move to the Midwest, I made a point of telling myself and every single one of my friends repeatedly that I was not making a major mistake. Instead, I was investing in my future.

That being said, I tried my best to keep an open mind during my flight to Nebraska, but still, upon arrival at the Omaha airport, I was shocked to see how different everyone looked. Not only did the locals seem bigger and bulkier, but they also were dressed like nothing I'd ever seen before. The worst weather in decades, the Blizzard of '78, had just landed, bringing icy winds, heavy snowfall, and subfreezing temperatures. There was no way to survive without thick, heavy apparel covering practically every inch of one's head, body, and face, especially for a Los Angeles native who'd barely ever experienced snow before.

My WOW coworkers were understanding and supportive in helping me adjust, but still, I knew from the moment I sat in the studio for the first time, giving the weather report at the tail end of my newscast, that I would need to start working my way permanently out of the station's front door as soon as I could. And despite the new Omaha friends I'd been able to make, a couple of whom I'm still in touch with even after all these years, plus the excitement that being live on the air generated, it was obvious the environment just wasn't for me.

That same first day I received a kind, congratulatory note from Paul Drew, the RKO bigwig who'd been the executive producer of our Beatles special. He made me feel so much better by reminding me that I was now at the number one station in mid-America and by wishing me success. Paul's letter, delivered to me at WOW, was dated February 1, and unbelievably, less than a month later, by February 28, I was already out the door and en route to Seattle, having been offered—and having accepted in a flash—a news anchor gig at KING-AM, thanks once again to KFRC's Les Garland. Never in a million years had I thought I'd be back on the West Coast in barely over a month, but WOW, was I excited to be leaving WOW!

—CHAPTER 14—

"California Dreamin'"

From the moment I found myself in Seattle, even though I couldn't help jonesing for my home state and knew I'd always consider myself a California gal, I felt things were going to work out just fine. That's why as job offers continued to pour in from remarkable Top 40 stations in Tampa, Houston, and other seventies radio hot spots, I turned them all down to stick it out in the Pacific Northwest. Sure, I knew it would be wet, but even in the pouring rain, I was able to adjust easily to the atmosphere. I was comfortable being so much closer to sunny California, and thanks to my cross-dressing college boyfriend, who came from Seattle, I'd become slightly familiar with the city several years earlier.

I found out right away that Seattle's exciting, emerging new music scene had inspired an assortment of cool local clubs and hangouts, and on top of that, there were major established venues where I'd be able to catch favorites like Blondie, the Ramones, and Southside Johnny and the Asbury Jukes. To say I was ecstatic is an understatement.

My new employer, KING-AM, was the Top 40 branch of a broadcast family that also included an FM classical outlet and a popular TV station. The company had been founded by Dorothy Bullitt back in the forties, when it was especially rare for women to play such a

Wearable proof of my return to the West Coast as an on-air newscaster at KING Radio.

prominent role in the industry. When Bullitt bought her first radio station, she immediately worked on changing its name to KING and raising its power output to the US maximum, fifty thousand watts. I took this as a sign that I was in exactly the right place at the right time to make my on-air mark in the world of music-radio news.

My first day on the job, I asked my new coworkers where the best place might be to catch live local music, and almost every single associate gave me the same answer: anywhere but downtown Seattle, which back in the late seventies had not yet been rebuilt enough to accommodate massive office buildings and skyscrapers and was still home to plenty of small storefront businesses like pawn shops and pubs. So of course that's exactly where I headed to spend my first night out on the town.

As I drove through the area, I heard the sound of a bluesy electric guitar coming from somewhere, but I couldn't tell where. I quickly parked the tiny red Honda I'd bought the day before and ran up and down the street to figure out my potential destination. I found that the music was emanating from a nearly hidden, funky little spot that seemed to attract mostly hard-core drinkers who were sitting at the bar but barely paying any attention to the performers on the other side of the room.

I headed back out to make sure I'd locked my car, and as I made my way once again to the watering hole, I stopped for a moment a couple doors down to stare into the window of the vintage tattoo parlor I'd just passed. To my surprise, the only person inside was a young woman, who quickly opened the door and introduced herself. She told me she'd learned the art of tattoo from the shop's original owner, who'd been in the business for decades. When she explained she had stayed late that night to practice her craft, I was pretty impressed, but I certainly had no idea that she would soon be considered "Seattle's First Lady of Tattoo," the world renowned Madame Lazonga. She encouraged me to stop by during the day to meet with her about designing the perfect piece of meaningful body art to celebrate this new phase of my existence, the thought of which fascinated me. As I said goodnight and headed back to the bar for a healthy dose of the blues, I couldn't help but laugh thinking about how horrified my fellow KING employees would be if they only knew how I'd completely disregarded their advice.

That was pretty much the direction I found myself taking during my entire time in Seattle, which amounted to almost a year and a half. Plus, thanks to having musical preferences that weren't accepted by the majority of my associates, I began to be teased on the air right from the start.

KING-AM's ultrapopular a.m. disc jockey Bruce Murdock, aka Murdock in the Morning, especially enjoyed making fun of me before almost every one of my newscasts. He would humorously introduce me to his listeners as the station's hard-core punk and tell them that I was wearing plastic pants and had safety pins stuck all over my face, which of course wasn't true.

Even though I really did dress quite a bit differently from my coworkers, there's no way Murdock could have known, since our KING newsroom was three floors below his DJ booth. Fortunately, this didn't put a halt to his sense of humor, since I truly enjoyed being the butt of his kooky jokes. Privately, he thanked me repeatedly for being such a good sport, but what he probably didn't realize was that he was actually boosting my popularity, not to mention helping me gain attention from Seattle's blossoming punk population. This was especially meaningful to me when it came to making friends with not only new-music fans, but also club promoters and even local punk/pop musicians.

One Seattle contact of mine is now a well-respected professional bagpipe player and instructor. I met Neil Hubbard long before his pro piper days, when he attempted to plug punk and new wave music by sending a letter to KING-AM's program director, Rob Conrad. Neil wanted to know why our station was sticking to a traditional Top 40 playlist and didn't seem open to playing new music by bands like Blondie and the Ramones despite their obvious popularity. "The one and only solution," Neil wrote, "is to play these fine records on your station in some sort of decent rotation."

Before responding, our PD called me up to his office and shared the letter with me, KING's so-called punk rocker. He asked me to contact Neil to explain how radio station programming worked. Instead, I made a point of letting Rob know I agreed with his correspondent one hundred-percent, and that's what ended up helping kick off my friendship with Hubbard, the well-known local music fan who'd cofounded Seattle's first punk rock club, The Bird.

Thanks to Neil, I was fortunate enough to meet up with a talented musician named Jim Basnight, at the time a recent high school graduate and leader of possibly Seattle's most popular local band, the Moberlys, typically described as new wave/power pop though they reminded me of the early Beatles and were my favorite weekend club band back then.

Strangely enough, I met my closest Seattle contacts—the friends I hung out with the most when I wasn't on the air—at one of the city's top tourist attractions. No, not the Space Needle, but the historic Pike Place Market in downtown Seattle, famous back in the day for its fish-flinging seafood shopworkers who tossed around everything from whole salmon to sea bass as part of their sales pitch to entertain customers. But since I was totally ichthyophobic, with an irrational fear even of dead fish, this wasn't my fave part of Pike Place by a long shot.

Instead, my number one meeting place for connecting with the friends I'd end up going to concerts or nightclubs with or simply spending time and having quality conversations with was Scotty's, a Pike Place Market juice bar. A local guitar player named Colin, an employee there, became one of my first Seattle friends, followed by his behind-the-counter coworker Susan Silver. Colin and 3 Swimmers, the band he'd go on to front, would open for the British post-punk/funk group Gang of Four in Los Angeles just a few years after we met. It was a great show but sadly the last time I ever saw him.

Susan, however, came down to visit and stay with me for a while a few years later once I ended up back in LA. She also built an awesome career herself as a music manager, helping to guide Seattle superbands including Soundgarden and Alice in Chains to success. Sadly, her marriage to Soundgarden's Chris Cornell wasn't as successful, ending in divorce just a few years following the birth of their only child.

My own most memorable romantic relationship during my Seattle days also ended disappointedly. It began thanks to another Pike Place Market spot I visited fairly regularly, usually on Saturdays, called Maximilian's. As I sat down and ordered my midmorning espresso, I couldn't help but notice a good-looking, fully bearded French waiter checking me out, especially once he started commenting on the men's necktie and jacket I happened to be wearing—my weekend uniform. We started talking, and it turned out that even though he was several years older than I was, he was in the US to complete his college studies as a civil engineer, which impressed me no end. When he found out I was a radio newscaster, that seemed to be the icing on the cake, and he asked me to come with him to a friend's get-together. I said yes, and that lustful night seemed at the time to be the beginning of a deep, fulfilling love affair.

WRONG. That turned out not to be the case, as he eventually let me know that in the back of his mind, he had quite a thing against starting a relationship with sex and hoped to have the strength to never do it again. In the farewell letter he wrote me, he said I was a good person, but he didn't want me to feel like I needed him, and he told me that giving one's body to another person should be a sign of something very special. "You can't just sleep with anybody that you like," he wrote, adding that he felt he wasn't respecting me or himself when we made love, which was probably the weirdest thing anybody had ever said to me, and it definitely helped me get over him. Interestingly enough, we've been back in touch over the past few years, and it's been a pleasure for me to know that he's in a long-term marriage and is the father of five adult children—something that wouldn't have worked out for me in a million years.

Just before being dumped by my seemingly super romantic French lover!
(Photo by Kate O'Neil)

On the other hand, something that definitely *did* work out for me during my time in Seattle was traveling, for both personal and professional purposes. Even though I had what seemed like more than a full-time job as a news anchor/reporter, I managed to freelance as a rock radio special writer and interviewer. This meant flying to San Francisco as many weekends as possible to work on a variety of projects, including updating and elongating our RKO Beatles special and kicking off a new twelve-hour show called the *Top 100 of the 70's*, a coproduction of RKO and radio syndication company Drake-Chenault that would highlight the decade's greatest songs and biggest hits according to US radio station airplay. The best part was all the interviews I got to conduct over a period of several months, even though a number of them were phoners, with megastars like George Harrison, Mick Jagger, and David Bowie.

On one Sunday night flight home to Seattle from San Francisco after a weekend of hardly any sleep but plenty of hard work and partying, I dozed off as soon as I boarded the plane, taking my seat in an otherwise empty row. I woke up a short time later and found myself lying on my side with my face buried in what seemed like a wild hairy animal. To my surprise, it turned out to be a black monkey-fur jacket worn by the bass player and cofounder of the Pacific Northwest's top rockers of the day, Heart's Steve Fossen. He looked at me and laughed, and when I introduced myself as an on-air KING-AM employee with an extremely early Monday morning start time, he suggested I close my eyes and fall back asleep while he continued puffing on his cigarette. I would have taken his advice, but I was a sometime-smoker myself back then, so instead I lit up and joined him.

The band's fourth studio album, *Dog & Butterfly*, had recently been released, and I was already a fan of Heart, especially the Wilson sisters. Women in rock, especially hard rock, was how I looked at Heart back then, and even though neither lead vocalist Ann nor guitarist Nancy had been original band members, they were to me the headliners whenever the group hit the stage. Speaking of women in rock, Blondie, fronted by vocalist Debbie Harry, gave one of the best performances I ever saw in Seattle. Their sold-out show at the Paramount Theatre made me wish I'd been able to see them back when they first started gigging at New York's number one punk rock venue, CBGB—the club I'd been dying to hang out at thanks mainly to my time with the Ramones and Talking Heads while at KFRC.

I finally did get to make my first trip to New York when I earned a week's vacation after spending several months working in Seattle. I stayed in Harlem with a musician I'd met through the *Village Voice* personals, and after greeting me at the airport, he made sure we headed straight to CBGB. This was early 1979, somewhat after the club's punk heyday, but I was still in heaven!

I'd been stealthily subscribing to the *Village Voice* ever since I was thirteen years old, and although my mother once made mean fun of me after getting to the mailbox before I did and discovering my secret, I managed to keep my subscription going for years. Mom had no way of knowing how much I loved reading the *Voice*'s revolutionary rock journalists and music reviewers opining on the latest record releases and shows; writers Robert Christgau and Lester Bangs, among others, have influenced me tremendously over the years.

That's why much later, in the mideighties, living on the Bowery in New York City, practically within spitting distance of CBGB, was yet another dream come true. Plus, it turned out I was barely down the block from Lenny Kaye, Patti Smith's cool guitar player and producer, whose apartment was just north of Houston, while I was just south. Thanks to our similar names, I would get his mail and even phone calls all the time, so I got to meet up with him not only to hand over his letters and give him his messages, but also to hang out with him and his wife at parties and performances. At the time, Lenny was also working with a folk music-inspired singer/songwriter whom he kindly kept inviting me to come see perform just as her first album was being released. Strangely enough, I could never remember her name back then, even though I considered her extremely talented and a total sweetheart too. These days I have no trouble remembering her name: Suzanne Vega.

Following my first, weeklong taste of the Big Apple, I found myself back in Seattle continuing to see as many live shows as possible, including, one night at a small bar called the Rainbow Tavern, the Ramones, who had somehow been booked there. As the band jumped up to stomp and play on the pub's tabletops, I felt like it couldn't possibly get any better . . . not quite CBGB, but still, so exciting!

Another memorable Seattle show was Southside Johnny and the Asbury Jukes, the Jersey group that followed Bruce Springsteen into the limelight in the midseventies. I'd been a big fan since first seeing them as a bar band in the '77 film *Between the Lines*, which I loved, since it was all about alternative journalists. Soon after the movie came out, I not only saw the Jukes play live, but also managed to start a groupie-type relationship with one of the sax players. This unexpectedly stretched out over the next few years, picking up again and again whenever they happened to play in a city I was living in or visiting.

When I first found out about the Jukes performing at the Paramount in Seattle, I immediately started prepping for our meetup by paring down my food intake. This ended up going far beyond just normal dieting, and even after our encounter, I continued eating barely enough to stay healthy. I realized I needed to see a doctor, and I ended up going to one who told me that it looked like I'd begun to develop anorexia nervosa and should see a therapist as soon as possible to deal with this dangerous eating disorder.

I found a psychologist whom I soon began to refer to as the Seattle Liar. He told me not only that he dealt strictly with adults, but also that he wouldn't be recording any of our sessions. However, when I got to his office for my first visit, I found it filled with stuffed animals and kiddie toys. Not only that, but I also caught him turning on a hidden tape player prior to the session. This therefore became my first and only appointment with him. Because my mother had always been concerned about her own weight, plus hypercritical of mine while I was growing up, I thought maybe talking to her about it might help. I was right.

When I brought up my eating issues to my mother, she seemed far more concerned than I ever would have expected. She told me she'd suffered from something similar when she was young and still living at home in Detroit and had started training to become a fashion model. Even though she was already super tall and thin in those days, she'd gone on a crash diet that radically upset her own mother, my Nana, who, she said, threatened to have her committed if she didn't start eating normally again. Apparently that's exactly what happened, and even though I'd never heard any of this before, I wasn't that surprised to find out that my mother had spent time locked up in a Michigan mental institution. Mom then admitted that when a nurse at that psychiatric hospital tried to force feed her, she'd deliberately knocked the plate into the woman's head and was immediately put in restraints and thrown into solitary confinement. This was followed by a series of electroshock therapy treatments, which have always been extremely controversial. The only way my mother was allowed to be released from the asylum was to agree to let Nana determine the direction her life would take from that point forward. This meant giving up her goal of becoming a model and going instead to secretarial school and joining the local Jewish singles group to find a husband as soon as possible. She did both, and ended up marrying the man who became my biological father because he agreed to make her dream come true and move to California—and whom I never met because he abandoned her as soon as she became pregnant.

Having Mom admit all this to me for the first time after so many years was definitely a wake-up call. I was able to use her story, at least for the time being, to help deal with my possible eating disorder and return to somewhat normal behavior. Although my relationship with my mother didn't actually ever change before she passed away years later, the respect I now had for her due to what she'd been through encouraged me to begin to overlook the way she'd treated me during my early years and gave me somewhat of a new outlook. Following her confession, I was able to get back to tackling my daily workload in full swing while making the most of my personal life as well.

It helped that soon after this, in December 1978, I landed a solo phone interview with George Harrison. This was doubly fortunate: one, I'd be able to update our RKO Beatles special, and two, because of my curiosity about George's longtime interest in India and his relationship with sitar specialist Ravi Shankar, I'd been hoping for a one-on-one conversation with him since I was a preteen. Plus, I wanted to congratulate him on his new baby boy, Dhani, as well as his marriage to Olivia Arias. George had first met Olivia on the phone while dealing with the label he founded, Dark Horse Records, and the couple tied the knot on September 2, 1978, almost exactly a month following the birth of their son, Dhani, on August 1.

As our conversation turned toward his latest creative work, George mentioned that his new album was being mastered at Warner Bros., so the first thing I asked was if he'd titled it yet.

"No, actually that's one thing I don't have is a title," he admitted, "so I'm just going to put the album out, just call it *George Harrison.* You can go in and say, 'Have you got the new George Harrison album?' That's what they usually say anyway!"

It was his first album in nearly three years, thanks to all of his other time-consuming projects, including cocreating the film company that financed/produced the feature film *Monty Python's Life of Brian*, and he described the songs on it as "optimistic."

"I don't think they're spiritual at all in the sense of 'My Sweet Lord' or something like that," George said, "but I think in many ways they're sort of typical George Harrison tunes. They have, you know, the same slide guitars, and it's still me singing, but the album is just a very 'up' album, and all the songs are . . . they're all melodious!"

When I asked if he had any favorites he wanted to tell me about, George responded that he'd probably come up with more songs that people would like than on any of his previous albums.

"There's a song which may be of interest called 'Not Guilty,' and it's actually a song I wrote for the Beatles' *White Album* back in 1967. It never actually made it onto the album, and I'd forgot all about the song until this last spring. I found an old demo I'd made, and actually I'm glad I never did it until now, because it's come out with a much nicer feel than I think it would have in those days." George's discussion of "Not Guilty" led him to look back on the days just after the Beatles broke up, when Capitol Records started repackaging and releasing new collections of the band's tunes.

"I wasn't too happy when they started doing that, because we no longer had any control of the packages or the artwork—they just put together what they felt. The thing about the Beatles is, it seems to have become in many people's minds that it's like public domain, you know? It's been so long now I just don't care at all; I look at it more like sort of Laurel and Hardy or Charlie Chaplin. I suppose, in a way, if there's that demand, you can't blame them for putting the records out. I hear there's a new package for about $120—everything seems to cost that much extra these days, but I don't know if they'll upgrade our royalties as well."

Even the possibility of not making every penny that he no doubt should have earned didn't seem to bug George that much at this point in his career. Money seemed to have little to do with the contentment he experienced from either his years with the Beatles or as a solo artist, and when I asked him which of the two gave him the most satisfaction, he jokingly responded, "I think gardening!"

"Staying home and planting flowers in the garden," he continued. "It sounds a bit fruity, but that period of all the noise and the acclaim and the tours and all that—that was fun at the time, y'know; when we were in our early twenties, that was fine. But I think looking back on it all, that was good for that period, but I wouldn't really like to go through that all over again. I think now I get most pleasure out of just being quiet."

Even though I was only twenty-three myself back then, I giggled in understanding and quickly brought up an interview done just a couple days before with New York disc jockey Murray the K, the self-proclaimed "Fifth Beatle," who'd mentioned rooming with George at one point during an early tour.

"It's hard to forget, really, because there's all the old newsreels. But when I look at it now, I must admit I look at it in a different light, because we were very naive at that time, and when we came into the States, they had us doing everything—you know, we were on every radio station. . . . I mean, we got tricked and conned into doing all kinds of things. And I must say, when you look at the old newsreel stuff then, Murray the K was a very nice, charming fellow, but he definitely took advantage of our naivety. But anyway, y'know—God bless him!"

I asked George if by any chance he'd read Alan Williams's book *The Man Who Gave the Beatles Away*. I'd spoken shortly before with Alan, who was the Beatles' first manager back in Liverpool, and was curious what George thought of his work.

"I did read it," George said. "I would say 98 percent of it was fiction . . . but I don't have any personal grudges against anybody, really. The Beatles were such a big thing, and a lot of people made a living, or if they didn't make a good living, they certainly are trying to make up for it now. There's probably about five thousand "Fifth Beatles"—Alan Williams and Murray the K were just two of them."

I laughed understandingly, telling George about the time I'd spent writing and coproducing our RKO special. "We had a running joke going around," I said, "'the Tenth Beatle, the Fifteenth Beatle,' you know."

"I still don't understand what happened, really," George responded. "If we knew what we know now, it wouldn't have been the same. I'm glad that we were naive and didn't know, because it made everything fun and innocent. If we'd have known about everybody screwing us down the line and ripping us off, which was really a large portion of the Beatles' career, then we wouldn't have been able to go about it with the spirit we had. I think that was the main thing apart from everything else that happened—that the Beatles' contribution in the sixties was that great—you know, joy—really!"

George's thoughts about the early years of the Beatles blew me away. He then sprang ahead, talking about hopefully taking a vacation in the start of the new year and possibly writing some new songs and ending up once again in the studio.

"A few people are trying to get me out on the road again," he told me. "Part of me would like to do that, but it's such an effort, to tell you the truth, not having a band. It's okay if you have a band; you can just go and rehearse new tunes, and everybody's on top of it. But for me, the whole thing is a bit much—I had to recruit a band and go through the whole thing again. And by the time you get to do some concerts, then you might as well keep going and tour for a year! But at the same time, I promised myself I wanted to stay home with this baby and have a look at what happens to babies as they grow up!"

This obvious link to John Lennon, who had himself become a househusband/stay-at-home daddy, triggered my next question: had George heard from or spent time with John, Ringo, and/or Paul?

"I saw Paul last week," he said. "He's just recording a new album for next year in England, so I see him occasionally." Little did I know that this upcoming Wings release from Paul and his band's latest lineup would be the one to prompt our RKO team trip to London in a few months for a McCartney interview!

"I see Ringo occasionally," George continued. "He's become an exile from England, and he only comes here for about two or three days, maybe five times a year. So I see him when he does pass through London, for a few hours. And John I haven't seen for about two years, since I was last in New York. I keep getting postcards from him in Japan and places like that, but I have no idea of what he's up to at all."

It sounded like George missed hanging out with his former bandmates, which I couldn't help but contemplate as our conversation came to a close.

"I want to thank you so much, George. Ever since we first started working on this special about a year and a half ago, it's just been a real ambition and dream almost of mine to get a chance to say hi to you and ask you a few questions."

Then, of course, I managed to come up with one more. I wanted to know if he'd had the chance to check out our Beatles special, since I'd just been interviewing him for the additional two hours we were about to tack on, taking the total up to seventeen.

"Wow, it's going to be that long?" he said. "No! Who did you send it to—I never heard it at all! If you send me a copy of the whole show, I'd love to hear it!"

He asked me to have it delivered to him care of Dark Horse Records at Warners in Burbank, and when I told him I definitely would, I couldn't help but gleefully add, "It's fabulous! I mean, I wrote it!" George laughed right along with me.

"Yeah," he said, "no doubt! And I hope all the people out there who liked the Beatles in the past are still enjoying their music. Maybe I'll speak to you in San Francisco if I get there, rather than on the telephone."

I was happy to hear him say that, since just like me, and of course the Mamas & the Papas, George seemed to be experiencing his own wave of "California Dreamin'." That's just one reason my biggest wish from that moment on was to be able to meet up with George Harrison for another interview, this time face-to-face!

—CHAPTER 15—

"London Calling"

Working in Top 40 radio news in the late seventies allowed me to cross paths with a lot of my longtime heroes, not just in music but also in politics and literature. Among them was President Jimmy Carter's mother, Lillian Carter, whom I'd admired since hearing she'd become a Peace Corps volunteer at the advanced age of sixty-eight, and essayist/novelist Joan Didion, whose work I found especially impressive because she was, like me, a native Californian.

Possibly the most thrilling of all the offers I had back in 1979 came just as I was starting to seriously consider making another major move by heading home to California from Seattle, despite the fact that I hadn't yet been given a start date for the news anchor job at KFRC I was hoping for and yes, to a certain extent, counting on. Out of the blue, as I was trying to make up my mind regarding what would work out best for me in the long run, I heard from RKO's Dave Sholin, who blew me away by telling me that if I was up for it, he hoped I'd head over to London with him and engineer Ron Hummel to interview Paul McCartney. Wow!

Needless to say, in no time at all I quit my newscaster position at KING-AM and rushed to California to get ready for the June trip, which was about to become my second conversation with a former

Beatle. It would be an astounding follow-up to my George Harrison interview just a few months earlier, which was in itself still unbelievable. The big difference was that I would be meeting and greeting Paul and his lovely wife, Linda, in person, along with the latest lineup of Wings. Plus, it would be my first trip to England. To say I was stoked would be putting it mildly; London was calling, and thanks to the dynamic Dave (the Duke) Sholin, I was on the verge of being able to answer! Wings' seventh studio album was just being released, and McCartney had expressed his appreciation of both punk and new wave, having cited Elvis Costello and the Clash among his favorites.

When we met up with Paul in London to talk about the new album, he told us, "We were always going to call it *We're Open Tonight*, which is sort of the theme going through the album, but in the end we decided we liked the title *Back to the Egg* . . . We thought it was a bit more striking."

And their next step, following the final title choice?

"You stick it in a shrink-wrap and release it, and then everyone criticizes it and says, 'Nah, it's not as good as the last one.' And then you say, 'Well, it's okay; we don't listen to the critics.' . . . and then you go on."

They'd recorded *Back to the Egg* in a handful of studios, including London's Abbey Road; a converted barn in Campbeltown, Scotland; and a medieval castle in Kent. This was all to "stop being bored," Paul told us. "It kind of tweaks you up a bit!"

Paul produced the album along with Chris Thomas, who'd worked previously with, among others, the Sex Pistols, Pink Floyd, and yes, the Beatles. Chris had been given that opportunity by Fab Four producer George Martin back in 1968, producing "Happiness Is a Warm Gun" while George went on vacation. Chris was officially uncredited for his work on the song, which, as things turned out, was said to be the favorite on *The White Album* of all four of the Beatles. Several months after our McCartney and Wings get-together I was able to set up a solo session in San Francisco with George Martin, right after his memoir, *All You Need Is Ears*, was published in January 1980. I was excited to welcome one of the best known record producers in the world to the KFRC newsroom studio for an interview that was both emotional and

Outside Abbey Road Studios with Ron Hummel
and Dave Sholin after landing in London.

educational. To top it off, George was super complimentary about my work on the RKO Beatles special, and he kindly wrote in my copy of his book at the end of our get-together, "It was great being with you!" I couldn't have agreed more.

Getting back to our impending interview with Paul McCartney and Wings, after arriving in London, Dave, Ron, and I checked into the Sheraton Park Tower hotel in Knightsbridge and wasted no time setting out to explore the area. The only reason I was even somewhat familiar with this district was the 1965 Rolling Stones song "Play with Fire," in which Mick Jagger refers to it as a playground mainly for the privileged.

On the eve of our McCartney meetup, we started celebrating by checking out a couple of London's best known nightspots, including the Marquee Club in Soho, which I'd read about for years. I knew everyone who was anyone had taken the stage there in the sixties and seventies, including The Rolling Stones, who'd played their first-ever gig there in 1962. The Marquee Club had started out as a jazz venue in the late fifties, but that night, June 14, 1979, the Knack, an LA-based new wave band, was headlining, following the release of their debut album, *Get the Knack*. Right before leaving for the airport, Dave Sholin had heard from his Capitol Records contact that the band's first single, "My Sharona," was about to come out. Because Dave's Hollywood RKO office was only a couple of blocks from the Capitol Records Building, he had had just enough time to get together with the promo rep in order to hear the song, which he immediately suspected was about to be a huge hit. And then in London, after seeing the Knack live, we were able to let them know what Dave thought. The minute they finished their set, we headed backstage with a bottle of champagne to congratulate and toast Doug Feiger and the rest of the group.

Needless to say, Dave was one-hundred percent correct. "My Sharona" cracked the top ten on the UK singles chart just a few weeks later and also became the number one single in the US for the entire year of 1979. That's why nearly three months later, in September, I ended up interviewing the Knack in San Francisco for our twelve-hour *Top 100 of the 70's* radio special.

We also brought a bottle of booze to Paul McCartney's office the next day as a big thank you gift for granting us our interview: a giant jug of Johnnie Walker Black Label, since we'd somehow heard that it was Paul's favorite alcoholic beverage. As we introduced ourselves and handed it over to him, he and Linda were both grateful and in a gracious mood. This was especially encouraging because shortly before leaving for London, I'd managed to sprain my ankle, which meant I'd been unable to exercise, and that in turn meant that I had put on more than a few extra pounds. Thanks to my mother's constant comments about my weight when I was a teenager, I was feeling extremely insecure about my heaviness. Fortunately, having both Linda and Paul ignore my fleshy appearance and still treat me as a friend and fan was totally flattering.

Paul acknowledged me right off the bat by laughingly repeating my name a number of times and then calling out "Hey, Laurie!" as he broke out in song after asking if I was familiar with that tune. Linda also seemed fascinated by my name and pleased to find out I was a Laurie from Los Angeles. She smiled as she instead laughingly began singing the 1963 number one pop hit "Hey Paula." She then switched over to the 1960s song "Tell Laura I Love Her," which Paul also began to croon, changing the lyrics to "Tell Laura I love him" as she and I both giggled.

"I get excited," he said, "a bit carried away."

"Do you? Then why don't you stay for a few days," Linda said, apparently suggesting that he hang out at his London office for a bit longer as opposed to returning right away to their rural family farm in Scotland. "You need a bit of excitement!"

So there we all were, five minutes in and even though our tape had already started rolling, the interview hadn't officially kicked off yet. It didn't matter; I was already happy beyond belief, feeling close to heaven as I looked straight into Paul's eyes, wondering when I'd have the chance to tell him that I'd first seen him in person back in 1966 when I sat practically in the top row at Dodger Stadium screaming my lungs out during almost the entire Beatles show. It took a while, but I was finally able to!

We wanted to know as much as possible about the newest members of Wings, guitarist Laurence Juber and drummer Steve Holley.

Along with original Wings guitarist Denny Laine and of course the McCartneys, they'd been confirmed for our mid-June appointment at Paul's London office, where Paul would end up facetiously telling us that instead of holding an audition, they'd added Laurence and Steve to the lineup after finding them camping out on Denny's front lawn. Ha!

We discussed how Paul and Linda managed to keep up with their musical career yet still maintain a close relationship with their family. "Super Glue!" Paul informed us. More laughter as Linda chimed in: "Super Glue and a nice deodorant!"

Paul then turned a tiny bit more serious on the subject, telling us, "We try and balance it out between working and the family. . . . They're good kids, and we try to keep them out of the business. They're big enough hams as it is!"

Ha!

"We don't take them on the road," he jokingly continued, "we try and LEAVE them on the road."

Paul was referring to his and Linda's four children: teenage Heather, his adopted daughter from Linda's first marriage, plus nine-year-old Mary, seven-year-old Stella, and sweet baby James, just over one year old. He said all were well aware of their parents' rock 'n' roll success.

"We'd have to shut them in a box for them not to be!" Paul informed us, smiling. "They know what's going on like anyone knows, and they have to put up with a little bit here and there about having famous parents. . . . . We just try and help 'em with that one."

"They NEED help with US as parents," Linda added.

When talk turned to *Back to the Egg*, I commented that Paul had made his mark not just as a singer/songwriter/musician, but also as the number one producer of every album released so far by Wings.

"Is it the song that counts the most, or is production the most important thing?" I asked, even though I was pretty sure I knew how he was about to answer.

"If you haven't got the songs, you haven't got anything, really," he told us. "I mean, there are the one or two odd instances where you can take a really nothing song and you can produce and make a really great record out of it."

At that point, Linda broke in by bursting out Chuck Berry's 1972 hit, "My Ding-a-Ling." "But I think those are the rare records," Paul continued. "Generally speaking, it's an idea, and that's the song, the original idea. And it's the idea that generally makes or breaks a record. That's what I think, but the idea has to be really good; it has to inspire people, 'cuz that's where all the juices come from!"

"How do you avoid the pitfalls of overproduction?" I asked him.

"Super Glue," he playfully answered yet again, before addressing the question more seriously. "You don't! You just overproduce some records, underproduce others, and get others right. You can't get it right all the time, you know. Sometimes you have what seems like a great idea, but I don't know—how do we do it, Denny?"

"Overproduction—it's a very easy thing to do," Denny Lane said, before Paul jumped in again.

"One of the modern buzzes, one of the things that technology's brought us, is multitracking. So, like Les Paul did back in the old days, you can play with yourself."

Linda chuckled, letting us know, "We all spend a lot of time playing with ourselves! Why do you think Paul seems so happy? He plays with himself quite a bit!" More laughter as Paul nudged Linda, saying, "Hey, it's a family show."

Working with coproducer Chris Thomas, Paul said, was a joy. "It's a bit heavy if you've got someone who's a sort-of awkward character and you work with them and you get a friction thing going—that's no use. But Chris is quite easygoing. We got used to him by the end of it, didn't we?" At which point Linda chimed in again, adding, "And he had good drugs, didn't he?"

Chris no doubt wasn't the only one with decent drugs in those days, since Paul himself was mere months away from being caught with nearly half a pound of pot in his luggage after landing in Tokyo for what was going to be Wings early-1980 Japan tour. Even though he made it clear to officials that the marijuana he was carrying was strictly for personal use, he was arrested and forced to spend nine days locked up in the city's Narcotics Detention Center. Needless to say, the Wings tour was canceled, plus their music was banned from every TV and radio station in Japan. Although McCartney didn't end up in court, he did get deported, and once he was back in England, he decided to separate himself from the band he'd put together nearly a decade before.

This happened just over six months following our London interview, which in itself took place a number of years after Paul had begun turning his wife into a performing musician so that they could hit the road and tour together.

"At first, people said, 'We hate it' and 'It's just stupid, and we won't accept it,'" Paul recalled, "but we just kept doing it. It's a weird situation, really. Some other people have said the last thing they would do is take their old lady on the stage with them. When we were forming the group for the first time, Wings, I just said to her, 'Do you fancy it, or would it be too much?' She fancied it, so we tried it to see if it would work at all."

For Linda, a photographer, this would be a completely new experience, and she was nervous about it at first. "In fact, there were a couple of gigs I really felt sorry for her," Paul told us, "'cause she cried before, and it was terrible." So what did he do? "I beat her about the head a few times and sent her on," Paul jived. "No, you better not say that for American audiences. You better ask HER that question, Laurie!" So naturally, I did.

"It was hard at first," Linda answered about her piano performances, "'cause I really couldn't play very well, and so to be playing with real musicians, it's a bit of a hang-up for them. I had fun all the time, mind you. It was a good laugh, and I started feeling comfortable after I'd done this a few times, once I started knowing what I was doing."

After admitting that it was especially difficult when she would get criticized for singing flat or being an amateur, Linda told us that Wings' first American tour helped her out a lot, since they performed so many shows. Her comments regarding concertgoers reminded me of what Talking Heads' Tina Weymouth had told me about how much she and her band preferred a rowdy rather than sedate audience.

"I really like that," Linda said. "When they're sitting down, you feel like it's a real concert and you're playing TO people. When everybody's standing up or has room to move, then it's more like you're playing WITH people—it's like you're all one!"

Paul added that Linda had gotten "as professional as she needs to get" by now, explaining, "You don't need to get too professional in rock 'n' roll, or else it's not rock 'n' roll anymore!"

Interesting comment, as were Paul's thoughts on the accuracy (or lack thereof) of people writing about his previous band. "It's weird, 'cause there's only four people who know what went on in the Beatles," he insisted. "No matter how close you were, the minute you weren't part of the four people who were going through it, you can't know really, because there's so much that happens off the camera or off the microphone, which is all the real stuff. So unless the four people sit down, unless it comes exactly from the horse's mouth, they're always a bit wrong."

I asked if he was referring to any specific books about the Beatles, remembering how George Harrison had told me they tended to be primarily fiction. "Oh yeah, I mean in books about me, I've never yet read any one book that kind of tells the truth. There's even one called *The Beatles: The Authorised Biography*, by Hunter Davies, where he came 'round and sat us all down and talked to us and got all our recollections, and he's got most of it there, but it's still not quite right. It still doesn't capture the real feeling of what went on, although it probably does the best job of all of them."

Then Paul unsurprisingly brought up the book I'd previously discussed with George, written by their first band manager, whom I'd been able to interview not long before.

"There's a book by Alan Williams," Paul said, "and he's just got us as the biggest lunatics on earth, doing all crazy things. And okay, we were crazy, but not in the way he described it.

"The thing about Alan, anyway," Paul continued, in relation to the author's interpretation of his early years with the Beatles, "he drove us over to Hamburg, and then he left, so I don't know where he got the story from. He must have got it at least thirdhand."

When I mentioned George's comment that the book was nearly one-hundred-percent fiction, Paul said, " I can't blame him. He's a good little fella. You know what people are like. You ask someone to tell you a story, and two different people who went to the same party will tell you two different accounts completely, 'cause they see it from their own points of view. That's what happens with stories about the Beatles, about Wings, our lifestyle, everything. They just pick up one little angle, and they play that up, you know. And, of course, just to the left and the right of that angle is the real story." Paul's attitude helped ease my own mind regarding my radio reporting about not just the Beatles, but also my impending script for our RKO special, *Paul McCartney and Wings, Their Words and Music*. What a relief!

That's probably what makes it a lot easier for me to talk about what else went on during the interview. I watched Linda as she rolled a number of joints and stuffed them in a shoebox; Paul began lighting them up and passing several around, sharing with not only his fellow band members but also the three of us from RKO. If anyone had ever predicted that one day I'd be smoking pot with Paul McCartney, I would have laughed my ass off, yet here I was taking hits off doobies that had been sitting between Paul's lips mere moments before, wondering if it would be too embarrassing to ask if I could hang on to one of his roaches so that I could keep it as a superhip rockstar souvenir!

One souvenir from that day I *was* able to hang on to, autographed records, books, and photos aside, was the McCartneys' interpretation of their relationship with each other. When asked what their secret was, Linda again repeated Paul's earlier wisecrack, saying "Super Glue!" before adding, "It's the drugs!"

Paul laughed, but he then addressed the question seriously: "What is it for us? We don't know. We may have been able to work it out for the last ten years, but the thing is, if it seems to work, we don't knock it."

"When people ask you about your marriage and stuff, it always comes out sounding like a fairy tale romance," he continued. "But like anyone who's got a relationship with another person, you have your ups and down, but I'm not going to go around talking about rows I have with my wife, 'cause you don't want to do all that. But it happens. We're the same as other people. We've managed to kind of work our way through it, and we still like each other."

So what advice did Paul have for other couples? Apparently, none. "I couldn't tell anyone how to do it, 'cause we're still trying to work out how to do it ourselves."

I found him to be refreshingly honest, which was true also when he switched gears and started commenting on disagreements he'd had with his record company over the years, with both Wings and the Beatles.

"Over here in England, we never released 'Yesterday' as a single," he reminisced, referencing one of his most famous songs, which he'd written solo back in 1965 even though it is credited to Lennon-McCartney. "And in America, everyone said, 'That's a real obvious single, wow!'" So true, and "Yesterday" eventually became one of pop music's most recorded songs of all time.

"When I was writing with John, our first songs ever, we were really trying to search around for what was going to be the next big thing, cuz we thought we could get in on it. We'd read papers, and they'd say calypso is gonna be the next big thing, and then they'd say Indian music's gonna be. Whatever it was, we could never discover it. And it turned out WE were the next big thing!"

Of course, what Beatles fans were still hoping for back in June 1979 was an onstage reunion, since the band had been broken up for nearly ten years at that point. When Paul mentioned the much publicized meetup of three of the Beatles the month before at the wedding of Eric Clapton and model/actress/photographer Pattie Boyd, who'd previously been married to George Harrison, we couldn't help but wonder whether one day a real Fab Four reunion might actually happen.

"So we all showed up, and we were in a marquee, and they had some microphones and stuff, so a few people got up. There was me, George, and Ringo," Paul said, along with several other well-known musicians.

"Is it a reunion, folks?" he asked. Apparently not, considering John Lennon wasn't even on the scene.

"It was just one of those things," Paul continued. "Everyone started jamming; it was mainly to get the kids off the mics."

Still, who wouldn't have loved to have been there?

"The newspapers heard about it the next day and said, 'Wow, super reunion group!' But it was actually just a crazy blow, you know? We all had a good time."

When asked if anyone rolled tape on it, Paul quickly said, "Let's put it this way: I hope they didn't!"

"It was really rough," he said. "It sounds better than it was. It sounds glamorous, but actually, it was just . . . 'YEHAAW!'" he said, screeching the last word to demonstrate his interpretation of what it sounded like. "It was a good laugh."

As our interview came to a close, Paul asked if I already owned an edition of his wife's first published work, *Linda's Pictures, a Collection of Photographs* by Linda McCartney. When I admitted I didn't, he jumped up and ran into their back room to grab me a brand-new copy, which featured fabulous, artsy photos she'd taken of such superstars as Mick Jagger, Janis Joplin, the Jefferson Starship and Brian Jones, not to mention the Beatles and John and Yoko. The book's cover featured a tenderhearted picture of Paul and their newborn son, James, and when he had Linda sign it for me with love and best wishes, I was blown away.

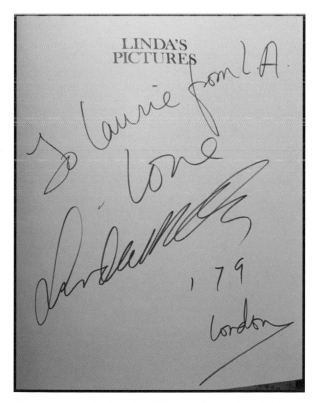

Linda autographed her book for me: Laurie from LA!

Then they both (along with Denny Laine) autographed a 45 of Wings' hit single "Silly Love Songs," with Linda writing, "love to Laurie" below her signature and Paul drawing a crazy cool cartoon character above his just before we all began to share goodbye hugs and kisses.

My autographed single "Silly Love Songs."

To my surprise, as Paul thanked me, he stood me up and bent me over backward like we were doing the tango and tenderly kissed me on the cheek. Suddenly, I wasn't a pro newscaster or rock interviewer any more! I was that preteen kid at Dodger Stadium back in the midsixties once again, screaming my lungs out when the cute Beatle and his cohorts, John, George, and Ringo, showed up onstage. Yes, I nearly lost it right there in front of Paul McCartney, and when I told him that, he laughed along with me while singing the chorus to "Silly Love Songs" and gently caressing me with his arm around my shoulder. Finally, he, Linda, and I posed for a photo.

Paul and Linda McCartney and me on the day we met. (Photo by Ron Hummel)

"Silly Love Songs," written by Paul and Linda, was going to be featured in the *Top 100 of the 70's* special I had already begun to write, along with three other Wings chart-toppers ("Band on the Run," "My Love," and "Live and Let Die"); Paul's solo hit "Uncle Albert"; the Beatles' final single, "Let It Be," which he also wrote and sang; and George Harrison's "My Sweet Lord."

The special ended up featuring twelve hours of the most popular music of the decade, also including number one songs by Stevie Wonder, the Rolling Stones, Donna Summer, the Eagles, Roberta Flack, the Bee Gees, David Bowie, the Commodores, the Knack, Rod Stewart, Linda Ronstadt, Barry Manilow, Simon & Garfunkel, and so many more! Lucky for me, I was able to interview and/or write separate RKO radio specials about a number of them, so the months following my London getaway were filled with thrills.

Two of the most exciting rockstar conversations I had during those days turned out to be last-minute phoners I had never even been guaranteed were going to take place. I was in the newsroom one fall day prepping for my last newscast of the afternoon when our KFRC receptionist paged me over the intercom. "Laurie Kaye," he called out, "David Bowie's on the line." I couldn't help but think I was being pranked and almost didn't pick up . . . but yes, it turned out to be the real deal!

Bowie was extremely polite, and though I tried my best to be as professional as possible, all I could do at first was giggle and gush as I let him know I couldn't believe I was on the phone with the one and only Ziggy Stardust. I began recording our call right away, asking my high school glam rock icon all about his 1975 *Top 100 of the 70's* hit "Fame," which he wrote and recorded with John Lennon and performed (mimed) on TV's *Soul Train*.

"The whole thing was done very fast," Bowie recalled. "We worked with Carlos Alomar and John Lennon at the studio, and that sort of—the actual writing of it—came together in about an hour and the recording not much longer. So I think the speed and the enthusiasm of the sessions added a lot to it."

I was ready to write off the rest of my day's work just to keep discussing anything David Bowie cared to bring up, but it turned out he had an upcoming appointment, so our goodbyes came much too soon. Just a few days later, our KFRC receptionist paged me out loud again, this time just moments before I was about to go on the air. "Laurie Kaye," I heard him call out from the speaker in the station's hallway, "Mick Jagger's calling!"

Again, I was somewhat unsure that I wasn't getting a phony phone call, but once again it turned out to be the genuine article. After quickly saying hi and thanking Mick for getting in touch with me, I had to let him know I had less than a minute before my newscast was set to start. I was about to tell him I could call him back shortly afterward, but instead he offered to stay on the line to listen to my report! I was super impressed, and of course I said yes. It was just going to be a quickie news brief, but still, the idea of a Rolling Stone tuning in made me quite a bit nervous.

When I got back on the phone following my closing lines, Mick was more than complimentary, and I took the opportunity to tell him about how winning tickets on the radio to the Stones Nicaragua benefit back in high school was a huge influence on my professional path.

Mick and I then talked about each of the band's singles that were going to be played on our special: "Exile on Main Street," "Miss You," and "Brown Sugar."

"Personally and as far as the band's concerned," Mick informed me, "we have quite a broad base in musical knowledge, but just what we like. So as far as I'm concerned, we're the greatest rock 'n' roll band in the world, and that's very nice and all, but we don't ONLY play rock 'n' roll, but we DO play rock 'n' roll!" This actually made a lot of sense considering the wide array of hits that had come from his band's bluesy approach to hard rock. Talking about music and sharing memories with Mick Jagger was another unforgettable experience.

Coincidentally, a short time later I had a somewhat interesting though undeniably gossipy in-person meetup with the gent known as "Spanish Tony." I'd booked an interview with Tony Sanchez following the release of his 1979 memoir, *Up and Down with the Rolling Stones: My Rollercoaster Ride with Keith Richards*, which thanks to a number of captivating but questionable stories about the Stones became a bestseller. Tony had spent eight years as Keith's errand runner, photographer, and yes, drug dealer, since he was able to supply the band with massive quantities of dope, including coke and smack, due to his underworld connections. I recorded him in our in-studio interview, but honestly never used it for anything other than background.

Just after that came the last of my *Top 100 of the 70's* interviews. Popstar David Cassidy had achieved hitmaker status nearly a decade before, back in 1970, after being cast in ABC-TV's *The Partridge Family*, about a musical family, also starring his stepmother, actress/singer Shirley Jones. Cassidy had attended the same West Los Angeles high school and junior high that I had—Uni and Emerson—although he'd graduated from both a number of years before me.

"I'd never been in a recording studio prior to 1970," David disclosed, "and I'd never actually seriously thought about doing it professionally. It came about because I did a pilot for a television show which happened to sell called *The Partridge Family*, and they didn't even ask me if I could sing! 'Okay, kid, I'm gonna make you a star,' and the first song I cut, the very first one, was 'I Think I Love You.'"

That bestselling 1970 single, which is what landed the Partridge Family in our special, kicked off Cassidy's music career as both a band member and then a solo act, which he called an amazing experience, although, he added, he was glad when the show came to an end after four seasons.

"It's a luxury for me at this point not to have the pressure of what I once experienced," he clarified. "When you have hit records and a lot of records in the Top Ten and you've got albums, you have that pressure from the record company, management, agents, and promoters trying to get you into more product. There are definite highs, but there are an awful lot of lows."

"I had no desire to be a teen idol," said Cassidy, who wound up becoming a heavy drinker. He also posed naked in 1972 for a *Rolling Stone* cover photo in order to distance himself from his young fans. Interestingly, his thoughts regarding his label's pressure to churn out new releases would be echoed just over a year later by John Lennon during our Dakota interview.

"After ten or fifteen, almost twenty years of being under contract and having to produce two albums a year in the early days and a single every three months regardless of what the hell else you were doing or what your family life was like or what your personal life was like, nothing counted," Lennon would say. "You just had to get those songs out!" Still, I have to admit that the Beatles' frequent releases brought me huge joy and played a crucial role in fostering my love of music, as they did for so many Fab Four fans.

—CHAPTER 16—

"Get Back"

As the seventies came to a close, I was filled with anticipation as I continued to live out my dream of being a KFRC San Francisco news anchor. Although my interest in day-to-day news took a back seat to my love of music and interviews with rockers and authors of newly released books, I continued to report both local and national news stories daily. One thing that helped a lot was being able to create and voice quite a few feature series from the interviews I was lucky enough to conduct. These short rock and pop-culture pieces, produced by the station's talented engineer, Ron Hummel, aired following my afternoon newscasts and got a great response from listeners and coworkers, which was certainly encouraging.

One of the most popular of these series was *Piloting the Jefferson Starship into the Eighties*, thanks primarily to a terrific session with native San Francisco rockstar Paul Kantner. Paul reminisced about the band's evolution since the sixties, when vocalist Grace Slick joined Jefferson Airplane, as it was known at the time, but just as impactfully for me, he offered insights that I identified with then and still remember to this day due to my devotion to rock 'n' roll and my childhood days spent staring into outdoor campfire flames at summer camp.

Kantner believed that all rock concertgoers shared a unique spiritual experience. "There's some odd tribal rite that I haven't quite figured out yet," he told me. "There's a lot of stuff there that I don't know what it is, but it's real enveloping, and drawing you in creates something like where everybody gathered around the old campfires. There's a lot of that in the rock 'n' roll ceremony." I couldn't have agreed more.

Slick, a former high school cheerleader and department store model who wrote the psychedelic anthem "White Rabbit," was another memorable interview subject, early in 1980. Her authorized biography, written by Barbara Rowes, had just been released, along with Slick's second solo album, *Dreams*, and China, her daughter with Kantner, had just turned nine. Grace signed the bio for me "Laurie—this book will put you to sleep!" It didn't.

In the mideighties, I interviewed her again and wrote it up for *Rock Magazine*, in a piece I titled "What Makes Slick Tick." One of my fonder memories of my days at KFRC is of nonstop champagne guzzling with her and several of my associates in a San Francisco hotel room when *Dreams* came out. To celebrate with me that night, I brought along my neighbor and dear buddy David, who was not only the same friend I was about to see Tina Turner's terrific comeback show with at the Fairmont Hotel's Venetian Room, but also the buddy I would make plans to meet and eat with in New York several months later, directly following the John Lennon interview. The tragic news that hit both of us at the tail end of that December dinner date was heartbreaking, but earlier on, in March, we had a delightful time drinking and hanging with Grace.

One of the final sets of short on-air pieces I put together at KFRC featured Linda Lovelace, whose shocking memoir, *Ordeal*, had just been published. I titled her series *Prisoner of Pornography*, since Linda claimed she had been terrorized into becoming an X-rated film star and then violently forced into prostitution, both by her former husband. The first thing I asked Linda was why she'd decided to tell her story. She responded that she would consider the book a success if even "one girl out there can be saved and helped and realize through my experience how degrading it was. I came out of it, and I'm a happy woman, and I can live a normal, decent life. I'm a happy human being again." She signed her book for me "To Laurie, God Bless you."

But my personal favorite of all of the series I created featured studio wizard George Martin, "the man behind the Beatles' sound," which is how I described him in the first episode. George had just come out with *All You Need Is Ears*, a memoir covering not only his work with the Beatles, but also his early life and production work he'd done with other pop/rock artists, including the Bee Gees.

"Brian Epstein walked into my office one day with this rather bad tape," George started his story by telling me, "but there was something about it that was different. It was a little more raucous, a little more, certainly, unusual." He said he let the Beatles manager know right away that he couldn't make a decision based on the tape itself and that he'd have to meet the group in person. "So bring them down from Liverpool," he told Brian, "and I will spend the afternoon with them in Abbey Road Studios, and I will give them a test."

Luckily, it turned out to be an instant click for George Martin and the Beatles once they met, although George's fellow executives at EMI, where he was head of studio production in the early sixties, weren't convinced. "When I came out and said 'I've got a group called the Beatles,' everybody fell around laughing. 'What a silly name for a group!'"

It wasn't until the band's second single, "Please Please Me," hit number one on the charts that their creative partnership with George Martin began to look like it could pay off, thanks to his insights as a producer.

"I think [producers] are pretty important people," George told me, "and I think we deserve lots of money. But I do not think we are superior to the artist." During the interview, he had many interesting insights to offer about the process of recording the Beatles, but the biggest surprise came when he admitted how little he'd been earning for his work early on with the group. He made a relatively small yearly salary and received no commission on sales. "I had to negotiate a royalty with them, which was pretty low. It amounted to about one-fifth of 1 percent." But even though he was making only about $7,000 a year at EMI, while others within the Beatles empire made millions, he thought it worked out well, since they were all still friends.

"I guess the unhappiest time was during the *Let It Be* period, when everybody was at each other's throats. I was quite surprised when Paul rang me up one day and said, 'Look, we want to get back into the studio, and we want you to produce us as you used to. Will you come and do another album with us?' That was how we did *Abbey Road*, and that was our swan song," George said somewhat sadly. "We kind of all knew that it was the last one, but it was a very happy recording, so we all ended happily ever after."

That fairy tale ending really resonated with me, especially because as summer drew closer, I couldn't help but feel that my time at KFRC was winding down. Just before leaving the Bay Area to move back to LA, I remember Ron Hummel calling me into his studio to listen in disbelief to an AC/DC song that was about to be added to the station's playlist: "You Shook Me All Night Long," which I fell in love with from the moment I heard it. I had to agree with Ron that playing the song on air might be considered quite controversial thanks to some supersexy lyrics. I was encouraged to check out the band's recently released seventh studio album, *Back in Black*, AC/DC's first LP featuring vocalist Brian Johnson, following the death of former lead singer Bon Scott. I credit *Back in Black* with helping to turn me into somewhat of a metalhead. Leaving San Francisco to return to Southern California meant, like the Beatles implied in their hit "Get Back," that I would be getting back to where I once belonged—even though my middle name is only Jo, not JoJo! The reason I was about to turn back into a SoCal gal was because Drake-Chennault, a radio syndication/production company launched in the late sixties by Bill Drake and Gene Chenault, had offered me what seemed like an exciting job at a significant pay hike. Because they were thrilled with the work I'd done for *Top 100 of the 70's*, they wanted me to come work for them as head producer and writer of an ambitious new radio special, *Satcon 1*, planned as a forty-eight-hour program featuring fantasy "live" rock concerts that were supposedly going to take place in twelve cities around the world linked by satellite. The idea was that we'd be creating the illusion of live music from what would actually be mostly studio recordings by huge talent, like Paul McCartney and Wings, the Rolling Stones, the Who, and the Eagles. Their so-called live shows would allegedly happen on stages in a number of major cities, including Honolulu, Los

Angeles, London, Tokyo, and Amsterdam. A final performance would take place in Moscow assuming we could convince listeners that we'd broken through the Iron Curtain.

I was intrigued by the concept, mainly because it was unlike anything I'd ever worked on before, although to be honest I couldn't see how any true rock fan would be happy to hear their favorite bands playing what were going to basically be phony live shows. That's what I considered the number one challenge as I went about building my production team. I hired engineer Rob Frankel, who was a relative newcomer back then compared with RKO's Ron Hummel when it came to creative audio production. Ron was the most talented and technically skilled engineering producer I'd ever worked with, but he was dedicated to his longtime radio station gig at KFRC, so the best I could do was persuade him to come down from KFRC to work for me temporarily on a Drake-Chenault studio session. That's when he created *Satcon 1*'s opening segment, a striking satellite launch that sounded authentic and worked out great.

I also was able to convince a gifted gal named Sue Steinberg to leave her RKO Radio office job to become my *Satcon 1* production assistant. She'd been working in Hollywood with Dave Sholin and other major network execs, so I knew she had all the important record company contacts we'd need to reach out to ASAP.

I began writing the script as soon as I could, coming up with the opening lines "Forty-eight hours of unbelievable concert performances. Forty-eight hours that will shake the world from its rock and roll roots to the height of space technology."

For concert hosts, Drake-Chenault wanted the standard radio personalities, but I also managed to come up with such talented performers as comedian/actor Phil Hartman, who at the time was one of the stars of LA's improvisational comedy group the Groundlings. Phil would go on to cocreate *The Pee-wee Herman Show* and then, most famously, join the cast of *Saturday Night Live*.

One of the other coolest parts creating *Satcon 1* was getting to meet, work alongside, and become friends with Drake-Chenault's Paula Jean Brown. Paula described her D-C gig as managing the company's music library along with researching record charts and coming up with songs to suggest that their on-staff radio dudes play. She was a talented musician as well, and just a few years later, in the mideighties, she joined the Go-Go's, replacing bass player Kathy Valentine, who had switched over to rhythm guitar. Sadly, the all-gal LA band, which started out as punk rockers but morphed into pop stars thanks to hits like "We Got the Beat" and tours with bands including the Police, broke up less than a year later. I'd originally seen the Go-Go's open for British male ska band Madness back in early 1980 at San Francisco's Old Waldorf while I was still at KFRC, but to be honest, I was much more into the boy band, and I especially enjoyed meeting up with them at the radio station before the show.

Two members of Madness I met up with in March 1980 at KFRC. (Photo by KFRC)

Another cool musician get-together I had at KFRC at just about the same time was with Peter Wolfe, lead singer of the J. Geils Band. The band had just released the album *Love Stinks*, and the title track, believed to be a reference to Peter's divorce from actress Faye Dunaway the year before, was about to become a Top 40 hit.

Peter Wolf telling me why he thought "Love Stinks." (Photo by KFRC)

Back in LA, I kept plugging away at my new job as I moved into a fairly expensive Bel Air apartment. The building was just off the freeway, which made the tedious daily schlep out to the valley from my new upscale neighborhood relatively easy. Not only that, but the apartment was practically right next door to the Bel Air Shopeasy—the local grocery store known for its celebrity customers, including musicians I encountered right off the bat like A&M Records cofounder Herb Alpert, the trumpet player who'd started the Tijuana Brass. Of course every time I saw Herb shopping for food, I couldn't stop myself from asking him why he wasn't buying *Whipped Cream & Other Delights*—ha! Another well-known Shopeasy shopper turned out to be Jan Berry of Jan and Dean, who'd been in a coma back in 1966 for over two months following his car crash near Dead Man's Curve, which coincidentally had also been the title of his group's top-ten hit just a couple of years before.

But the best part of my move to Bel Air was eventually having Brian, one of my best buddies from high school and college, as my brand-new neighbor once he found his own place just down the street from me. Bri and I were able to socialize whenever we both had time off from work, which unfortunately wasn't often enough, since I was spending a number of evenings each week late at the office, while he was just starting out as an editor of a TV series. But one afternoon in mid-October, I convinced him to come with me to check out a show at the Comedy Store on Sunset Boulevard, and we were able to meet up early enough to drive over together to have what we hoped would be a much needed night of fun and laughter. Sadly, that's not how it turned out: the experience turned out to be a terrifying nightmare when a young couple stopped us on a cross street just off Sunset, pretending to be lost and asking for directions. Before either of us could respond, the guy pulled out a gun and aimed it at Brian's forehead while the woman grabbed a long, sharp knife and held it up against my throat. They demanded I hand over my purse, which I reluctantly did, and that my friend take off his watch and give it to them along with his wallet, which he didn't—at least not until the woman traded weapons with her male so that he could begin stabbing Brian in the chest, right around his heart.

I was not only horrified, but I was also beginning to feel guilty for bringing us out there in the first place. I was afraid to start yelling, since I knew that if I did, I'd be next. Besides, it didn't seem like there was anyone around to hear me. I watched Brian fall to the sidewalk bleeding heavily as the two criminals looked at each other and hustled down the street. I left him alone for a moment, running into the middle of the road to scream for help, and apparently someone heard me through their window and called the cops. The police came quickly and looked fearfully at Brian's wounds while we waited for an ambulance to arrive to take him to the emergency room. Meanwhile, the cops came across a car with the wicked couple and a number of their apparent accomplices inside and were able to grab both my purse and Brian's wallet and watch back as they arrested them. Once Brian was finally loaded into the ambulance, I hopped in to hang with him and hold his hand all the way to the UCLA Medical Center. My tears were flowing, as I expected nothing but the worst.

My close, longtime friend had to spend the next few weeks in the hospital's intensive care unit, but eventually Brian fully recovered physically, and it took me just as long, if not longer, to come to terms with the emotional ramifications of the attack.

Photo booth shots of Brian and me following his recovery from our freaky attack.

I was terrified to spend even a few minutes outside after dark or to try to persuade friends to come out with me if they weren't one-hundred-percent into it or it wasn't their idea in the first place.

To help deal with my fear and guilt, I ended up making an appointment with a well-respected local therapist recommended by another high school friend. I continued to see Dr. Tom Grant at least once a week through early December, which is when I told him I'd be heading to New York to interview the artist he let me know had always been his favorite Beatle.

Although I also let Drake-Chenault know I'd be out of town for a few days, I didn't reveal the real reason I was traveling to the Big Apple. I suspected I'd already done as much RKO freelance work as my contract with D-C permitted, so I didn't want to risk upsetting them or causing any legal problems. Of course, they eventually found out anyway once news of John's death broke (and yes, it did end up causing contractual issues).

But that was definitely not my main concern as I headed to LAX to fly to New York with our RKO team on Sunday, December 7. With our conversation with John Lennon and Yoko Ono scheduled for the next day, I was more nervous than I'd ever been prior to an interview, mainly because they were extremely intellectual and had both been away from the music business for just about five years.

Once our RKO team of Dave Sholin, Ron Hummel, and myself arrived, along with Bert Keane of Warner Bros./Geffen Records, we made dinner plans for later that night with former KFRC News Director Jo Interrante. Jo was now a New York-based RKO Radio Network executive, and she, along with Conni Gordon, KFRC's former public affairs director, who'd also been a friend back in my San Francisco days, was wonderfully encouraging and supportive. Plus, I was also able to invite my former boyfriend Jim, the Bay Area bass player I'd met in an elevator, to join us, since he too lived in Manhattan, so all in all it was a beautiful evening, full of optimism, warmth, and reassurance . .. just what I needed.

The only awkward thing for me about our group dinner was that it happened to take place at a steak restaurant where almost all of the dishes included some form of beef. Because I hadn't eaten red meat since getting back from Bali, where I'd had no choice but to devour far too many mammal meals, I stayed hungry for nearly the next twenty-four hours. Later that evening, as our four-person interview team hung out in one of our hotel rooms at The Plaza to prep for the upcoming Lennon-Ono get-together, I took advantage of the opportunity to fill my tummy with a couple of large cups of cocoa. I then headed a few doors down to sleep in my own comfy bed and dream of the day ahead.

—CHAPTER 17—

"#9 Dream"

What strikes me most about our John and Yoko interview when I listen back to it all these years later is how it turned out to be anything but a traditional artist interview. Yes, we covered basics like the release of their latest album and the state of music in general, but we also chatted about women's rights, politics, religion, hangovers, headaches, fatherhood, parenting, and even junk food.

Asked why he didn't want his young son watching TV commercials, John replied, "They're selling the sugar. We don't eat sugar, mainly, although I'm guilty of it when I make records because it gives me energy. But for the most part, since I met Yoko, in 1966, I have not taken sugar as part of my diet. And the damn commercials, it's that constant sugar, sugar, sugar, sugar, sugar, sugar! And the only break is hamburger, cheeseburger, hamburger, cheeseburger!" I couldn't help but laugh as I thought back to the night before, when supersweet hot chocolate had been my main meal.

But before we talked about diets, including the nearly nondairy one John tried hard to get Sean to follow despite the fact that he referred to his five-year-old's nanny as the "dairy queen," I had the chance to chat with Yoko about relationships while waiting for her husband to show up.

"It was bigger than both of us," she said regarding her original connection with John. She let us know she believed marriage is more of a spiritual bond than a commitment, especially their own marriage. In relation to creating their first album together in years, *Double Fantasy*, Yoko told us, "Both John and I felt that dialogue is necessary between men and women again." She added that it was time for men to extend their hands to women. "It's their turn to understand the situation and say, 'Hey, let's start all over again.' In 'Starting Over,' that's what John is saying."

I asked about her gut reaction to hearing 'Starting Over' for the first time, which she described as a beautiful experience. Yoko added that every time she heard that song, the first single released from the album, she choked up. Remembering her emotional response that day, I wouldn't be surprised to find out that decades later, that would still be the case.

When John joined us, apologizing for being late but blaming what had seemed to him like a never-ending photo session for causing his delay, I gasped as he settled right down next to me on the office loveseat. The subject of our group conversation changed when Dave asked what a typical John Lennon day was like.

"When we're not making records and being up late, I get up about six, go into the kitchen, get a cup of coffee, cough a little, have a cigarette," John said. "Sean gets up at 7:20, 7:25. I oversee his breakfast—don't cook it anymore. Got fed up with that one."

He said Yoko, whom he labeled a workaholic, often spent hours on end dealing with their business in the office while he generally stayed in their bedroom playing records or musical instruments.

"I used to say, 'If you can't do it in bed, you can't do it anywhere.' I'm a bit like Hugh Hefner; it's like the bed controls the whole thing," he joked.

Continuing on about his typical day, John said, "I'll buzz down to see what Yoko's doin' downstairs. If the day's not too hectic, we can meet for lunch, go out to lunch. If not, if I haven't got anything outside of the house to do, I would go back in at twelve to see that Sean gets a good lunch, and then it just goes on like that."

Lennon obviously loved talking about raising Sean, who, like John, was born on October 9, "so we're almost like twins." Finally, after a number of questions about his son and the joys of fatherhood, John asked, "Are we talking about child-rearing or records here?"

To be honest, as excited as I was to be chatting with John and Yoko, I did find it difficult to relate to the emphasis on raising children. I had made the rock-hard decision way back when never to have kids myself, based on my own unsteady upbringing. Although I was impressed that Yoko had given birth to Sean while in her forties and that John was finally working on becoming the father he'd never been able to be for his son Julian during the early Beatles years, I was more than happy to hear that John was ready to change the subject.

"I want to ask you about getting the urge to make music again," I said.

"Oh, it came over me all of a sudden, LOVE!" he replied in a voice that was superloud, funny, and affectionate. " I didn't know what came over me!"

Everyone laughed, and I responded confidently, "I know. Like you were possessed!"

"I was possessed by this rock 'n' roll devil, you know!" More laughter.

"Was that the question?" he asked politely. "Did I interrupt you?"

"You got it!" I told him, smiling.

"Just suddenly, I had like— if you'll pardon the expression—diarrhea of creativity!" John said, describing his earlier conversations with Yoko about the inspiration for their songs. He said, "We had discussed going back in the studio, but I didn't have the material. But I wasn't worried about it, because I thought, 'Well, I haven't done it in a long time; maybe if I switch into that, there'll be something there.' But it just sort of came, and I called her 'cause I was in Bermuda with Sean and she was here in New York, and I called her and said, 'Well, look, we were talking about recording, and it must have triggered something off here, because I'm getting all this stuff!' And I started singing it to her down the phone or playing the cassette." Then John echoed what Yoko had told us just before he'd arrived—that she would call him back a couple of hours later and tell him how when he sang a song to her like "I'm Losing You," she'd been inspired to come up with 'I'm Moving On,' which she would then sing to him. "And then I'd be swimming," he added, "and something else would come, like 'Starting Over.'"

"It was really, truly a dialogue in that sense," Yoko had said earlier, "that I would make one song and sing it to him over the phone, and then he reacts to that in a way and then he would write another song, and vice versa. I'd say, 'Oh all right, that's how he feels. Okay, how about this!'"

What were Yoko's favorite *Double Fantasy* songs?

"'Starting Over,' 'Woman,' 'Watching the Wheels'— those three songs, especially 'Watching the Wheels.' Even now when I hear them, and this is after remixing and hearing them over a hundred times, it really makes me choke up. You know why? Because 'Watching the Wheels' is a song that sums up what he was doing these past five years, and I went through it with him. It was very hard for him, because people were very suspicious about it. Like, 'What are you doing now? When is your next album coming?' That sort of thing."

Yoko went on to say that even following the release of *Double Fantasy*, whenever John declares he's a househusband, he ends up embarrassed because of the reactions he receives. So, she said, it took courage for him to label himself that way.

"I'd been so locked in the home environment," John said about his househusband years, "that I didn't really think about music at all. My guitar was sort of hung up behind the bed, literally, and I don't think I took it down for five years." No doubt he was exaggerating, but now that he was inspired again to write and record with Yoko, things were different. "I wasn't always *on*; it was switched off. And when I sort of switched it on again, ZAP—all this stuff came through. So now we're already half—well, we did enough material for the next album, and we're already talking about the third. So we're just full of VIM and VIGOR!"

Did that mean he and Yoko were also getting ready to hit the road?

"I'm so hungry for making records that because of the way I feel, I wanna make some more records before I tour," John said. "So I'd like to make at least one more album before actually making that final decision of calling those very expensive session musicians and taking them on the road, you know?"

He said that when he originally started recording again, he had no intention of going live but that once they'd been playing 'Starting Over' in the studio, the musicians he'd hired began saying, 'Can we do this again? I mean, let's take it on the road!'

"That was the first time that this came out, thinking, 'My God, this would be fun, wouldn't it?'" John said. "And if we can do it the same way we've done the album, which is have fun, enjoy the music, enjoy the performance, be accepted as John and Yoko, then I'd be happy to go out there!"

He acknowledged, however, that he truly had no desire to think about what type of venues they'd be booking.

"I don't know whether Madison Square Garden is what I really want to do, but then can I really go into a small club and am I going to have to deal with 'Oh, he couldn't make Madison Square Garden anymore'? Do I have to care? Do I care? I don't know."

But he did say it was a real possibility that once their next album was tucked away and people already knew the songs from *Double Fantasy*, they could go out and perform music from both instead of having to go back to material from *Imagine* or even earlier. "I don't really want to go out and do 'Yesterday,'" he told us jokingly as he began to sing Paul McCartney's huge Beatles hit. "I really don't want to get into that, you know?"

John was clearly pleased that his original motivation for making music was returning. "I started out to do rock 'n' roll because I absolutely liked doing it. And that's the part of me that's coming out again, and that's why I'm enjoying it this time. I'm not trying to compete with my old self or compete with the young new wave kids or anything like that. I'm trying to go back and enjoy it as I enjoyed it originally, and it's working."

"That's another thing," Yoko added. "We both enjoyed it so much, and that's really good, isn't it?" She'd mentioned earlier how nervous they'd been before heading back into the studio with each other, but at the same time they were excited about the songs they were about to record. This, plus the fact that John was talking about both his past in general and specifically his time with the Beatles, was breathtaking considering that we'd been warned not to bring up anything other than his then-current life and work, and especially not anything about his history with his former Fab Four band members.

"There's only two artists I've ever worked with for more than one-night stands, as it were," John said, bringing the topic up completely on his own. "That's Paul McCartney and Yoko Ono. I think that's a pretty damn good choice, because in the history of the Beatles, Paul met me the first day I did 'Be-Bop-a-Lula' live onstage, okay?" He told us how a mutual friend had brought Paul to see his group, the Quarrymen, back then and that he and McCartney met and talked after the show.

"I saw he had talent, and he was playing guitar backstage, doing "Twenty Flight Rock" by Eddie Cochran. And I turned around to him right then on first meeting him and said, 'Do you want to join the group?' And I think he said yes the next day."

"George came through Paul, and Ringo came through George, although of course I had a say in where they came from, but the only person I actually picked as my partner who I recognized had talent and I could get on with was Paul. Now, twelve or however many years later, I met Yoko. I had the same feeling, so I think as a talent scout, I've done pretty damn well."

Considering John's and Yoko's unique personalities and their history as one of rock's most maligned but creative couples, the tale of their first meeting, followed by their earliest erotic session, eventual eighteen-month separation, and finally their romantic reunion had always made perfect sense to me and totally warmed my heart. The story that John and Yoko were about to tell us was far more personal and detailed than what I'd expected to hear from them when I first found out that we had been approved to conduct the only US broadcast interview with the two of them for the release of their first album in years. Why us? I couldn't help but wonder about the answer to that myself, until I heard a rumor later on that John had actually called his old pal Paul to ask if there were any radio interviewers he might recommend based on McCartney's experience promoting Wings in the late seventies, after changing record companies and band members. Assuming the rumor was true, apparently Dave, Ron, and I had made quite the impression on both Paul and Linda the year before when we spent the afternoon with them and the latest Wings lineup in London. So unofficially, the word was out: for a good time, hang with the gang from RKO!

Even though I was already aware of the story behind John and Yoko's first meeting, I asked them to relate it to us. The meeting had taken place at John Dunbar's Indica Art Gallery in London in November 1966. Dunbar had been married to Marianne Faithfull and was about to host an art show that he described to John beforehand as featuring "this fantastic Japanese girl coming from New York," John recalled. "It's going to be this big event, something about black bags, and I thought, *Ooh, orgies!*" However, when he arrived he found the opening party was actually quite sedate, with tons of what he called "very peculiar stuff" on display. "An apple on a stand for £200 when the pound was worth eight dollars or something, and hammers saying, 'Hammer a nail in.' All this very peculiar stuff. A ladder with a painting on the sky—what looked like a blank canvas on the ceiling with a spyglass hanging from it." So John climbed up the ladder, looked through the spyglass, and saw that the ceiling said "Yes."

"I took that as a personal, positive message, because most of the avant-garde artists of that period were all negative," he said. "But here was this crazy little message on the ceiling. And then the guy introduced me to her, and she didn't know who the hell I was. She had no idea!" John admitted that while he now understood what concept art means—"the idea is more important than the object"—he had no idea at the time. When he asked Yoko if he could hammer in a nail, she said no, which blew him away.

"Because it's before the opening," Yoko explained, and John told us that's when the gallery owner had a word with her, no doubt informing her she was dealing with a huge celebrity. "Then she comes over to me and she says, 'All right.' No smiling or anything, because you know how she is—she's not runnin' for office." Then, after Yoko said to him, "Give me five shillings and you can hammer a nail in," John told us he looked at her and said, "I'll give you an imaginary five shillings and hammer an imaginary nail in, okay?"

"That's when we connected, really," he revealed, "and we looked at each other like something went off." Still they didn't see each other again for a few weeks, before they happened to run into each other at another art opening, this one featuring the work of sculptor Claes

Oldenburg.

"We're both very shy, believe it or not," John said. "We didn't really get together until eighteen months later. We didn't make love 'til two years!" Yoko was quick to correct him, saying they didn't get together at all for two years. To explain why, John told us how easy it was for him to deal with one-night stands and groupies, but he was so paranoid when it came to real relationships that he needed to wait quite a while before he and Yoko could get close to each other physically. He then brought up his first wife, Cynthia, telling us that their relationship had been a different thing altogether, since it had started when they both were still kids.

"It was quite a long trip," he reminisced about his courtship with Yoko. "People always think, *Well, John and Yoko just got together and the Beatles split.* And we've been together longer than the Beatles!"

"How did your music start reflecting your meeting and your spiritual bond with Yoko?" I asked John. "Was it immediate?"

"It was IMMEDIATE! I used to have a place where I worked in the house— again upstairs, in my first incarnation, with my other wife— and I used to make kinda freaky music at home. You would hear it coming through on things like 'Tomorrow Never Knows' on *Revolver* or 'Rain' and some little backwards things, but I never made that the whole track. But at home, I would make far freakier stuff, you know? I would take the sort of most usable and add it to the Beatles, or to my tracks on the Beatles, like 'I Am the Walrus' or 'Strawberry Fields,' whatever— fiddled around a bit or put loops or something funny. But at home I was really far-out, and I had a kinda little studio, which was really just a lot of tape recorders, and we made *Two Virgins* that way. She came over for a date, as it were, and I didn't know what to do, and she didn't know what to do, so I said, 'You wanna go upstairs and play with the tapes?' (Yoko had a good laugh at this recollection.)

"So 'cause we didn't know what to do, we did play with the tapes all night, and we made *Two Virgins*, and I was showin' her all my different tape recordings and how I made the funny sounds. I was runnin' around pushing buttons and playin' the mellotron and she was—she started into her Yoko Ono stuff, which is now stuff you hear on B-52's or Lene Lovich and all that stuff. She started doin' this 'OOOOH

OWWW' and all that," John said, passionately imitating his wife.

"And I was goin' 'BLOOP BLOOP' on the tapes, and she was goin' 'OWWW.' And we did—we made a tape all night, and in the morning we made love, as the sun came up. But we'd made this album's worth of sound together without consciously setting out to make something, and that was the first togetherness. We shot the cover ourselves, privately. We just got somebody to set the camera up, took the shot, and put out *Two Virgins*. And that was the start of the whole shebang."

But once their relationship was basically blamed for the breakup of the Beatles, it couldn't have been all romance and roses, right? "So the multiyear process that went into this evolution to *Starting Over* . . . well, obviously you had a lot of bad stuff as well as good stuff," I commented, and when John agreed, I asked him, "What was the worst for you?"

"The worst was bein' separated from Yoko and realizing I really, really needed to be with her, wanted to be with her, and could not literally survive without her as a functioning human being," he said. "I just went to pieces. And I didn't realize that I needed her so much."

"What do you think of the work that reflected this period?" I wanted to know. "Well, that period I did the *Walls and Bridges*, which—"

"Which wasn't bad," Yoko interrupted, referring to his 1974 album.

"— was technically okay," John continued. "If you pull it apart as a production or, you know, format the songs, there's nothin' wrong with them, but there's an air of loss. It's a positive/negative, you know? It's saying, 'This is where I'm at; this is how it's going.' And you could say it's a film where you came out crying from that movie. *Walls and Bridges* has this sort of misery, but you can't put your hand on it. There's this kind of cloud 'round it. If you look closely, you can say "Bless You" is a nice song, nothin' wrong with it. Good construction, good harmony. You know, you can go into it and look at it, and you can't find fault as a piece of art. But overall, there's some horrible confusion and loneliness in it that—that is apparent from the whole album—that it gives off."

When I told John that "# 9 Dream" always hit me as a super wistful song, full of longing, he responded, "That's how I felt, my dear, 'cause I realized that I needed her more than she needed me, and I always thought the boot was on the other foot, you know? And that's as honest as I can get." John was of course referring to his eighteen-month-long "lost weekend" away from Yoko in Los Angeles. "I didn't go off on a 'I'm gonna be a rock 'n' roll bachelor,'" he said, elaborating on their period of separation. "Yoko kicked me out. She literally said, 'GET OUT!' And I said, "Ooooh, okay! I'm goin'!' I'd been married all me life, you know? I was married before Yoko, and I immediately married Yoko, so I'd never been a bachelor since I was twenty, or something. So I thought 'Whoo-hoo, ha-ha!' But it was god-awful. It was awful."

"Amazing isn't it?" Yoko chimed in. " Oh, but the other thing is— John explained it, so I have to, uh, explain my side of it. It's almost like, maybe it's almost like John and I are sort of the prototype of that situation, but because the world was pressuring me so much, I mean really too much, really suffocating me in the sense that I can't work anymore. And, uh, when John was in LA, I really had enough space to think about it and all that, and realize it was the society. It wasn't John so much; it was the society that's really messing the whole thing up, you know? And when John came to New York once to sort of, wanting to come back, and I said—"

"Not quite on his knees, but one knee," John interjected.

Yoko went on to say that John sang "Bless You" to her, and that's when she started crying—actually, they both did, as they held onto each other.

"But still I thought, *No, no, no, let's not get emotional; let's not get tricked again, because if I accept him back, the whole shebang is gonna start again. So let's be cool about this.* I was cryin', but I said, 'Okay, look, I'll see you later.' And it was hard for me too. And what I'm saying is that maybe—on a different level, maybe—most women are in that position that I was in. And so if men and women are gonna come back together again, then man has to really make a big step forward. So it's hard for men too. But that's the only way, I think, that it's gonna happen, you know? Because, um, I mean, I tried my best, but still, if I were to just be normally healthy, I have to get that from John. If I didn't, I would've gone crazy, anyway. So, you know, it wouldn't have been a relationship. He would have had the wife that accepted him back, but I would be in a mental hospital, you know?"

"I would've visited," John said.

"That's true," Yoko joked back. "But what I went through when we were separated was amazing. I mean if I was outside, reporters would ask, 'Well, do you think John's gonna ever get back to you?' Or 'Poor Yoko—lonely in the Dakota all by herself because her husband is . . .' Or whatever. And it's that image that is so humiliating. But I wasn't gonna stand up and say something, because that would humiliate his macho image, you know? But the other thing is, well, so he was having a headache because he got drunk or something, and he had a hangover."

"For eighteen months!" John admitted, as Yoko let us know that she was having a headache as well during that time, "because of all these people saying, you know, sort of nonsense."

After hearing their thoughts in person on the most difficult part of all their years together, I was even more impressed by their ability to reconnect with each other and repair their relationship, although John emphasized, "We're not presenting ourselves as the perfect couple, because we don't want to get into that bag either."

I can't say I was the least bit surprised at this point that neither John nor Yoko had brought up his relationship with May Pang, the former assistant whom Yoko had introduced John to in the first place. Yoko eventually encouraged the two of them to hang out together and then head off to live and love in Los Angeles, kicking off what John ended up referring to as his "Lost Weekend." To me, May's most important contribution to their relationship was reconnecting John with his son Julian, followed by her work on *Walls and Bridges*. That's May warmly whispering John's name on "#9 Dream."

I was surprised to run into May Pang myself at a party shortly after I moved to New York in the mideighties. I introduced myself as the coconductor of John Lennon's last interview, but she didn't seem at all interested— no doubt because she'd apparently been celebrating her birthday since earlier that evening and had already seemed quite drunk upon arrival. I watched and listened as May laughed like crazy while playing with a handheld paddleball toy that someone had just given her, smacking the attached ball and exaggerating the sound it made by loudly declaring "PANG! PANG! PANG, PANG, PANG!" That was my first and only encounter with her.

No matter what topic any of us brought up going forward, John had plenty more to say about his relationship with Yoko. "There's something about love that's fantastic," he said. "Even though I'm not always a loving person, I want to be as loving as possible. Or, in the Christian sense, as Christlike as possible. In the Hindu sense, as Ghandi-esque as possible. And when I met her, even though we're from two different schools of thought, as it were, we found that was the common denominator. That's why we became the love-and-peace couple. Before I met her, she was protesting against war in a black bag in Trafalgar Square. And when we met and we discussed what we wanted to do together, what we wanted to do was carry on—me in my 'Love, Love, Love' and her in her 'Peace, Peace, Peace.' Put it together and that's how we came out with the bed-in, because I couldn't go down as John Lennon and lie down in a bag in Trafalgar Square, because I might get attacked." (An eerie comment, considering the later event of that night.)

"I'm not aiming at sixteen year olds—if they can dig it, please dig it," John told us. "But when I was singing and writing this, I was visualizing all the people of my age group from the sixties being in their thirties and forties now just like me. I'm singing to them. I hope the young kids like it as well, but I'm really talking to the people who grew up with me. I'm saying, 'Here I am now; how are you? How's your relationship going—did you get through it all? Wasn't the seventies a drag? Well, let's try and make the eighties good. We're going into an unknown future, but we're still all here. While there's life, there's hope!"

I responded: "So it sounds like instead of the down litany of the early seventies, with all the things you don't believe in, now it's—"

"Exactly!" John cut in. "I always consider my work one piece, whether it be with the Beatles, David Bowie, Elton John, Yoko Ono. And I consider that my work won't be finished until I'm dead and buried, and I hope that's a long, long time."

If only that had been the case.

John Lennon, Yoko Ono, and me at the end of our interview.
(Photo by Ron Hummel)

—CHAPTER 18—

Paperback Writer"…"Everyday I Write the Book"

Looking back on what I consider the most memorable day of my life, I still experience the same rush of excitement when I picture myself sitting next to John Lennon on his love seat as he lifted my spirits with positive reinforcement, making comments like "You hit the nail right on the head!" "Exactly!" or "Yes, LOVE!" as he slid his circular, wire-rimmed glasses down his nose and looked straight into my eyes with admiration. Never before had I felt so appreciated or validated. Since music had been my emotional escape from my mother and her husband and their lack of praise while growing up, this moment was life changing.

"I love the way this went," I told him. "I really had a good time!"

"It was enjoyable," John agreed, prompting me to quip, "Same time tomorrow?"

"When's this gonna be on, or whatever?" John asked. "I like to listen to these." I promised to send him a copy.

"Oh, yeah," he said, "but I like to . . . I like to listen to it. It's like the record—I listen to the test pressing, but I don't really listen 'til they put it on the radio."

"Well, I'll call, John, and find out exactly what stations in New York and what time," Bert Keane said.

"Okay, great! Because it's always—I'd love to have it, but it's not real unless it's on the radio," John said. "It's like the record!"

So mind-boggling to hear that John Lennon was looking forward to the airing of our interview via the special I was writing.

As we all sat in what was primarily Yoko's office realizing that the tail end of our Q & A session was approaching, the desk phone began to ring a few times, and it turned out to be one of their assistants, calling to remind John and Yoko that their recording session that evening was coming up soon. The last time the assistant called, it was with the news that their car and driver were for some reason not going to be available to take them over to the studio. That's when Yoko asked whether we could, if necessary, give them a ride to the Record Plant. They were ready and eager to get back to work with Jack Douglas, with whom they had produced *Double Fantasy*.

Years later, in the nineties, I co-owned a small recording studio situated behind my home in Los Angeles. One day, Douglas dropped by to check it out for a band he was working with. I mentioned my interview with John, but the emotional impact of the memory seemed to overwhelm him, so I backed off and said goodbye, feeling sorry that I'd said anything about it in the first place.

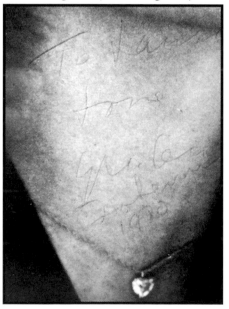

Back at the Dakota, the guys told Yoko of course they'd give her and John a lift on their way to the airport (I was the only one in our group not returning to the West Coast immediately). Their flight was coming up soon, so we needed to wind everything down if we wanted enough time to take Lennon/Ono friendship photos and ask them to autograph our copies of *Double Fantasy*.

For some strange reason, hardly any of the ballpoint pens

John and Yoko's barely legible autograph on *Double Fantasy*.

or felt-tip markers we'd brought seemed to work very well, but we kept at it, and when I brought out my copy of Yoko's book *Grapefruit* to ask for her autograph, John was excited, commenting that they hadn't seen a copy up close for years.

"I'd love to sign it!" John said. "I did the introduction, you know?"

He'd written it for the 1970 edition of the book, originally published in 1964, and a short time after that, she'd written the intro for the rerelease of his 1964 book, *In His Own Write*.

John had this to say about Yoko's book of conceptual art and poetry in relation to his '71 song "Imagine":

"It should really have said Lennon-Ono on that song, because she contributed a lot. 'Imagine' was a straight lift out of her book *Grapefruit*. There are pieces in there saying 'Imagine this, imagine that.' So I didn't give her credit."

As he began to laugh and sing "Tra la la la a" sort of apologetically, Yoko started laughing and added that instead, he'd dedicated the entire album to her. John had also included the song "Oh Yoko" on *Imagine*, to show what a major part she played in his life and how convinced he was that no matter when or where he would ever call out her name, his love for Yoko would continue to turn her on. He then chimed in, "I dedicated the album to her, which is a cop-out, but I was only as honest as I could be then, you see?" So even though John was admitting he was being somewhat self-involved, he was so moved by what Yoko referred to as her series of "instructions" in *Grapefruit* that it had inspired his most successful single as a solo artist. "Imagine" that!

At that point, John spotted the crazy little fire-breathing monster plaything I'd brought along and asked, "What is THAT?" Then he picked it up and started checking it out.

"It's a present from Laurie," Yoko said.

As John wound up the dragon, I said, "It's for Sean," and they both chuckled as the Godzilla-esque toy traveled noisily along the entire length of their coffee table.

"Oh wow, he'll love it!" John predicted. "They love monsters, you know? All this peace and love talk—he loves weapons and space fights and all that!"

As Yoko picked up the phone to answer another call related to the

My now nearly fifty-year-old copy of *Grapefruit*, which I brought with me to the interview.

recording session, John signed my copy of *Grapefruit*, adding a cartoon of the two of them. When I thanked him and told him how much it meant to me, he responded, "Oh, it's a pleasure! I'm a fan of people too, you know? I like people to sign their books when they give them to me and all that. "Well, when I come out with MY book—" I began, thinking how cool it would be to be able to sign and send John a copy of my own volume.

"Yes!" he responded. "Great!"

As we headed outside the Dakota, we saw quite a few more people standing around the building's entrance than had been there earlier. I was surprised there weren't even more, like you'd find outside Apple headquarters in London back in the day. Right off the bat, one guy started harassing us by asking why we'd been with John and Yoko and what they had told us. Bert, assuming the dude was a Lennon fan, attempted to shut him up by handing him a copy of *Double Fantasy* and asking John to sign it for him once he and Yoko had come out of the Dakota on the way to the limo.

While the two of them stepped toward us on their way to our car, John quickly autographed the album; then he and Yoko got in along with Dave, Ron and Bert. I hugged each of them and stood on the sidewalk waving farewell as the car pulled away. I couldn't help but think about the San Francisco get-together we'd begun to plan with John and Yoko, figuring I'd fly up from LA once they let us know exactly when they were coming to town. I was already anticipating not just the Japanese dinner John and Yoko told us could take place within a couple of weeks, but also the chance to talk with John about our experiences in Bali. I was also hoping to ask Yoko for advice about romantic relationships, since she had told us during the interview that "the eighties is going to be another step up, and be beautiful." The interview had gone so well that I felt certain this was the beginning of a lasting friendship with John and Yoko.

Before I could take a single step backward and start walking away, I was accosted by the same obnoxious guy as before, who now stood in my path and was attempting to trap me in front of him. There was something deeply disturbing about the way he kept asking me "Did you talk to him? Did you get his autograph?" I couldn't wait to get away and was ready to push him aside if necessary, but even when I had managed to step around him, he kept slinging questions at me and then actually started following me as though he really expected me to turn and answer. Finally, I turned my head and shot him a dirty look over my shoulder, telling him with my eyes to get lost and leave me the fuck alone. I sped up the block, thinking how creepy he'd been and how someone like that should be barred from bothering people and hanging outside the Dakota.

As I continued walking, I began to feel like I was floating several feet above the sidewalk thanks to the joy I'd felt during my afternoon with John and Yoko. I wanted to call every one of my best friends and tell them what a wonderful day I'd just had, but when I finally reached the office of the friend I'd planned to have dinner with, it hit me that I was starving, so I gave him a quick recap and we went right out to eat.

Afterward, we headed over to his apartment, and as my pal (also known as Dave) began to unlock his front door, he explained to me that he'd left the radio on so that if anyone would have the nerve to try and break in, they'd assume someone was home and head off somewhere else instead. It made sense, but as the door opened, the first thing we heard was a radio bulletin with the shocking news that John Lennon had just been shot upon his return to the Dakota from a recording studio.

I gasped in horror and disbelief, and when the reporter said that John had been rushed to Roosevelt Hospital, I ran immediately out onto the street to catch a cab. I remember that when I arrived at the hospital, I looked through the big glass front door, and the first thing I saw was Yoko Ono sobbing as she hung on tightly to someone who was obviously a close and loving friend. As much as I wanted to run in to hug and help soothe her, I knew it would be inconsiderate, since it was evident that the situation was far more serious than what had been publicly reported up to that point. I felt certain that John had been fatally shot, so I headed into the phone booth outside the hospital to call RKO's Jo Interrante, telling her where I was and what I somehow knew was really happening. When Jo told me to meet her as soon as possible at the network headquarters to file reports and discuss the interview I'd been part of earlier, I hurried over.

For the next several hours, I fought through my grief as the tables were turned; *I* was now the interviewee, peppered with questions from newspeople from all over the country—in fact, all around the world. I recalled comments John had made about life and death; at one point, he had shared that while he hoped to live as long as possible, he didn't want to outlive Yoko.

By this time, news had broken that the police had already arrested the killer, and I had the gut-wrenching feeling that I knew exactly who that assassin was. I found out from briefly watching the news and seeing the suspect on camera that I was right, and that's when it hit me, hard as a rock: the overwhelming guilt that would consume me for so many years.

I had already been feeling somewhat at fault for being part of the radio team that kept John and Yoko in town that day rather than heading off to Hawaii, as they'd previously planned on doing. But now it was much worse, because even though I'd unknowingly come in close contact with the creep who was about to become John's killer, I hadn't thought to tell the security staff at the Dakota how shady I'd considered him. Had I done so, perhaps they would have noticed that he was carrying a gun. That thought haunted me me again and again, especially every time I listened to what John mentioned during our interview regarding his '71 Plastic Ono Band single "Power to the People": "In retrospect," he had said, "if I was trying to say that same thing again, I would say that people have the power—I don't mean the power of the gun—they have the power to make and create the society they want."

Unfortunately that evil character outside the Dakota DID have the power of a gun, so I made up my mind from that moment on that I would NEVER, EVER mention (or even write) his name any time or anywhere for any reason. The publicity he'd been seeking would never come from me; I knew that from that point forward, I would already be consumed by guilt.

In the wee hours of the morning, after putting together a short feature for the RKO Radio Network and other stations to air, I was informed by Jo that RKO had been contacted by the *Today* show, and I was instructed to head over to NBC to take part. She admitted that I looked as if I hadn't slept in the last two weeks and asked if I had any makeup with me, and although normally I would have been extremely nervous about how I looked before guesting on a national TV show, this time my appearance was the least of my concerns. I didn't care about anything except being able to speak clearly about my experience, which turned out to be terribly difficult, as I tried my best to make sense and finish my sentences. Hosts Tom Brokaw and Jane Pauley seemed to understand, but that didn't make it any easier, and I spent the entire time on the air hoping it would end soon.

About fifteen minutes in, I was featured along with a couple of other journalists, plus Richard Lester, director of *Help* and *A Hard Day's Night*, who appeared via satellite from Oslo. Brokaw introduced me as "Laurie Kaye of RKO Rodeo—uh, Radio. She was the last person to interview John Lennon, yesterday," and he began our group conversation by asking me what John had to say about death.

"He did bring it up," I answered. "He mentioned that if he were to be left alone, if Yoko were to die before he would, he wouldn't be able to cope with it—he wouldn't be able to survive. And he said that he hoped to God that he died before Yoko."

As I was about to tear up, Pauley joined in, mentioning how I'd also let them know that John was "essentially full of life and very optimistic about his future." I responded by saying he'd hoped he had many years of creativity ahead. Thankfully, Jane's attempt to change the tone of the interview helped me wake up a bit and remember more direct quotes from John and Yoko. But still, when Tom asked each of the show's guests "to do something difficult," as he described it, by briefly giving them our most memorable impressions of John Lennon, I was overwhelmed and had no idea how to reply. For some reason I brought up how at the end of our interview, John had suddenly started singing a classic rockabilly guitar lick by Johnny Burnette, and he then began comparing it to some of his favorites. Looking back, this seems to have been kind of a weird memory for me to emphasize considering everything else John had come up with during our multiple-hour session, but it obviously had made quite an impact on me.

Finally, a half hour into *Today*, I was able to leave and hurry off to the airport, knowing that rather than flying home to LA I needed to head to KFRC San Francisco and get started the minute I arrived writing the radio special that was already scheduled to air in just a few days.

The station booked a room for me at a nearby hotel, and I stayed in bed twenty-four hours a day for at least two full days listening to our Lennon interview and creating the script for the special, the most difficult and emotionally devastating piece I'd ever written. I came up with the title *John Lennon—The Man, The Memory*, which basically amounted to the story of the best and worst day of my life, and I dedicated it at the start of the three-hour program to Yoko Ono. From there I quoted a lyric line from John's song "God," off of his *John Lennon/Plastic Ono Band* album, saying "The dream is over," which is exactly how I felt.

When I wasn't writing, plumping up my pillows, or wiping tears from my eyes, I was remembering what John had told us about being able to do anything/everything while on his and Yoko's bed in their room at the Dakota. This inspired me to keep going without hardly any sleep at all and finish the script in time for Dave Sholin to voice my words and for Ron Hummel to wrap up the technical production with music and sound bites. All this had to happen before our air date, just a couple of days away: Sunday, December 14—exactly two months from the day we originally planned to air the Lennon/Ono *Double Fantasy* interview as a Valentine's Day special.

I headed over to KFRC to return the cassette player I'd been using and drop off my script, then headed back to LA to face what I knew would be an extremely difficult meeting with executives, aka my big bosses, at Drake-Chenault. Not only had I neglected to tell them the true reason I was leaving town in the first place, but during my appearance on *Today* I had been identified on-screen only as an RKO Radio Network employee. My D.C. bosses were so pissed off that they threw me out of the office and canceled my year-long contract.

Thankfully, Jon Davidson, my good friend from high school who was now an attorney at a top entertainment law firm, was able to help. Although I didn't get my job back, which wasn't necessary anyway, since I'd completed work on *Satcon 1* and the special had already aired, RKO agreed to give Drake-Chenault several minutes of our Lennon interview to use in its upcoming *History of Rock and Roll* show update. I in turn was allowed to maintain my writer's credit on *John Lennon— The Man, The Memory* and eventually, following a legal battle and thanks to the hardworking Jon Davidson, get paid the rest of my full year's salary despite the fact that I'd been terminated.

Just after *John Lennon—The Man, The Memory* aired, my career as a writer/producer of rock specials took a sharp turn for the worse, mainly due to the emotional repercussions of that day at the Dakota. I was wrapped in guilt. Although I'd dealt with plenty of remorse throughout my life, this was something entirely different. I felt torn apart, unable to process or accept what happened. I felt chronically tired, alienated, and dissociated from life.

Strangely, receiving RKO Radio Network's check for my freelance interview of John and Yoko and then writing the three-hour special following John's murder only intensified my guilt. Rather than deposit the money into my bank account, I decided to invest in the memory of John Lennon. "Bag One" was a series of primarily erotic lithographs John had created to give Yoko in 1969 to commemorate their marriage and honeymoon. An exhibition of this artwork followed early the next year at London Arts Gallery. Only 300 sets of John's limited-edition fifteen-piece series were printed, numbered, and hand signed.

I was especially fond of a litho made up of John's written words rather than his sexually explicit artwork. Titled "Poet's Page A to Z," it depicted letters of the alphabet and linked each letter with a bizarre but meaningful memory and/or association that John himself had written directly onto lithographic plates. He ended the piece with the lines "This is my story both humble and true. Take it to pieces and mend it with glue."

I bought one as soon as I could—not to be among the mere three hundred people on the planet to own it and not only because I wanted to contribute as much as I could to John Lennon's remembrance, but also because I'd begun to relate so strongly to everything he had to say in "Poet's Page A to Z." I simply couldn't help myself. I had the poster-size lithograph handsomely framed, and it's been hanging on every living room wall in my life since.

Even though I resumed meeting with my therapist as soon as I returned to Los Angeles, my guilt inflected every interview I conducted from that point forward. I still needed to complete a number of them right off the bat for RKO specials I'd agreed to take on prior to my trip to New York, but it became more and more difficult for me with each session. First up was my interview with Neil Diamond.

This was followed a few days later by my meetup with Barry Manilow, which was especially meaningful because I couldn't help but think throughout the interview about how John had cited Manilow's mellow-pop contributions. Even though Barry sent a lovely letter after the program aired—"probably the best radio special I've ever been involved in," he called it—describing how flattered and moved he was, I have to admit I was still having major problems for quite a while following our conversation.

Meeting up with musicians became more and more difficult; I even considered getting out of the business before it became impossible for me to continue. Nothing seemed to matter any more.

My first interview after the John Lennon tragedy, with Neil Diamond.

I tried to take a break from work, but instead found myself getting and accepting more offers as a freelance writer, producer, and interviewer than ever before. I also took an on-air gig for a company called The Creative Factor that involved writing and voicing a weekly syndicated music magazine/rock column.

The Creative Factor, where I also ended up writing network superstar specials, was located in the same building back then as Motown Records, at the intersection of Sunset and Vine in Hollywood. One morning on my way up to the office I happened to hop in the elevator alongside funk rocker Rick James, and without thinking I began singing his biggest hit to him, telling him I knew he was a "Super Freak." He laughed and joined in, giving me what may have been my first truly enjoyable meetup with a musician since that day at the Dakota.

I took it as an encouraging sign, even though I'd been allowing the outcome of December 8, 1980, to continue to corrupt my career choices, as I avoided applying for a number of promising musician-related jobs. Maybe I could find positivity and move forward if I was somehow able to stop dwelling on my own role in the events of that day. I made a point of rarely if ever mentioning that I'd coconducted

John Lennon's final interview, hoping it might help.

It did, but at the same time it didn't.

I decided to focus on seeking off-air work with longtime idols like Dick Clark. I was hired to write his radio countdown show, and thanks to his frequent offers to add everything to my original gig from writing his syndicated weekly newspaper column to ghostwriting a book for him, working with Dick became the major step toward regaining not only my confidence, but my career direction as well.

Surprisingly, about five years after the John Lennon interview, I headed back to New York—this time, to live there while writing a USA Network music video countdown show called *TV 2000*. Once there, I realized that even driving past the Dakota or heading over to Yoko Ono's John Lennon memorial in Central Park, Strawberry Fields, would profoundly affect me, so I made every attempt to leave that time behind and concentrate solely on my present and future.

I did, however, attempt to get in touch with Yoko, but didn't hear back from her, which was understandable considering the circumstances. I figured she must associate me with what had turned out to be the most tragic day of her life.

In retrospect, I no doubt should have begun to tell my story way back when. Not only would my memories be sharper, but doing so probably might also have helped me cope better with the guilt that was haunting my life and work. However, I didn't really want to write this book while my mother was still alive, since she would have no doubt felt quite insulted had she bothered to read it. Our relationship had improved somewhat over the years, but sadly deteriorated again before she passed away, which left me emotionally conflicted.

That's why, as I mentioned right from the start, becoming a "Paperback Writer" is something I've had to work my way up to, with the time to finally put my story in print being NOW. And thanks mainly to Paul McCartney, although John Lennon was of course also credited as the song's cowriter back in 1966, here are a couple of questions I have for everyone:

"Dear Sir or Madam, will you read my book? It took me years to write, will you take a look?"

Thank you!

—ACKNOWLEDGEMENTS—

I'm so grateful for the help I've received from everyone I've met and/or worked with both recently and over the years, starting way back in high school with B. Mitchel Reed—the first disc jockey I ever met in person, who instantly complimented me and encouraged me to put my voice on the air and start a career in radio.

Just a few years later, Jo Interrante became my first radio station news director, and to this day she is the best I ever had. She not only recognized my writing ability right off the bat but also helped me become even better when it came to creating news stories and specials. Big thanks to Jo for recommending me back in 1976 to Dave Sholin to write what turned out to be the nation's longest Beatles special. Sholin was KFRC-AM's music director when I started there and the fellow most responsible for making sure I was able to continue interviewing rock stars for years to come, in addition to creating and developing radio specials. Thanks to Dave for moving my career from news over to rock 'n' roll, along with Ron Hummel, the station's supertalented technical producer, whom I was lucky enough to work with right from the start and learn from for years. We spent hours together not only in Ron's studio, but also on so many spectacular on-site interviews.

Shortly after I finally began writing my manuscript, Ken Womack, the well-known author of multiple bestselling Beatles-related books, provided continuous inspiration, enthusiasm, and support when it came to helping me finish my memoir and eventually getting it published. Fayetteville Mafia Press's David Bushman and Scott Ryan are two talented authors and editors who created their own independent publishing company and thankfully responded right away to my initial inquiry and submission with intense support and the desire to publish and promote my book.

Mick Haggerty, the Grammy-winning designer of rock 'n' roll album covers and music video director, deserves much appreciation for creating the amazingly cool front cover for my book from my original photo with John and Yoko.

I also have Madeline Bocaro to thank—she's the writer of the intriguing *In Your Mind—The Infinite Universe of Yoko Ono*. Madeline's encouragement and her introductions to a number of podcast hosts who've interviewed me to promote my book long before it was released have been extremely helpful.

Plus, I'd like to acknowledge my longtime friend Kat Dillon for her initial reads and helpful, thoughtful, congratulatory comments on the first draft of my memoir. Kat's a former TV production manager who has also been a member of multiple book clubs for years.

So much help from so many superb people has been what's enabled me to move forward!

—ABOUT THE AUTHOR—

Writer/producer Laurie Kaye began her career in radio while still in college as an intern in the news department at RKO's KFRC-AM in San Francisco, for years Billboard magazine's number one Top 40 station. She eventually quit school to work there full-time in radio news, followed by newscaster gigs at WOW-AM in Omaha and KING-AM in Seattle before eventually returning to KFRC in an on-air position. Kaye wrote, coproduced, and interviewed some of the world's most famous rock stars for long-form radio specials, including the fourteen-hour *RKO Presents the Beatles* (originally released in 1977, later expanded to seventeen hours and retitled *The Beatles from Liverpool to Legend*) and the twelve-hour *Top 100 of the 70's*. In 1980 she wrote and produced the forty-eight-hour *Satcon 1, A Space Age Radio Fantasy Concert*, and that December she found herself an inadvertent participant in history when she interviewed John Lennon at the Dakota Apartments in New York City just hours before his death. This resulted in the radio special *John Lennon: The Man, The Memory* but also upended her life and career due to the trauma she experienced. Eventually she went back to work, writing Dick Clark's weekly radio countdown show and nationally syndicated newspaper column. Kaye next became a television and film promo writer, producer, casting director, and location manager. Never one to sit still, she cocreated the horror movie video magazine *Gorgon* and the BMG video magazines *MetalHead* (hard rock), *Slammin'* (rap), and *Country Music Video Magazine*. Several years later, she headed to New Zealand to lead the location production of *The Lord of the Rings: The Return of the King's Special Extended DVD Edition*. She continues to work in television production, handling both creative content and line producing for network docuseries pilots.

Author Laurie Kaye prior to her June 2023 interview for the John Lennon tragedy episode of the European true crime docuseries *Red Crime*. (Photo by Maddie Khalaf)